AS SHE LIKES IT

As She Likes It tackles the question of how the unruly women at the centre of Shakespeare's comedies have been embodied in performance.

Unique amongst both Shakespearean and feminist studies, *As She Likes It* asks how gender politics affect the production of the comedies, and how gender is represented, both in the text and on the stage. Penny Gay takes a fascinating look at the way *Twelfth Night*, *The Taming of the Shrew*, *Much Ado About Nothing*, *As You Like It* and *Measure for Measure* have been staged over the last half-century, when perceptions of gender roles have undergone massive changes. She also interrogates, rigorously and thoughtfully, the relationship between a male theatrical establishment and a burgeoning feminist approach to performance.

As illuminating for practitioners as it will be enjoyable and useful for students, *As She Likes It* will be critical reading for anyone interested in women's experience of theatre.

Penny Gay is a Senior Lecturer in English and Performance Studies at the University of Sydney. She has produced and acted in numerous university Shakespeare performances.

GENDER IN PERFORMANCE
General Editors: Susan Bassnett and Tracy C. Davis

The *Gender in Performance* series reflects the dynamic and innovative work by feminists across the disciplines. Exploring both historical and contemporary theatre the series seeks to understand performance both as a cultural and a political phenomenon.

Also available:
CONTEMPORARY FEMINIST THEATRES
To each her own
Lizbeth Goodman

ACTRESSES AS WORKING WOMEN
Their social identity in Victorian culture
Tracy C. Davis

Susan Fleetwood as Rosalind, John Bowe as Orlando,
As You Like It, 1980, directed by Terry Hands.
Photograph: Reg Wilson.

AS SHE LIKES IT

Shakespeare's Unruly Women

Penny Gay

822.
33
DG

London and New York

First published 1994
by Routledge
11 New Fetter Lane, London EC4P 4EE

Simultaneously published in the USA and Canada
by Routledge
29 West 35th Street, New York, NY 10001

© 1994 Penny Gay

Typeset in Bembo by
Ponting–Green Publishing Services,
Chesham, Buckinghamshire
Printed and bound in Great Britain by
TJ Press (Padstow) Ltd, Padstow, Cornwall
Printed on acid free paper

British Library Cataloguing in Publication Data
A catalogue record for this book is available from
the British Library

Library of Congress Cataloging in Publication Data
Gay, Penny
As She Likes It: Shakespeare's Unruly Women / Penny Gay.
p.   cm. – (Gender in Performance)
Includes bibliographical references and index.
1. Shakespeare, William, 1564–1616 – Characters–Women.
2. Shakespeare, William, 1564–1616–Political and social views.
3. Feminism and literature–England–History–16th century.
4. Feminism and literature–England–History–17th century.
5. Women and literature–England–History–16th century.
6. Women and literature–England–History–17th century.
7. Shakespeare, William, 1564–1616–Comedies
8. Women in literature.   9. Comedy.
I. Title.   II. Series.
PR2991.G38   1994
822.3'3–dc20   93–40997

ISBN 0–415–09695–2 (hbk)
ISBN 0–415–09696–0 (pbk)

CONTENTS

PLATES

PREFACE

To a young Australian postgraduate student arriving in London in the late 1960s, the theatrical experiences on offer were, as we used to say, mind-blowing. There wasn't much Shakespeare on in Sydney or Melbourne in the 1950s and 1960s: in particular, I had never seen a Shakespearean comedy – I had never laughed at a Shakespearean joke, nor been moved by a Renaissance image of young lovers rejoicing in their future.

What astonished me – and still does today – was the power of performance to make alive and infinitely varied those over-studied texts. As the 1960s turned into the 1970s, and we all became caught up in the social revolution instigated by the new wave of feminism, I became more and more fascinated by the performances of women in Shakespeare – especially in the comedies, which (with few exceptions) centre on female characters, and give them a great deal more to say than do either the tragedies or the histories (the Cleopatra play always excepted). Yet it was these latter two categories which were considered by my teachers – both at school and at university – as important, *serious*, dealing as they did with weighty matters of politics, government, and religion, and offering us poetic meditations on 'life'. That this was a male-imposed cultural perspective, which elevated men's experience and interests and devalued women's as secondary and inferior, only became evident as feminist literary theory developed in the late 1970s.

Feminist theorising about theatre and performance has come even later on the scene, and is still in its early days. I hope that this analysis of five Shakespearean comedies in performance may make some contribution to it, as a set of case studies of the way gender (and other) divisions in British society of the past fifty years are reproduced, or challenged, by their embodiment in actresses and actors performing these classic texts. The Royal Shakespeare Company is unique in its concentration on Shakespeare – on average, each play is done once every five years – and it is itself the national monument of the national writer. To study its performance of Shakespearean comedy is to encounter a continuing dialectic between theatre practice and English social and political history, since theatre will always in some way reflect the general culture of which it is a part.

I begin my study of each play after the Second World War, in order to provide a context for the developments of the last twenty-five years, of which I have been a fascinated witness. The two most popular 'transvestite' comedies – *Twelfth Night* and *As You Like It* – were an obvious choice, since every production, whatever its other emphases, will unavoidably foreground the question of what is proper feminine behaviour. To balance these, I look at three of the most commonly performed woman-centred comedies in which the heroine does not get into male dress – *The Taming of the Shrew*, *Much Ado About Nothing*, and *Measure for Measure*. Each of these three plays has a 'problematic' woman at its centre – one who is too talkative, or who behaves in a way that denies patriarchal authority. In all five plays the disruptive behaviour of the heroine is finally contained by the prospect of marriage – or so the text indicates. In performance it may be otherwise.

Plays exist most fully in performance, and classic plays such as these exist in a historical continuum of performance. This book is an attempt to write theatre history from a feminist point of view, and thereby to provide new points of entry for those who are reading, watching and thinking about Shakespeare.

ACKNOWLEDGEMENTS

The research for this book was undertaken, during several periods of study leave from Sydney University, at the Shakespeare Centre Library, Stratford-upon-Avon. I am grateful to the librarians of that unique institution, especially Sylvia Morris and Mary White, for their unfailing helpfulness and erudition. The staff of the Performing Arts Library, the Sydney Opera House, were equally helpful at the 'tidying-up' stage. Talia Rodgers at Routledge and the series editors, Susan Bassnett and Tracey Davis, provided the enthusiastic support and judicious commentary that every author needs. I also wish to express my thanks to the Academic Board of the University of Sydney for granting me a year's leave from teaching in order to undertake the research. Colleagues and students in the Department of English and the Centre for Performance Studies, University of Sydney, provided a supportive environment and occasional inspiration in discussion of the book's general issues, as did my family. A special thanks must go to Meg Gay, reader, editor and caterer extraordinaire.

The extracts from *Clamorous Voices* by Carol Rutter, reprinted on pages 78–82, 91, 109–14, published 1988 by The Women's Press Ltd, 34 Great Sutton Street, London EC1V 0DX, are used by permission of The Women's Press Ltd. I am grateful to Fiona Shaw and Michael Billington for permission to reproduce extracts from unpublished correspondence and interviews. For permission to reproduce photographs, I thank the Shakespeare Centre Library (plates 2, 4, 6, 9, 14, 17); David Ball (for the Angus McBean photos, plates 1, 7, 10, 13, 16); Reg Wilson (frontispiece and plate 5); Morris Newcombe (plate 3); Zoë Dominic (plate 8); Laurence Burns (plate 11); Donald Cooper (plate 12); Clive Barda (plate 15); Gordon Goode (plate 17) and Chris Davies (plate 18).

INTRODUCTION

SHAKESPEARE'S COMEDIES AND SOCIAL HISTORY

'You must not, sir, mistake my niece. There is a kind of merry war betwixt Signor Benedick and her. They never meet but there's a skirmish of wit between them.' Thus, in the opening minutes of *Much Ado About Nothing*, Leonato encapsulates my theme in this book. As the visible representative of patriarchy – governor of Messina and head of an extensive household – he feels obliged to explain (to another male, even one as lowly as the Messenger) the odd behaviour of a young woman under his protection, and to assert her normalcy: 'You must not *mistake* my niece', he says, evidently worried that his female relation might prove impenetrable to the 'normal' male gaze. Yet the behaviour that he is so busy explaining is intrinsically paradoxical and transgressive of norms, 'a kind of *merry war*'. Beatrice's demeanour towards Benedick cannot be described by ordinary (that is, male-defined) linguistic usage, though Leonato tries to contain it by his oxymoronic metaphor drawn from the masculine military world (from which the Messenger and Benedick have just arrived). What Leonato sees in the 'skirmishes' of Beatrice and Benedick is what is traditionally known as 'the battle of the sexes', masculine and feminine genders in continual opposition (and here 'tradition' might be thought of as the product of a patriarchal culture, that can *only* think in this way about relations between the sexes). However, the element of 'merriment' in this conflict disrupts traditional assumptions about the proper behaviour of young men and women: Beatrice and Benedick – Beatrice particularly – via their verbal wit and the laughter it generates seem connected to a source of energy that cannot be fully contained by social forms.

Let us consider Leonato as a type of the critic, literary or theatrical. Observing a young woman performing beyond the bounds of the normal decorum of her gender, he registers puzzlement, or anxiety (the critic may not be a biological male, but in such cases he/she is responding from the culturally-dominant masculine perspective). He himself is obliged to spend a good deal of energy in response to hers, attempting to explain or contain or censure her behaviour. Something which helps the critic, which Shakespeare chose not to make available to Leonato,[1] is the literary theory of comedy. From the scores of books written on comedy, and on Shakespearean comedy in particular,[2] – all of them impelled by the critic's impulse to explain/contain – we can draw half a dozen points which are common to the plays under consideration here. The major plot centres on a young woman of wit and intelligence, apparently ripe for marriage (*ipso facto*, a virgin, and therefore a valuable commodity in the patriarchal economy). There is a roughly parallel low-life plot, which abounds in the figures of carnival: clowning, 'cakes and ale', bawdy sexuality. Song or dance will irrepressibly occur, even in the 'darkest' of comedies. One or more characters in the play will figure as an outsider, a non-joiner, a scapegoat perhaps for the guilt-for-excess that the play cannot quite banish. The major plot will involve courtship and end with the prospect of marriage for the heroine.

From these structural elements, theories have been developed which suggest that comedy represents the ultimate triumph of the idea of the community: an organic entity close to the rhythms of nature, whose principal icon is the young heterosexual couple on the verge of marriage and reproduction. Any occurrence of evil is seen as disrupting, or rather disobeying, these persuasive rhythms, and a scapegoat figure will usually, in the course of the play's plot, be expelled from the community represented on stage so that at the end we may join in, via our proxies the actors, the dance or feast which signals the community's confidence in its self-ordering. Comedy, according to such theories, is profoundly conservative: it allows the topsy-turveydom of carnival – the transgressions of gender and sexuality involved, for instance, in the transvestism of some Shakespearean heroines, or even in their talkativeness – as a way of 'letting off steam'. The community or audience thus permitted to enjoy its fantasies of disruption will then, after the carnival event, settle back happily into the regulated social order of patriarchy – of which the institution of marriage is one of the most powerful symbols.

2

By looking at the history of the *performance* of five Shake-spearean comedies over half a century in one theatre, I want to challenge this essentialist and immutable definition of comedy. Performance is always potentially disruptive of received readings, because in order to hold an audience's attention it must respond in subtle (or not-so-subtle) ways to the changing *Zeitgeist*. It may not always be what the audience likes, but it represents what the audience at least subconsciously *knows* is happening in their world. This is particularly the case when the plays in question foreground the idea of gender,[3] since the representation of gender is bound up with the culture's ambivalence about sex, that powerful and un-predictable force. 'Woman', especially, because she is the unknow-able Other of patriarchy, can make her marginal position a source of disruptive power: though politically powerless, she can refuse to obey the rules of appropriate gender behaviour, flaunting her sexual mystery as if to point out that the patriarchy cannot do without her. It is around such transgressive female figures that Shakespeare chose to centre these comedies.

Lesley Ferris points out that 'the absence of women in [Eliza-bethan and earlier] theatre created the notion of woman as a sign, a symbolic object manipulated and controlled artistically by male playwrights and male actors':[4] unavoidably, it would seem, the Shakespearean text presents its female characters from a male point of view. Certainly the fact that they are almost invariably recuper-ated into the patriarchal economy via marriage would suggest this. There are exceptions: the Princess of France and her ladies in *Love's Labours Lost*, the silent Isabella at the end of *Measure for Measure*. But more pertinently, there is the major cultural difference between the theatre for which Shakespeare wrote and the theatrical practice of our own day: women now play those roles written for the boys who played the idea of 'woman',[5] and women can choose, to a certain extent, how far their performance will embody – or perhaps more accurately, refuse to embody – their culture's idea of femininity (the limitations on their choices within the structure of the Royal Shakespeare Company are discussed below).

The peculiar materiality of drama, its *embodiment*, is always potentially disruptive of the conservatism of critical theory, whether it is that of the study or that of the audience. Beautiful, grotesque, sweaty, shouting, whispering, crying, laughing, moving bodies are, first and last, the producers of the texts of drama; how the audience reads these texts will depend on their own attitudes to the body and its decorums. The play will in every production, at every performance, be retextualised according to what is available, or fashionable, at the time of its presentation – and this includes the actors and actresses. Female actors[6] are perhaps more subject than men to the sway of fashion because control of woman-as-image is essential to patriarchy's continued dominance. Women's efforts to free themselves from patriarchal control are easily absorbed by the culture and turned to its own ends. For instance, changes in women's dress – particularly the increasingly common wearing of trousers for greater freedom of movement – will almost invariably be echoed in the costume design of a production, yet the heroines of Shakespeare's cross-dressed comedies are almost always discussed by reviewers in terms of their conformity to some notion of essential womanliness that the critic holds – as though it didn't matter what her clothes 'said', he could gaze right through them to her heart, and there see played out the cultural fantasy of the perfect heterosexual marriage in a self-regulating community.

Yet a determined actress (or actor) can disrupt such voyeurism; not by 'playing against the text' – there is no such thing as the 'text itself', unmediated by cultural assumptions – but by investing all the textualities of the production (speeches, costume, body language, how she inhabits the stage space and how she relates to the other performers) with her own individual energy; in a sense, by fighting for her role, as the embodiment of a *particular* woman enclosed in a narrative that pretends to be universal. Interview any modern actress of the classics about her craft, and you will find that she sets about 'creating a character' by finding an explanation for all her speeches and actions in terms of a consistent and comprehensible psychology. Despite the magisterial pronouncement of the anonymous critic of the *Birmingham Post* (7 May 1952) – 'Viola, Beatrice, Portia, to greater or lesser degree *all* Shakespeare's great comic heroines set their interpreters the self-same problem – that of protecting against the glitter of their more brilliant qualities the essential womanliness that makes them lovable' – the modern actress does *not* aim to embody the abstractions of 'femininity'; graciousness, warmth, radiance, tenderness, and so on. What evidence there is suggests that this is also true of the great pre-Stanislavskian actresses and actors – in all ages they have aimed for what they think of as realism of representation. As the contemporary actress Fiona Shaw says, commenting on the general feminist consciousness of her generation, 'It's not my right or the

4

right of any actress to define what women are. We are merely trying to understand the circumstances that bring about what they are'.[7]

One consistent feature of Shakespearean drama – not just of comedy, despite the influential arguments of Bakhtin – is that it proceeds by way of *inversion* of the norms of behaviour (if Rosalind is not behaving normally, no more is Lady Macbeth; both are figures of excess). This suggests that the plays can indeed provide 'the exhilarating sense of freedom which transgression affords', a dream in which glamorous, charismatic people do in public things that we cannot or would never dare do. Perhaps, as Stallybrass and White argue, such transgression is often 'a powerful ritual or symbolic practice whereby the dominant squanders its symbolic capital so as to get in touch with the fields of desire which it denied itself as the price paid for its political power.'[8] But 'to get in touch with the fields of desire' is fraught with danger, however much it is apparently controlled by the conventions of bourgeois theatre-going. It is possible that one or many individuals in the audience, disturbed and excited by the play of the possibilities of human bodies before them, may go out of the theatre politically changed persons, their consciousness of the discourses circulating around us heightened.

How transgressive a particular production may be depends to a large extent on the conscious politics of the director and to a lesser extent those of the actors. When the performance is that of an institution such as the Royal Shakespeare Company, there is obviously the danger of stultification, of reproducing the same sort of 'safe' product for a known audience. Yet there is also a challenge peculiar to such a situation: the challenge to creative artists to produce a striking and exciting performance of these received texts that is 'of the moment'. By studying the variations in production styles of one play over a number of years in the same theatre, under the aegis of the same company, it will be possible, I hope, to identify some aspects of what makes theatre speak for the culture at large.

The Royal Shakespeare Company has always had a generally leftish image, insisting on the 'relevance' of Shakespeare for today.[9] Its predecessors, the annual companies formed to present seasons at the Shakespeare Memorial Theatre (under the three- to five-year artistic directorships of such people as Anthony Quayle and Glen Byam Shaw) would no doubt have labelled themselves and Shakespeare apolitical. They offered productions which pretended to exist in a historical vacuum, aspiring to present 'universal', 'timeless', 'essential' Shakespeare, which was more often than not cant for productions which were no more than elegant and well-spoken, pandering to the tastes of a conservative Midlands audience.[10] 'After three centuries of reverential abuse', the American Charles Marowitz wrote feistily in 1962, 'Shakespearean production has become a glorious kind of music rather than a powerful kind of drama . . . . The popular image of a Shakespearean play is of a dozen lengths of exquisite poetry backed by spectacle, interrupted by swordplay, and relieved by intervals' (*Plays & Players*, January 1962).

Signalling a change of theatrical philosophy, Peter Hall – the first of the university-trained artistic directors[11] – remarked in 1964,

> an actor's expression is a synthesis of the times *he* lives in and the audience he is acting to, and that changes and it changes radically.
>
> A nation's vocabulary, its accents, its whole culture, are always shifting, and . . . [t]he means of expressing Shakespeare's intentions must vary with these developments.[12]

Not that the director who thought he was presenting 'the essential Shakespeare' disappeared from the scene entirely – but that form of artistic egoism was largely replaced by the belief that Shakespeare's plays could be made more immediately relevant to an audience that was changing under the influence of the 1960s 'youth revolution'. Hall's own production of *Hamlet* in 1965 starred the youngest Hamlet for many years at the Royal Shakespeare Theatre, the unknown and uncouth David Warner, who looked exactly like the long-haired, untidy, long-scarfed students who crowded every performance. Throughout most of the 1970s this audience remained, growing older but retaining their enthusiasm for things radical. Productions were done cheaply, most commonly by using a basic 'empty space' set for a whole season, cleverly transformed with a few superficial design elements. The productions relied for their success on the extraordinary energy of the performances of a group of actors – including Janet Suzman, Judi Dench, Alan Howard, Ian Richardson – who returned season after season to try their hands at other major Shakespearean roles, growing more confident in their own performances year by year. (Commenting on 'the difference in styles, both of verse-speaking and acting' between RSC performances of the 1960s and those of the 1970s, Sally Beauman wrote: 'The Seventies approach is freer, more romantic, and more passionate'.)[13]

Under the Thatcher Tory government the inevitable move to boost the tourist market occurred; Ralph Berry records 'a sense of change' in the RSC style beginning in mid-1981:

> At that point the Governors of the RSC, the makers of manners, determined that there was an urgent need to increase investment in production. So there was; box-office returns had fallen very substantially. More money, then, was allocated to productions, starting with the final production of the 1981–2 season, Trevor Nunn's *All's Well that Ends Well*. This change of policy coincided with much better business in 1982.[14]

The government's insistence that the company pursue business sponsorship was a challenge that it rose to with great success, though the sponsorships that it gained did not seem to lessen the financial crises that dogged the RSC throughout the 1980s.[15] In the early 1990s there were a number of glitzy and popular productions of the early comedies (*The Comedy of Errors* (1990), *The Two Gentlemen of Verona* (1991)), which might be thought of as directed largely at the tourist trade; but they also had the beneficial effect of popularising Shakespeare for a new generation of school-children and student theatre-goers. Adrian Noble's new regime, beginning in 1991, had considerable achievements in these areas, and also produced some impressive work in the histories and the tragedies, and in non-Shakespearean plays at the Swan Theatre, but the women-centred comedies failed to spark. This situation is the culmination of the cultural process which I have tried to trace in this book.

WOMEN AND MEN IN THE PROFESSION

The result of institutionalisation as a 'flagship' of British culture is that the RSC has become the principal embodiment of the 'Shake-speare myth', the notion that 'Shakespeare' represents the spirit of England itself ('this precious jewel set in a silver sea'); that in his works all that is spiritually necessary for us is already spoken. This is clearly a dangerous situation, reinforcing the patriarchal status quo, for anyone – especially a woman – working in theatre with the hope of changing society for the better through theatre's play-ful transgression. It breeds an unconscious assumption that only patriarchal males can truly interpret the Shakespearean text (the priest and Bible syndrome) – a text which is already imbued with patriarchal attitudes which might more profitably be deconstructed. The RSC has offered work on its main stage to scandalously few women directors, considering its liberal credentials (though in this it is no worse than any other theatre company in England).[16] In an impassioned article in *Drama* (1984, 2) asking 'Why aren't there more women directors?' Margaret Sheehy wrote:

> If you want a career as a director in British theatre there is a definite advantage in being a man – an even better one for that matter, is being an Oxbridge educated man . . . .
>
> Directors mostly get on by receiving the patronage of older, more established directors who are less likely to identify with or to see themselves as the young woman assistant as they do the young man. This pattern is particularly obvious in the history of both the National Theatre and the RSC. Moreover, young women directors are likely to be given a much harder time than the young men. They are consistently offered high risk productions with small budgets and are forced to work under constricted conditions – in the studios and on tour. Of course this happens to men, too, but the evidence suggests that it goes on happening to women far longer and further into their careers.

Little has changed since this was written. It is only as some aspects of feminist thinking have been accepted into the general culture – mentioned, for instance, in the rhetoric of politicians – that attitudes have changed in theatrical practice so that it *almost* seems natural to engage a woman to direct a Shakespeare play. Fiona Shaw says of Deborah Warner, who has directed several plays for the RSC (but as yet no comedies), that for her women's issues are not particularly important: 'She comes under the heading of the generation after – who get it for nothing'.[17] Shaw herself in 1985 organised a forum at Stratford for women concerned with acting and directing Shakespeare – 'an inconclusive event which had more power in its symbolic value than its actuality . . . the best of what ensued may or may not be directly related' (letter to the author, January 1993).

The only woman director who has worked at Stratford on the main stage on a comedy in recent years is Di Trevis, whose 1988 *Much Ado About Nothing* was fairly comprehensively panned by the critics (but see my discussion of it in chapter 5). Trevis is consciously a feminist, and in a 1985 article she discussed illuminatingly the situation of women in the conventional theatre. She began her career as an actress:

> I . . . felt disgusted by the passivity of the actor, waiting to be chosen, wanting to please, trying not to offend. This appalling situation I felt in some ways echoed my experience of being a woman in the world. By being an actress I was being a woman *twice*.

She managed to make the move to directing at the Glasgow Citizens' Theatre:

> I knew I'd found my real career. I could only wonder why it had all taken so long. I could only wonder what many women in our decade were wondering: was it because of something personal, individual within me, or was it because I was a woman?
>
> (*Drama*, 4, 1985)

Conscious of these questions and others asked about her rare achievement, she approached her first commission for the RSC (the inevitable touring production), *The Taming of the Shrew*, as an attempt to 'examine the dual aspect of being player and character, of being a woman, and a woman paid to act a woman's role written by a man (albeit for a boy!), as well as more profound questions of whether power resides in gender or wealth or both'. Critics reported a 'good-humoured' production which made its point by using the play-within-a-play structure of the Induction, and showed the travelling players as exhausted refugees from the Napoleonic wars; at the end, said Robert Hewison, 'when the women revert to their subservient refugee roles, and Sian Thomas's sparky Kate is once more in rags with a baby at her breast . . . the implicit social criticism of the production is made clear' (*Sunday Times*, 13 October 1985). As Trevis's experience shows, making feminist sense of patriarchal play-texts within an organisation perhaps best described as paternalist is not easy.

Actresses since the early 1980s, also conscious of feminist thinking, have made the same complaint.[18] Two of the most vocal of them are Fiona Shaw and Juliet Stevenson, whose comments on roles they have played for the RSC can be found in the excellent and thought-provoking set of interviews by Carol Rutter, *Clamorous Voices* (1988), from which I quote gratefully in the following chapters.[19] In an earlier interview (*Plays & Players*, October 1987)

Juliet Stevenson spelt out the Shakespearean actress's particularly difficult situation:

> Nine times out of ten, women are in the minority in the rehearsal room. Quite often I've ended up being the only woman . . . . Most directors are men. Their experience and their world view is the one that's going to predominate but their experience does not correspond to your own if you're a woman. If there are areas in the play touching on your areas of life you know about as a woman, you will find yourself trying to justify the choices you want to make and battling for them; trying to explain or apologise for those choices even if it is unsettling for other people. Men have a far greater range of choices available to them and those choices are instantly recognisable because the director is male and his experience of life is similar.

And Fiona Shaw points to the implication not only of the director, but of the designer in this marginalisation of women: 'Images projected on stage tell us what to think about the women in the play. And about the women in the audience. What is a production saying about Portia if it puts her in blue chiffon and ribbons? How can we take seriously a woman who looks like that?'[20] (It is encouraging to see that Sinead Cusack as Katharina in 1982 at least managed to persuade her designer, Bob Crowley, that an elegant dress she'd been given was wrong for her conception of the character: they mutilated it together to get the 'right' look.)[21] The dominance of men in all areas of decision-making at Stratford, while it does no more than echo the general cultural situation, is the principal factor which must be taken into account when considering the production history of the women-centred plays of Shakespearean comedy. The actresses who perform these major roles must always feel outnumbered – patronised or disregarded – and respond at some level of their performance to this disempowerment, with submission, aggression, defensiveness, or irony.[22]

REVIEWERS, HISTORY, FASHION

'Any perception of a character's struggle to understand his or her own experience must be conditioned (and limited) by a reader's or a viewer's sense of the issues at hand', argues Philippa Kelly. 'A reader may tease out connotations and allusions in reading a text, whereas a playgoer simply does not have the time to disentangle manifold, abstruse meanings'.[23] The theatre critic is not a simple 'playgoer', nor is he (more rarely, she) usually an academic with a profound textual understanding of the play. He stands somewhere between these two positions, having probably seen most Shakespeare plays several times, and knowing them, from this perspective, better than most members of the general public.

The reviewer for the daily or weekly newspaper sees himself as a 'mediator' between the performance and the public, and between the audience and the performers (Benedict Nightingale, *Plays & Players*, July 1982). However, these are inevitably partial judgements, influenced by the reviewer's age, class, education, gender, sexuality, political views, and previous experience of the play. Much of the evidence about the style and effect of specific productions in this book is drawn from newspaper reviews; the theatre historian has to learn to read between the lines, sifting and analysing agreements and disagreements among the critics, searching for the sub-text. This is particularly important for the feminist historian, who needs to be aware, as Lyn Gardner points out, that

> the Fleet Street Cosa Nostra exerts considerable power and influence: not only do they fill or darken theatres but they are also the arbiters of 'good' theatre. When the majority is male, it follows that even with the best will in the world, that [*sic*] the cultural climate is inevitably determined by their male perception.
>
> (*Plays & Players*, April 1986)

To this general awareness of criticism's male,[24] white, middle-class, Oxbridge-educated bias, one needs to add that Shakespeare is a special case. The 'Shakespeare myth' is always in operation, and as I have argued, male intellectuals tend to believe they have special access to the true meaning of Shakespeare's plays. The reviewer of a Shakespeare performance does not see himself as 'representative' of the audience, but as an educator of the audience. Frequently also, he is telling the director and actors what they ought to have done with the play – that is, he has a Platonic idea of the play ('a perfect *Twelfth Night* laid up for us in heaven'),[25] and he is irritated when a production fails to conform with this, or even to approach conformity. Related to this is the idea of a 'definitive' production, seen (usually) in the distant past, and adopted by that particular critic as a touchstone for all subsequent performances. But I suspect that if that critic were able to see the remembered production once again he would find it strangely dated (as one finds, for instance, old film and television versions of the plays dated, recognisably 'of their time', though they may contain fine performances). Undoubtedly they would still offer wonderfully moving performances (my own choice for revisiting would perhaps be John Barton's *Twelfth Night*, with the young Judi Dench's heartfelt Viola), but they would speak to a different world from ours (was Dench as resilient a Viola as we now expect our solo heroines to be? Isn't Malvolio a victim of class-structures, and not just as hilariously self-important as Donald Sinden made him?).

Nevertheless theatre reviews are of immense value, once we are alerted to the conventions under which they operate. Cary M. Mazer points out that 'even the worst theatre review speaks with the voice of its own time . . . a period's definitions permeate the way critics sum up their experience in the playhouse'.[26] And some are very illuminating indeed, both about details of the performance and about the meaning of the play at that time and in that place. Harold Hobson, critic of the *Sunday Times* for many years until 1976, though he had recognisable idiosyncrasies like any other critic, saw clearly from his retirement the political and historical significance of his job:

> The theatre is at all times socially relevant in that it is in general subservient to, or reflective of, the bases of power. It is towards realising this fact, and watching this process that the whole of my professional career has been devoted . . . .
>
> My theory of the theatre was such: that on each visit to the theatre something happens. Something happens to the critic's mind and heart and the thing becomes a sort of historical event, therefore my criticisms are records of how I feel at a particular play . . . they are the founding of a historical record more than the passing of a judgement. They're the narration of something that happened to me in the theatre rather than a judgement passed on the merits of the thing I was seeing.[27]

It is for the reasons implicit in Hobson's 'theory' that I have largely avoided referring to the surveys of a whole season published annually in *Shakespeare Survey* and *Shakespeare Quarterly*. Useful though these are for an overview, they are already historical essays rather than the record of 'something that happened to me in the theatre'; and they are, of course, the views of academic Shakespeare scholars written for other scholars to read, rather than an immediate communication with a mass public (though here, as ever, one needs to be aware of who the 'public' is: readers of the *Guardian* differ from those of the *Daily Telegraph* in their expectations of theatre).

There is no criticism, no history, that is not written from a specific perspective and for a specific imagined audience; as a materialist feminist,[28] I am aware that 'gender' is not an isolated construct, but dependent on the matrix of discourses of nation, race, class, and age in which it is embedded. This is true both for the Shakespearean text and for its embodiment in any one production. Because 'Shakespearean comedy' foregrounds the fiction of 'the community' (both dubious but useful generalisations), productions of these plays offer an easily readable text of the dominant hopes and fears of the society to which they are presented; in this case, England in the second half of the twentieth century.

In the immediate post-war period, the euphoria of survival and the hope of renewed prosperity produced comedies – most notably the much-revived Gielgud *Much Ado About Nothing* – which were unashamedly aristocratic and elegant, in which no hard questions were asked about the structure of society, and actors and audiences alike revelled in material splendour. This period lasted right through the 1950s, barely touched by the modern theatrical revolutions represented by Brecht, Beckett and Osborne (what could *they* have to do with England's Bard?); but in 1960, as Peter Hall took over the fledgeling Royal Shakespeare Company and declared his first season to be dedicated to exploring 'the development of Shakespearean comedy', signals of intellectual adventurousness emerged. Hall was the first of the 'Cambridge connection' at Stratford: influenced by Leavis and George Rylands, he brought to Stratford the idea that there could be a sub-text to these light-hearted comedies, and that if it was to be found, it would be by careful attention to Shakespeare's language. Thus Shakespearean production became more reflective, more self-conscious, and ultimately more questioning, at the same time as Britain began to look seriously at restructuring itself and its social contract. The 1960s generation found a representative voice in the political activist Vanessa Redgrave's youthful Rosalind, barefoot and denim-capped; between performances she was a vocal presence at 'Ban the Bomb' rallies. Throughout the 1960s the RSC's apparent radicalism, particularly on the sexual front, increased: the play of desire was highlighted in the young Trevor Nunn's *Much Ado* of 1968. By 1974, with Peter Gill's bisexual *Twelfth Night*, sexual relations (indeed, all relations) had been problematised as a narcissistic generation looked anxiously to R.D. Laing and other gurus to resolve its doubts of identity. Feminism was beginning to challenge entrenched gender roles, both inside and outside the theatre: Bogdanov's daring exposé of the power-abuse of a capitalist patriarchy in his 1978 *Shrew* only lacked an empowered Kate. Other productions in the 1970s and 1980s occasionally allowed strong feminist actresses to make their mark on Shakespearean comedy, where earlier their roles had been contained by a male notion of the feminine. But the 1980s also brought the three terms of Thatcherism, and a corresponding pessimism from the ranks of left-liberal directors that 'the community' could ever be a positive fiction again. Dark (and often wintry) productions – Hands's 1983 *Twelfth Night*, Caird's 1989 *As You Like It* – reflected the grim state of the individual oppressed by the power games of monetarism.

These historical shifts are reflected – either consciously or reactively – in the performances of gender and sexuality, and of the idea of the community (its structuring via class, wealth, race), which audiences are willing to pay to see. The authority and continuity represented by the 'Shakespeare myth' make it easy for this transaction to take place; but productions only succeed in wooing and winning the audience if they tread the always-perilous path between boredom and outrage – and if they allow space for the unique power of the performer to work its magic.

THE EROTICS OF PERFORMANCE

'As I look back on fifty years of playgoing, I more often recall what the actor has done with the part than what the director has done with the play'.[29] There would be, I expect, few exceptions to Robert Speaight's observation among theatre-goers. Brook's *Midsummer Night's Dream*, Barton's *Love's Labours Lost*, and a few others among the comedies present themselves to the memory as an ensemble governed by a directorial concept, but those concepts would not remain in the mind if they had not been performed with panache, if the actors had not exerted their personal magnetism to their utmost; if they had not, in short, seduced the audience into passionate attention.[30] We go to the theatre for many reasons; but I suggest that those who go for something more than a mere social outing are there hoping to experience yet again the magical attraction of human beings enacting a story which momentarily fulfils their fantasies of transgression.[31]

It is not simply a matter of voyeurism but of a particular circulation of erotic energy between actors and audience:

> Presence, as the word suggests, has to do with being totally present in the moment – we spend much of our time as human beings living in the past or the future. The actor fills the moment, and his or her energy radiates out into space to draw in the audience with the power of the magnetic field set up .... This energy, this life force which the actor brings to performance, is partly rooted in sexual energy and owes some of its chemical attraction to that. There is an animal quality about powerful acting. There is an omnivorous voraciousness about it, a territoriality that claims all space and consumes all within its reach.[32]

Shakespeare's comedies, more than any other group of his plays, offer the actress the potential to put forth this extraordinary transgressive energy, to assume power, whatever the ultimate containing pattern of the play might be. In particular, these plays are fascinated by the possibilities of sexual transgression, which is euphemised as temporary transgression of the codes of gender. As Stephen Greenblatt argues, Shakespearean comedy

> constantly appeals to the body and in particular to sexuality as the heart of its theatrical magic .... More than any of his contemporaries, Shakespeare discovered how to use the erotic power that the theatre could appropriate, how to generate plots that would not block or ignore this power but draw it out, develop it, return it with interest, as it were, to the audience.[33]

The plot centres on romantic love, thus allowing an 'innocent' reading for more repressed times (such as the Victorian age or the 1950s); but what really activates it is the circulation of desire among all the characters. Desire is amoral, sometimes benign, sometimes destructive, always going at full tilt to engage, confuse and delight the audience. Like Orlando, we would – if we had time in the bustle of the plot and the excess of linguistic riches – stop and ask ourselves, which do we fancy more, Rosalind or Ganymede? Does it matter? The pleasure of the actor's multi-gendered presence (for that safe, enclosed moment of performance time) is delicious.

The fact that we are no longer obliged by theatrical convention to watch adolescent boys playing Shakespeare's female roles is one of the imponderable differences between ourselves and the audience for whom Shakespeare wrote, whatever its constitution may have been. Instead, in the latter half of the twentieth century, we are invited to contemplate a changing image of 'woman', for whom a refusal of the codes of femininity offers exciting possibilities for the liberation of physical, psychic and erotic energy. But whether the heroines' transvestism or other disguise (nun's habit, shrew's habits) is protective, evasive, empowering, or simply a game depends on the perceived relation between women and the patriarchy at the moment of the play's embodiment.

1

TWELFTH NIGHT
Desire and its discontents

Twelfth Night's alternative title is *What You Will*. What's in a name? we might ask with Juliet. A parent's impulse to play? In Will Shakespeare's 'romantic comedies' *will* – meaning, for the Elizabethans, both the assertion of power and sexual desire[1] – is the principal concern of the characters and motivator of the plot. *Twelfth Night*, in particular, offers multiple images of 'the mobility of desire'[2] – a theme which was taken up enthusiastically in performance in response to the 'sexual revolution' of the 1960s and 1970s, but was increasingly sidestepped in the more conservative atmosphere of the 1980s.

In performances of the last fifty years, the figure of Malvolio – 'ill-will' – begins as that of the traditional puritanical killjoy, denying 'cakes and ale' to the drunken Sir Toby, but develops into a disturbing image of the madman who cannot reconcile his sexual fantasies and the realities of his class position. Gender, in this play, becomes an ever more unstable mask: Orsino and Olivia behave increasingly 'improperly' as the play's interest in the fluidity of sexuality is explored in performance. Viola always exists in the margins between genders: claiming first that she will present herself as 'an eunuch' to Orsino, she is called by him 'boy', wooed by Olivia who thinks she is male (or thinks she thinks so), and never herself changes out of her male costume once she assumes it after I.2. That she has an identical twin in the male Sebastian is of course a biological impossibility: it is a fantasy of desire undifferentiated, uncontrolled by the constraints of gender: the play 'enables not only the fantasy that one need not choose between a homosexual and a heterosexual bond but that one need not become either male or female, that one can be both Viola and Sebastian, both maid and man.'[3]

17

The 'play' of desire in *Twelfth Night* is a game for leisured people, not for those who must work for their living (here again Viola's position is liminal – the role she takes on is that of a page-boy who will grow up to be a leisured aristocrat). Hence the impropriety of Malvolio's fantasies about Olivia in her day-bed, and the play's lack of interest in the precise nature of the relation between Maria and Sir Toby. But it might be argued that as an audience we are, for the moment, the equivalent of 'leisured gentry', and that we watch the behaviours of Orsino, Viola, and Olivia in love with an empathetic interest. The *mise-en-scène* of the performance mediates our reading of their behaviour: though the actors may wear Elizabethan or Caroline costumes, they will behave more, or less, 'historically' according to subtle choices made by director and designer, and the audience will feel with varying force the relevance of the performance to their own lives. *Twelfth Night* is (with *The Taming of the Shrew*) particularly prone to the sort of production which induces nostalgia for 'merry England' – its aristocracy gracious and unthreatening, its comic roisterers devoted to the cakes and ale of traditional Christmas festivity. It is easy enough for directors and even actors to avoid the questions about sexuality and gender which its narrative proposes.

1947–60

In the first post-war production (1947) of *Twelfth Night* at the Shakespeare Memorial Theatre, directed by Walter Hudd, who also played Malvolio, the *Guardian* reviewer observed a 'most notable abatement of traditional burlesque' in Hudd's performance of the role: 'he emerges, like one of Meredith's tragic comedians, as betrayed by what is false within as well as by the machinations of Maria' (26 April 1947). Ruth Ellis commented that he portrayed a

cranky, crotchety creature, 'sick of self-love' indeed, but without the inward looking eye, the sepulchral voice and the almost tragic megalomania that some actors give the part. The last exit is not a stormy curse but a creeping away of a man somewhat restored by Olivia's petting.

(*Stratford Herald*, 25 April 1947)

Another (unidentified) comment in the cuttings book records,

The scene behind the grill is too painful for comedy nowadays, but that is not Mr Hudd's fault, and he plays so well that when we arrive at his final outburst . . . we feel ourselves to be included in the condemnation, for did not we, too, laugh at his discomfiture in the garden?

Arguably these critics are recognising a nascent attempt to portray Malvolio as though he were part of a social context, not just the stereotypical killjoy of light comedy. The Sir Toby (John Blatchley), was also considered to be less gross than usual, and the same fresh impulse may be recognised in the casting of the 19-year-old Daphne Slater as Olivia: according to the *Guardian* 'less the madonna and grand lady [of tradition] than the impulsive and warm-hearted girl, both in her eager wooing of Cesario and in her natural and unforced concern for the bemused Malvolio turned fantastic.' Ruth Ellis thought her 'an endearingly foolish little wench, enjoying grief, petulantly put out by Cesario's indifference'. These are notes that will re-emerge over a decade later,[4] in Peter Hall's first production; and it leads one to think that had artistic director Barry Jackson been encouraged to stay on at Stratford, instead of being hounded out by the local establishment, there might well have been a Royal Shakespeare Company, doing genuinely innovative work, from the beginning of the 1950s.

The most strikingly unconventional casting was that of Viola – the 44-year-old Beatrix Lehmann. Since her debut in 1924, she had made her name as an actress of modern 'strong' roles, those of Tennessee Williams, for instance. She became president of Actors' Equity in 1945. Lehmann had not played Shakespeare professionally until this Stratford season, when her roles were Portia, Isabella, Viola, and the Nurse in *Romeo and Juliet*. She was a strong-chinned, short-haired, modern-looking woman despite the Caroline costume for Cesario (photographs give the impression that she looked more 'masculine' than Sebastian, which opens up charming possibilities in the cross-gender comedy). The critics were surprised, but pleased:

> One may say of Miss Lehmann that her Cesario is every inch a man . . . . If you will put by any preference for the openly wistful, Miss Lehmann seems here superlatively well cast and well spoken: here may be the nearest thing to the Violas that Shakespeare saw since the part ceased to be played by boys of flesh and blood.
>
> (*Guardian*, 26 April 1947)

19

('*Every* inch a man'? This delightfully naive response, relying as it does on outward signs of gender, has already been deconstructed by Viola's 'A little thing would make me tell them how much I lack of a man' (III.4).)

> she laughs at Olivia more readily than she sighs for Orsino, and would obviously have much pleasure in trouncing Sir Andrew if the text allowed. She greets her brother with cool, sisterly affection, and the betrothal to the Duke seems a comfortable settlement rather than the realisation of the heart's desire.
>
> (Ruth Ellis)

This was a production not intent on foregrounding sexual confusion, but confidently presenting an image of the emotionally-independent, self-reliant, and rather interestingly 'masculine' woman whom the social disruptions of the Second World War had brought into being. At the same time it reasserted, through the marriages and the ultimately unthreatening Malvolio–Olivia axis, an ideal of a mutually interdependent (though still strongly hierarchical) community able to heal itself and to find a place for all types and conditions of people in the post-war world.

The famous Shakespeare Memorial Theatre production of *Twelfth Night* in 1955, directed by Sir John Gielgud and starring Laurence Olivier and Vivien Leigh, came after a gap of eight years in the SMT production record – the longest gap recorded between twentieth-century productions at Stratford (before or after this date). The new production was clearly intended as an indicator of a confident, newly self-indulgent society, for whom the austerity of the war was now thankfully past.

The design, by 25-year-old Malcolm Pride, was 'particularly pretty', according to Philip Hope-Wallace: 'settings which suggest a Persian court as an Italian old master might have imagined it' (*Manchester Guardian*, 13 April 1955). Other reviewers confirmed this impression of luxury – a world in which there is no poverty or distress, and very little social or erotic unease: 'Always there were within the proscenium arch rich pictures of Shakespeare's dream country, Illyria' (*Wolverhampton Express and Star*, 13 April 1955). There were, as was still usual in the 1950s, two intervals, and much set-changing between scenes – to the relief of some critics, who avowed themselves bored with the 'fetish' of the single set, which was obviously thought of as a sign of austerity rather than an attempt (beginning in advanced theatrical practice after the First World War) to approximate the swift and uncluttered pace of Elizabethan production.

Keith Michell's Orsino was heavily made-up, coiffed, and be-jewelled – a 1950s image of the 'Renaissance prince' – and his acting style was swaggeringly romantic. We may safely say this was an Orsino who never doubted his sexuality. Similarly, most reviewers commmented approvingly on the warm 'femininity' of Maxine Audley's Olivia: no questioning *her* maturity or good sense. In this Gielgud and his actress were simply following tradition: Trewin and Sprague point out that Olivia 'used to be a stately Countess. In London, earlier in the century, one reason for this was the average age of the leading actresses. It was a more mature theatre world than today's, and Olivia could never have been allotted to the company's *ingénue*'.[5] Or at least, not unless it was in a company directed by the always unconventional Barry Jackson, as was the case in 1947.

Most critical attention was paid to the star couple, Laurence Olivier and Vivien Leigh, as Malvolio and Viola. Leigh had done little Shakespeare previously, and Olivier came fresh to Malvolio. Olivier showed the virtuosity that the world expected of him in the role: at one point he leapt onto a sundial; he cut capers; he 'exchange[d] doubts, through winks and grimaces [at the audience] on the correct pronunciation of "slough"' (*Leamington Spa Courier*, 15 April 1955) – he may indeed have invented this business, commonly used in more recent productions. Almost all critics remarked, beyond the virtuosity, a new interpretation of the role. It began with the costume, that of a respectable Puritan steward (contrasting the Spanish grandee look favoured by earlier actors): a realistic class perception here enters the production. Gielgud, who felt that 'somehow the production did not work' ('partly because of the scenery, which was too far up-stage'), commented that 'Olivier was set on playing Malvolio in his own particular, rather extravagant way . . . he played the earlier scenes like a Jewish hairdresser, with a lisp and an extraordinary accent'.[6] Michael Billington remembers him as 'a bumptious arriviste with a faintly Hebraic appearance and an insecurity over pronunciation';[7] Philip Hope-Wallace noted the 'wonderful costive voice which exactly expresses the touchy knowingness of the character and is a most refreshing change from the usual parade of crude self-esteem'.

Others saw him as far more sinned against than sinning: 'not . . . a pompous bore but . . . a tight-lipped effeminate Shylock with an inferiority complex' (Ronald Barker, *Plays & Players*, June 1955). Perhaps Olivier's choice of a Jewish and 'effeminate' persona was playing subconsciously on collective guilt about England's pre-war complacency regarding the Nazis' brutalities; Barker goes on to remark, '*The Merchant of Venice* presented in this light would be a revaluation [*sic*: for "revelation"?]'.

Reinforcing this sense of vague discomfort about Malvolio, the reviewer of the *Coventry Evening Telegraph* (13 April 1955) found himself 'disturbed' by Malvolio's last scene: 'it may be said to stand outside the dimension of the play'. This critic is evidently working with the old assumption of uncomplicated romance and fun in the play; others were more aware of Olivier's revolutionary effect on the role:

> it remains a terrible thing to see a man stripped of the image of his dream uttering futile threats of revenge at the end. At the same time, Sir Laurence does not make the mistake of over-shadowing the play. His Malvolio is not a tragic figure.
>
> (Ruth Ellis, *Stratford Herald*, 14 April 1955)

Olivier's performance, even more emphatically than Hudd's, brought a disturbing realism to moments in the play, though his extra-ordinary comic inventiveness at other moments worked against this.

If Olivier's Malvolio reflected contemporary unease about judgments based on class and race distinctions, and thereby influenced all major actors of the role up to the present day, Vivien Leigh's Viola was of the moment only. Dressed in a 1950s interpretation of an Elizabethan boy's suit, wasp-waisted, with the bosom clearly outlined, she looked at all times uncomplicatedly 'feminine'. This is not to say that she acted incompetently as Cesario, but rather that she was untroubled by the ambiguity of the role: 'She may some-times suggest the modern miss in jeans, but she is never really out of period' (*The Stage*, 14 May 1955). On the other hand, the 'modern miss' of the 1950s liked to get into a nice frock for formal occasions – which is what Leigh did for the curtain calls, wearing a full evening gown, with jewels and tiara, a cross between the 1950s 'New Look' and Queen Elizabeth I. Philip Hope-Wallace wanted Leigh's Viola to be more old-fashioned: struck, as most critics were, by her air of cool confidence, he was surprised that 'this Viola does not change her mood back to frightened femininity when she is

lone and can drop the facade' – that is, when she could have shown
he audience the 'real woman'. The critic of the *Daily Worker* (15
April 1955) also found something wanting in Leigh's restrained,
beautifully-spoken performance: Viola, he said, should be 'a be-
wildered, even tormented creature. Miss Leigh was about as be-
wildered as a practised society hostess giving a successful party';
and from the other end of the political spectrum the *Spectator*'s
critic made the same complaint: he wanted 'warmth, uncertainty, a
capacity for being embarrassed' (22 April 1955). 'Embarrassment'
s an ambiguous condition, and the critics' desire to see it in a female
protagonist may reflect their own discomfort with a changing image
of woman. 'Retreats into maidenly frailty were not for her', said the
Leamington Spa Courier (15 April 1955): and a good thing too, one
might reply – audiences did not need to have their most reactionary
fantasies reinforced.

Gielgud's production was followed in 1958 by the young Peter
Hall's, a reading (revived in 1960) which many found 'definitive'.
Hall, with his designer Lila de Nobili, had sought for and found the
'dark side' of this comedy: the visual tone was autumnal, the
costumes Caroline rather than Elizabethan, the whole had a 'faint
air of over-lushness' (*New Statesman and Nation*, 28 May 1960).
Clearly, for Hall, the 1950s dream of a brave new world had faded.
Max Adrian, the Feste, an ageing Pierrot,

> set the tone of the production: of comedy become wistful and
> enervated, of the lyric falling into the decadent, of jokes on the
> edge of turning sour. It was not for nothing that every scene
> was played through a filter of gauze drops; the play, too, came
> across as darkened and unexpectedly serious.[8]
>
> (*New Statesman*)

Various critics disliked what they called the production's 'modern-
ism': John Wain launched a typical diatribe; bemoaning the 'neurotic'
approach of modern actors, he complained with heavy irony:

> Malvolio in his dungeon was allowed to give us ten minutes of
> pure tragedy, complete with hysterical laughter, anguished
> groaning and broken appeals for pity. Feste, singing his final
> song, had to break down and sob in case anyone had missed
> the point that his character was meant to be rather sombre.
>
> (*Observer*, 27 April 1958)

His final complaint that Sir Andrew was played as 'a paranoid manic-depressive, strongly reminiscent at times of Lucky in "Waiting for Godot"' would no doubt have delighted Hall, who had been the director of the first English production of *Waiting for Godot* three years earlier; under his direction, cross-fertilisation from contemporary drama and theatre became an important part of the agenda of the Royal Shakespeare Company. Another critic, commenting on Max Adrian's Feste, was more favourably impressed with this contemporary flavour:

> it would be possible to make a case for Feste as the ancestor of the modern anti-hero – a resounding tinkler, a caretaker, a mad mother all rolled into one . . . . In fact, Feste is much the most interesting character in the comedy; he provides in his own person the interplay of light and shadow which makes it memorable.
>
> (Alan Pryce-Jones, *Observer*, 22 May 1960)

The most controversial 'modern' aspect of Hall's production was the playing of Geraldine McEwan as Olivia. In earlier reviews – and here the Gielgud 1955 production was typical (where Hudd's of 1947 was not) – Olivia would barely rate a mention, and then it was simply to congratulate the actress in question on her 'warmly feminine' performance. But McEwan, encouraged by Hall, put a bombshell under the role, to the great delight of the more open-minded critics. J.C.Trewin wrote:

> the susceptible *poseuse* . . . has needed a candid performance . . . . This pouting doll, this gawky, giggling coquette with the voice that crackles and squeaks . . . [T]he verse is utterly lost . . . [but] Olivia needed this exposure.
>
> (*Birmingham Post*, 23 April 1958)

What Hall achieved by putting McEwan into the part was the sexualizing of Olivia – and that, of course, has a ripple effect on the rest of the play's dealings with sexuality. The relation between Olivia and Viola now becomes genuinely interesting to the audience, providing a *frisson* of unorthodox sexual play which is recorded in Felix Barker's comment: 'this pert puck-faced girl pouted, smirked, simpered and bit her lip as she pined for the disguised Viola' (*Evening News*, 23 April 1958). *The Times* (23 April 1958) commented that this Olivia is 'a little amused at Viola's earnestness and a little amused also at her own surprising response to it.' In a similar vein her response to Sebastian seems to have provided a precedent for all later Olivias: 'Her exclamation of "Most wonder-ful!" when at the end she saw *two* Sebastians – two handsome husbands for the price of one! brought down the house' (Barker).

Of course there were objections from the traditionalists: *The Stage* (24 April 1958), invoking its Platonic ideals, said that McEwan was 'totally foreign to the character of this dignified, melancholy lady'. John Wain, again signalling his consciousness of the pervasive effect of a lively contemporary theatre, said that the first dialogue between Olivia and Viola sounded 'as if it had been written by Tennessee Williams' instead of being 'spoken quite simply'. Obviously a sexually-aware Olivia was 'not Shakespeare' for some members of the audience. Yet McEwan spoke only Shakespeare's lines.

M. St Clare Byrne, an academic critic reviewing the whole 1957–8 season, also had her own ideas about the play's proper style and meaning, and took Peter Hall to task for

> an Olivia socially demoted from the Elizabethan great lady to the Jacobean citizen-heiress, with the coquettish airs and urban graces of upstart rank . . . . [It] adds up to a general impression that though it was brilliantly done it was produced right against the grain of the play. It belonged to another world, another convention. Sophistication and the romantic mood do not take kindly to each other.[9]

This critic may have hit upon a more sustainable objection to the production, that its 'modern' conception of Olivia was out of kilter with a style that was otherwise darkly beautiful and nostalgic. Certainly Dorothy Tutin's Viola required little comment from the critics: universally admired for her wit and charm – she won the Evening Standard Drama Award for this performance – photo-graphs show her looking very 'feminine' as the page-boy Cesario (plate 1). Tutin is a small woman; in her Cavalier satin and lace, and with shoulder-length hair, she looked very like Gainsborough's romanticisation of the Caroline period in 'The Blue Boy'. She presented an almost pre-pubertal character, thus to an extent desexualising Viola's equivocal presence in the play. Michael Billington remembers Tutin as 'the first cheeky and mischievous Viola that I ever saw' [10] – modern at least, this suggests, in her wry self-mockery, her sense of the ironies of the theatrical game she is playing. M. St Clare Byrne's assessment of her performance, while complimenting Tutin, indicates, however, the comfort that it gave to audiences who did not care for the notion of 'contemporary' Shakespeare:

> Dorothy Tutin's Viola was warm, eager and lyrical, touchingly young and boyish in her page's garb. The simplicity and sincerity of her playing probably comes nearer, in its total effect, to the Viola of the Shakespearean stage, than do performances of greater emotional depth.[11]

Contrast this use of the 'true Shakespearean' criterion with that of the comment on Beatrix Lehmann's admirable mannishness in 1947. Fashions in gender performance are as much subject to historical change as any other fashions.

Malvolio (Mark Dignam in 1958, Eric Porter in the 1960 revival) was played as a dignified civil servant, and as in Olivier's performance of the role, his humiliation was genuinely disturbing. But neither of these actors brought to the role even the *frisson* of sexual ambiguity that Olivier had. Derek Godfrey's Orsino similarly continued in the traditional unexploratory mould: 'He made a fine striding figure of a lover who would certainly have had the guts to do his own wooing with that persuasive voice' (Caryl Brahms, *Plays & Players*, July 1960).

T.C. Worsley summed up the moderate changes to tradition made by Hall's production: 'Mr Hall's solution is not to take the lovers half so seriously at one end of the comedy line and to cut down on the buffoonery at the other' (*Financial Times*, 20 December 1960). No new production was attempted at the SMT for six years: Hall's elegant autumnal show, with just a hint of modern irony and gender-disruption in the Viola–Olivia scenes, seems to have satisfied – or sated – the market.

1966–74

In 1966 Clifford Williams cast as Viola one of the great popular icons of the Swinging Sixties, Diana Rigg, whose high-camp adventures in television's *The Avengers* had imbued her with a strong aura of sublimated sexuality; as B.A. Young put it, somewhat patronisingly (forgetting perhaps that Rigg is a classically-trained actress who had, for instance, played a disturbingly tough Cordelia in Peter Brook's revolutionary *King Lear* of 1962): 'her rough-and-tumble experiences on television have made Diana Rigg into the ideal Viola – a big strapping principal boy with a gift for romance as

Plate 1 Geraldine McEwan as Olivia, Dorothy Tutin as Viola,
Twelfth Night, 1958, directed by Peter Hall.
Photograph: Angus McBean.

well as comedy' (*Financial Times*, 17 June 1966). Thus Rigg had already established in the public mind an image of a confident active woman who wore breeches with perfect ease; quite unembarrassed by her 'tightly-tailored behind'.[12] The contrast (plate 2) was with Ian Holm's tiny martinet Malvolio, affecting a 'phoney-genteel accent' and 'revealed mercilessly in hair-curlers' in II.3 (Hugh Leonard, *Plays & Players*, August 1966) – a male effeminized by his class-uncertainty in a house ruled by a young woman.

Rigg's sensual presence was matched on stage by Alan Howard's Orsino: Williams's production did for that role what Hall's did for Olivia (Estelle Kohler's Olivia in 1966 was coquettish and giggly, following McEwan's reading). The *Spectator*'s critic Hilary Spurling (a rare woman in the largely male camp of theatre journalists in the 1960s) was one of the few who recognised the significance of this, and her review deserves to be quoted extensively, for it illustrates a changing consciousness of *Twelfth Night*'s treatment of the body and desire:

> Orsino stands before a row of slender columns, listening in an attitude of conscious ecstasy – a rose in one outstretched hand . . . . Orsino is a prince of the Renaissance; and Clifford Williams's production is built round that assumption, which is perhaps why it has been received with such a notable lack of enthusiasm . . . . Part of the trouble is no doubt a sentimental disappointment. There is nothing fanciful about this particular Illyria: that severe colonnade, that gleaming floor, the tall, slim, sallow-featured gentlemen of Orsino's court, all belong specifically to the Italian High Renaissance . . . .
>
> Alan Howard's delivery of the famous first speech . . . shows a Renaissance delight in luxury and artifice. Also more than a hint, in his glistening eyes and sensuous lips, of Renaissance barbarity . . . .
>
> (*Spectator*, 24 June 1966)

Rehearsal pictures include some striking images of Orsino lying at full length on the floor, as if inviting 'Cesario', who first stands, then leans over him, to make love to him (the promptbook shows these moves remained).[13] Spurling reinforces this impression of barely-controlled eroticism:

> An aura of desire, narrowly and deliciously averted, hangs over all the scenes between Orsino and his 'dear lad', Viola/ Cesario. At one point, as his page, she undresses him, draws

28

Plate 2 Diana Rigg as Viola, Ian Holm as Malvolio,
Twelfth Night, 1966, directed by Clifford Williams.
Photograph: Tom Holte.

off his gloves, takes his hat and cloak, half-caressing, half-shrinking from the touch. For both, pleasure and pain are intensified by the role she plays as go-between in his formal courtship of Olivia.

Spurling's sense that the triangular relationship of Orsino–Viola–Olivia is 'the central ambiguity of this strangely ambiguous play' is supported by Alan Brien of the *Sunday Telegraph* (19 June 1966), who, if we read between the lines, perhaps would have wished it otherwise:

> all the males in Illyria seem besotted by an innocent, school-boyish affection for their own sex. Sir Andrew snuggles up to Brewster Mason's Sir Toby like an enormous, idiot dog, and even Norman Rodway's plump and business-like Feste is given to hugging his pals. In this matey dukedom, the disguised Viola's sheep's eyes for her boss no longer look suspiciously effeminate.

The bluff heartiness of Brien's voice represents perhaps the last cry of the old-fashioned reviewer determined to see an apolitical 'timeless' performance of the play. But Williams deliberately subverted such a naive stance by a conscious mixing of styles (including the high camp of Rigg's 'Emma Peel' television persona). The programme – the first such self-consciously 'literary' programme at Stratford – contained a number of quotations from Barber's *Shakespeare's Festive Comedy* (1959), which were embodied in the *commedia dell'arte* antics of the low-life characters, and Hugh Leonard reported:

> An ill-assorted bunch of fools, decadents, swingers, melancholics, time-servers and transvestites is dropped into the deep end to sink or swim in defiance not only of dramatic unity but of the guiding principles of the Royal Shakespeare Company. The immorality of it all is that the mixture succeeds.
>
> (*Plays & Players*, August 1966)

For all its world-tour fame and its many revivals, John Barton's acclaimed 1969 production was conservative by comparison with Williams's treatment of the play (and its audience); indeed, it looked back consciously to the emotional ambience of Hall's 1958–60 production.[14] Through his designer, Christopher Morley, and the associated lighting design (by John Bradley) and music and sound effects, Barton achieved a unity of tone that Williams's more disturbing production lacked. This was a subdued, late afternoon Elizabethan world, typified by Emrys James's Feste: a 'courtly jester, ageing now and wistfully wise' (John Barber, *Daily Telegraph*, 22 August 1969), whose music and snatches of song interpolated many points in the drama, as did the sounds of the sea (most notably under Orsino's opening speech and in the long pause before Viola and Sebastian started their duet of recognition).

The beautifully detailed naturalism of the two households' scenes was achieved with a minimum of setting, and all took place within a long narrow wickerwork 'hall' through which sunlight intermittently penetrated – beyond which could be imagined and heard the sea. Peter Roberts described the 'subtlety' of the design, suggesting that Barton and Morley had managed a unique combination of the nostalgically 'historical' and the generally 'poetic': 'At times exterior lighting transforms [the set] from a solid Tudor Chamber into a frail fairy-tale structure that looks as though it might float away on the next whiff of poetry' (*Plays & Players*, October 1970). Viola's arrival on the shores of Illyria, as a number of critics noted, gave the impression that she was arriving, through mists, in 'a dream tunnel, a journeying place of the mind' (Sheila Bannock, *Stratford Herald*, 29 August 1969). This slightly surreal aspect was also evident in the 'dark house' scene, when only Malvolio's head was seen, 'a talking head, desperately rolling its eyes' (Ronald Bryden, *Observer*, 24 August 1969). The resultant defusing of the cruelty of Malvolio's treatment was reinforced by the tricksters' obvious remorse by the end of the scene, as though they – we children all – had been caught indulging in sadistic fantasies.

It was a production with heart rather than sex or sensuality. Olivia (Lisa Harrow) was very young: according to Ronald Bryden (*Observer*, 9 August 1970) she found Viola/Cesario attractive because she/he had 'none of the adult danger and urgency of sex'. Judi Dench's acclaimed Viola responded with wonderful comic naivety to the various complications of her situation (the wildly athletic duel scene with Sir Andrew was the funniest I have ever seen); critics spoke of her 'sunniness', her 'untarnished freshness'. Nevertheless she also plumbed depths of emotion. 'She is never just a jaunty boy, she is desperately vulnerable and there are tremendous areas of great sadness in her although she is the catalyst in the play', was Dench's own assessment of the part,[15] and the critics agreed, noting particularly her effective use of the natural catch in her voice.

Her assumed persona was not a confident game, but a condition in which she was always in danger of discovery – from Valentine's friendly slap on the chest, or from Feste's knowingness. Her physical attraction to Charles Thomas's Orsino (another sensuous and self-indulgent Renaissance duke) was less openly expressed than Diana Rigg's, but it was seen in a memorable image from II.4: as Feste sang, mocking love's self-absorption, Orsino lay languishing on the ground; on a chair immediately behind him sat 'Cesario'. His arm was on her knee, her hand hovered near his shoulder – her desire to cradle this self-indulgent child in her arms was manifest (plate 3). As Harold Hobson remarked, 'Viola knows that for Orsino she is little more than a consolation prize' (*Christian Science Monitor*, 17 April 1971). This theme was repeated in the marriage of plain, middle-aged Maria to an ageing, somewhat subdued Sir Toby, and in the pathos of Sir Andrew's attempts to woo Olivia.

Stanley Wells concludes his finely detailed essay on this production with a summary with which it would be difficult to disagree: 'it is its beauty that I remember. Not especially – though partly – a visual beauty, but a beauty of communication, of sympathy, understanding, and compassion. It had a Chekhovian quality . . . '.[16] For many critics, indeed, Barton's production achieved a comforting benchmark status, eclipsing even Peter Hall's. Nevertheless the dissenting voice of the young playwright Simon Gray is instructive:

> Viola . . . is far too delightful to take advantage of Olivia or in any way embarrass the audience . . . . Shakespeare's Viola, in fact, is a much more knowing girl than Mr Barton's, much more complex, and consequently the comedy in her relationship with Olivia is both more intensely erotic and altogether more dangerous.
>
> (*New Statesman*, 28 August 1969)

Here the nostalgically 'Chekhovian' is implicitly contrasted with a *contemporary* reading of 'Shakespeare's Viola' as one who exists in a tougher world, where class-decorums no longer protect the young girl from knowledge of the potential dangers of sexuality.

In a similar 'Chekhovian' vein, Donald Sinden played Malvolio as a dignified steward whose comic qualities arose from his attempts to maintain his dignity, and who ended with pathos[17] rather than a threat to the future happiness of the dream lovers, who exited from the play at the back of the Alice-in-Wonderland tunnel, whereas the

Plate 3 Judi Dench as Viola, Charles Thomas as Orsino, *Twelfth Night*, 1969, directed by John Barton. Photograph: Morris Newcombe.

'everyday' characters left the stage nearer the audience, via the wings. It was a beautifully balanced production, but its theatrical impact was just a little remote from the present: 'Chekhovian' was indeed the *mot juste*, but only if we interpret that as 'English' Chekhov, stressing the mild melancholy, the sense of a society in gentle decay, the perceived need for tolerance of all human foibles. (That this may well be a cultural appropriation of the *Russian* Chekhov, we are only just beginning to recognise.) Both Chekhov and Shakespeare are reduced in potential transgressive power by this implicit claim that they are 'apolitical'.

Barton expounds his views on this matter in *Playing Shakespeare*:

> I believe that 'Contemporary Shakespeare' . . . is rarely justi-fied . . . . In performance it distorts Shakespeare more often than it illuminates him. It is usually a way of avoiding grappling with a problem of getting in touch with the play itself . . . . Shakespeare is timeless in the sense that he anatom-ises and understands what is in men and women in any age, and what he has to say is always true and real. It is this element that is truly contemporary and which the wise actor or director will try to bring out.[18]

Barton's essentialism ignores the fact that 'what is in men and women' is always a construct of the age – how it views gender, class, and sexuality – and of the individual's own perspective on these; in this case, that of a middle-aged male Cambridge don. A tendency towards a comfortingly quietist view of Shakespeare's text might perhaps be expected.

That could not be said of Barton's successor, Peter Gill's 1974 production, which confronted both actors and audience with the full range of ambiguities, psychological and sexual, to be found in the play as seen by a young director of the 1970s. The set (by Bill Dudley) was dominated by a huge picture of Narcissus on the back wall; on one of the front walls was scrawled in red chalk the message, 'learn to read what silent love hath writ'. Robert Cushman in the *Observer* (9 February 1975) noted the 'distinction between those characters who habitually turned themselves upstage and those – most notably Jane Lapotaire's Viola – who boldly addressed the audience, seeking a sounding-board rather than a mirror'. Irving Wardle explained: 'All are intoxicated with their own reflections, and the function of Viola and Sebastian is to put them through an Ovidian obstacle course from which they learn to turn away from

Plate 4 Jane Lapotaire as Viola, John Price as Orsino, *Twelfth Night*, 1974, directed by Peter Gill. Photograph: Joe Cocks Studio.

the mirror and form real attachments' (*The Times*, 23 August 1974). 'The emphasis is on the play's erotic metamorphoses, and this means underplaying the comedy', he continued. Frank Thornton's Sir Andrew was sad, and David Waller's Sir Toby a cynical bully: age – losing out in the sexual game – affected them both.

The young actors' bodies were much in evidence: the males (including 'Cesario') wore tights and short breeches; Orsino (John Price) was frequently seen barelegged and barefoot, in a loose gown, and as in the 1966 production he spent much of his time lolling on the floor, but now fondling whichever favourite happened to be closest in a conscious display of bisexuality (plate 4).[19] For Peter Thomson, Jane Lapotaire as Viola, tiny, with a boyish figure (no bosom at all evident under her open-necked shirt), 'backed up her director's concept by reaching the audience's bisexuality';[20] Wardle perceived her as 'a neutral androgynous presence, a blank screen on to which others project their fantasies'. Certainly this production, very much in tune with the sexual consciousness of the 1970s, insisted that the audience see the play as addressing contemporary issues – though by keeping the costume at least generally Renaissance in style, it made its claim also to be 'genuinely Shakespearean'. Michael Billington (*Guardian*, 6 February 1975) catalogued the disconcerting differences from Barton's 'classic' production:

> Orsino hugs Cesario to his breast with rapturous abandon; Antonio is plainly Sebastian's longtime boyfriend; and Viola all but tears her hair in anguish at Olivia's unfulfilled passion for her . . . the almost novelistic detail that characterised Barton's magnificent 1969 production is here totally lacking.

Billington's epithet 'novelistic' is indicative of the cultural comforts Barton's production offered: familiarity and an essentially private pleasure – not a public anatomy of the psyche of a society that might be contemporary. Other critics also signalled their preference for Barton; but for Peter Ansorge in *Plays & Players* (October 1974) Gill's production

> provided . . . a sense of innovation, of fresh attitudes and individual tastes – largely absent from my experiences at Stratford over the last couple of seasons . . . . [The production] is the first in my experience (which includes John Barton's famous version of two years ago) to show us exactly what kind of shape Illyria might take.

As with Barton, the production centred on an outstanding Viola, who made her mark with her first 'zestful' entrance rather than the usual doleful appearance. For Ansorge,

> Jane Lapotaire's Viola is a brilliant, white-costumed emblem for this self-enclosed, self-deceiving society . . . . This Viola is fondled, in turn, by both Orsino and Olivia delicately, softly, and treated as a kind of intellectual love object. There is no hint here of the kind of tom-boy tactics normally employed by our stage Violas in order to disguise the real nature of the role. This Viola accepts the double nature of her sexuality – yielding to Orsino's embraces as a page boy, even wanting to satisfy Olivia as a woman. Indeed both Jane Lapotaire as Viola and Mary Rutherford's Olivia are the aggressors in their relationships (at one point they turn angry, sterile circles of frustration on a darkening stage).

We note, in passing, a new essentialism to suit the new age: Ansorge talks of 'the real nature of the role' – an interpretation fuelled both by the 1970s post-censorship sexual revolution and by the increasing prominence of what was then called 'women's lib'. If Michael Billington missed the 'boyishly mischievous . . . Tutinesque manner', what he got instead was a 'perplexed' modern young woman, accepting and exploring her own sexuality.

A further deconstruction of conventional ideas of gender was effected by the playing of the young male roles: Ansorge reported 'It's Orsino and Robert Lloyd's Sebastian who are the more feminine, passive receivers of love (the latter weeps more tears on Antonio's shoulders than ever did this Viola on her Captain's after their shipwreck).' Gender is perceived as an unnecessary constraint on the fluidity of sexuality in the 'love-in' atmosphere of the 1970s. Even as the play ended, Orsino and Olivia each turned momentarily to the 'wrong' twin. 'Equally, Olivia is clearly delighted at the prospect of a ménage-à-quatre: doubleness adds piquancy to desire' (Ansorge). The play's ending resolved very little: the mysteries, delights, and confusions of human sexuality are – according to Gill – perennial, as is the self-induced misery of a Malvolio whose desires (both sexual and social) are for the impossible. Early in the piece, Olivia, an autocratic 'ice-princess', 'embracing Malvolio with Illyrian [i.e., 'narcissistic'] carelessness, unwittingly primes him for his downfall' (Robert Cushman, *Observer*, 9 February 1975); at the end, Nicol Williamson 'moves the house to heartbreak . . . by his delivery of his final unforgiving words through the hands with which he is covering his face in shame' (B.A. Young, *Financial Times*, 23 August 1974). For Wardle, he was

> an eternal outsider wearing the uniform of someone who belongs . . . . The garden scene, where he tortures the MOAI conundrum into experimental Welsh words, has an almost unbearable privacy. And his cross-gartering fits poignantly into the production's scheme as a planned metamorphosis that fails to work out.

This Welsh Puritan (or, according to Thomson, 'a pinched, Scottish elder of the kirk with the distorted sexual aspirations of the "unco' guid"') was in the same authoritarian mould as Ian Holm's Malvolio, but, a decade on in the sexual revolution, much more obviously disturbed by the indecorous antics of the young, and recognising in himself the same impulses, consumed finally with self-disgust. There was no reconciliation hinted at, no place to be found in this narcissistic world for one who is only a 'distorting mirror to [him]self', as the programme's quotations from pop-psychology guru R.D. Laing put it.

1979–87

The contemporaneity of Gill's production was also reflected in Ron Pember's Feste, the bearer of the production's political conscious-ness, who 'hinted always at a radical's social distaste for the antics of privilege . . . . He was discomforting, an outsider, almost male-volently saturnine . . . [he] sang his songs with the gritty voice of the modern unaccompanied folk-singer'.[21] Billington found him 'savage, sardonic, teeth-baring . . . rasping out his songs as if it were "The Threepenny Opera" . . . startlingly effective.' This deliberate, confrontational anachronicity was not a line to be followed by the next RSC production, by Terry Hands in 1979. Yet it had its own contemporaneity. Hands's university-trained interest in Shake-speare's comedies as structured on seasonal myth led him to place the play firmly in winter – the literal season of Twelfth Night – moving to early spring:

> The festive moment has passed, and this is now the cruellest point of the year. The old leaves are going to come off the trees, but the young ones are going to come through strongly,

and the oldies are going to be humiliated and lost. *But* you feel that the cycle will continue, the wind and the rain, that it will start all over again . . . . I saw it as a natural cycle, and within the womb of the sea.[22]

The wintry set and drab white and black costumes (vaguely Caroline, suggesting a band of refugees from the Civil War) was a design few critics liked: 'rather predictably schematic', said Sally Aire (*Plays & Players*, July 1979). Yet the visual symbolism spoke of a society on the edge of despair: with this production Hands and his designer in fact began the series of dark (not just comfortably melancholy) readings of the comedies of the 1980s, as the liberal-humanist establishment saw its moral power base undermined by Thatcherism.

John Napier's set was a deep snow-covered vista of 'bare ruined choirs'; much of the action took place at night, lit by a street lamp and hand-held lanterns. As the audience returned for the second half, they found the snow retreating, and in its place clumps of early spring daffodils and snowdrops. Indeed, those who returned early enough saw that the ragged, ill-looking Feste, who seemed to have the role of tutelary god in this production, was planting them. Feste was present on stage throughout the whole play – when not taking part in a scene, he was at the edge, watching, or with his back turned, simply a natural presence in the bare woodland set. (The programme carried, as well as a page of descriptions of Elizabethan Twelfth Night customs, a set of extracts from Enid Welsford on the wise Fool.) Despite the promise of spring, the play finally balanced hope with despair. Robert Cushman described the final scene: 'the stage gradually filling with seated, disillusioned figures: Andrew nursing his broken head, Toby subsiding beneath alcohol and marriage, Antonio lonely, the lovers apparently more oblivious by the minute' (*Observer*, 20 April 1980).

As for the lovers, Gill's ground-breaking insistence on their problematic sexuality was not ignored:

In Illyria love is a sudden and alarming affliction, a variety of glandular fever . . . . Antonio seems much more than ordinarily besotted with Sebastian, and Gareth Thomas's Orsino is not the usual droopy musicophage but a grizzled gentleman-pirate dangerously likely to succumb to his unpredictable impulses and cut a throat or two.

(Benedict Nightingale, *New Statesman*, 22 June 1979)

Kate Nicholls as Olivia, a tall jolly-hockey-sticks type, 'flirtatiously rubs up against Malvolio . . . and proceeds to astonish Cesario–Viola with the physical frankness of her unruly emotions . . . leaping at her, cuddling her, and pursuing her pellmell through the garden.' Nightingale's choice of pronoun is apt: Lunghi's Viola, even in disguise, looked more like Olivia than like Sebastian: both late-adolescent girls in a hothouse of emotion (plate 5). The *Daily Telegraph* (14 June 1979) considered that the two players of Olivia and Orsino 'firmly set the tone of sexual frustration as it can seldom have been set before.'

Cherie Lunghi's Viola, however, was for me (and others) most reminiscent in style of Judi Dench. She 'exudes an air of guileless innocence', said Sally Aire; like all the characters she is 'in search of an emotional wholeness . . . . She plays the role with a straight directness and childlike charm, but I missed the toughness Jane Lapotaire brought to the role five years ago'. Michael Billington corroborates:

> an exquisite mixture of fun and melancholy . . . For me the high spot of the evening is the moment when she shrouds Orsino in her cloak as they listen to Feste sing, and she gazes at her master with an enslaved intensity.
>
> (*Guardian*, 13 June 1979)

> Cherie Lunghi is a magical Viola: she actually listens to everything that is said to her and you can see her choking back a feminine fury at Orsino's blithe dismissal of women's love and discovering for herself that Olivia is filled with vain pride.
>
> (*Guardian*, 14 April 1980)

Lunghi, under Hands's direction, was clearly taking her place in a conservative tradition of femininity: the production's more disturbing aspects arose from the violently egoistic behaviour of the males. Hands's exploration of masculinity foreshadowed a decade of cultural fascination with the image of the aggressive, grasping male in high society ('Greed is Good', said its icon, Gordon Gekko of the 1987 film *Wall Street*). The production's interest in masculinity did not leave Malvolio untouched: John Woodvine, in the now-standard Puritan dress and 'insecure about his class origins', was, according to Billington's 1979 *Guardian* review,

> grotesquely funny; he emerges not just in yellow stockings but in a saffron body-stocking with bulging cod-piece which he

Plate 5 Kate Nicholls as Olivia, Cherie Lunghi as Viola, *Twelfth Night*, 1979, directed by Terry Hands. Photograph: Reg Wilson.

periodically flashes . . . . in its combination of downright lust and social panic, it is the best Malvolio since Sinden.

But as we have seen, Barton's production with Sinden downplayed 'lust': the word, in fact, belongs to the power-driven 1980s just as surely as Woodvine's slicked-back hair indicated the upwardly-mobile yuppies who were just arriving on the world scene. No amount of hopeful gesturing towards the seasonal cycle of renewal could obliterate this unpleasant sense of a world in which the sexes were brought together only on power-trips, and the old, the poor, and the dissident (Antonio) are brutally brushed aside.

Both new productions of *Twelfth Night* by the RSC in the 1980s demonstrated a strong directorial interpretation, and both may also be read as further reflecting the weariness and cynicism of Britain in the 1980s. Of John Caird's 1983 production, Victoria Radin asked,

> Will love come again, in the decadent, perverse world of Illyria, where tears are wasted on what one should not have? John Caird's production, a very contemporary one despite its turn-of-the-century look of Pre-Raphaelite medievalism, says that it's not so certain.
>
> (*Observer*, 24 April 1983)

Similarly Nicholas de Jongh: 'I cannot remember a *Twelfth Night* so steeped in an atmosphere of autumnal rejection, or one which shows so graphically people withering under the strain of hopeless love' (*Guardian*, 24 August 1984). These comments suggest that Caird viewed the play as an example of *fin-de-siècle* weariness (ours *and* Shakespeare's), in which the energy of desire that fuels 'romance' has been oppressed and dissipated. According to Sheridan Morley (*Plays & Players*, October 1984), 'this may not always have been a play about the impossibility of sex, but Mr Caird has successfully turned it into one about a group of exiles who can support anything except reality' – the reality being, presumably, the contemporary failure of romantic love.

Robin Don's single set, a reminiscence of Giorgione's 'La Tempesta' in russet, sand, and black shades, was dominated by a huge, twisted, bare-branched tree (lit strikingly by David Hersey), which had a 'transforming effect on the play', according to one member of the audience[23] – surprising in its insistence on the seriousness and transience of life, and on the state of permanent exile of the play's protagonists. Underscored by the sound effects of sea, wind, and rain, this emphasis put the Viola, Zoë Wanamaker, 'at a disadvantage in a show that reserves its main sympathy for the losers', said Wardle: she 'never takes over the emotional centre' (*The Times*, 21 April 1983). James Fenton saw her as 'concentrat[ing] on the sad truth of Viola's experience' (*Sunday Times*, 24 April 1983); John Barber remarked that she 'never even permits herself to look happy when she has won her duke' (*Daily Telegraph*, 21 April 1983). Wanamaker's own comments on this are instructive:

> Perhaps the problem was just being a woman in 1983: putting out a hand to say I am going to marry you seemed an anti-climax . . . . I don't think we ever resolved [the last scene's] complexity or found the play's real ending. But then came the clap of thunder that marked the end of our production, and the returning darkness, and Feste finding the ring on the tree and singing of the wind and the rain.[24]

As Morley asked, 'Is Olivia really going to be happy with a monosyllabic refugee like Sebastian? Is Orsino really going to settle down with a wife who was infinitely sexier when disguised as a man?' These are the questions of a modern perception of the (im)possibility of romance; but Morley also commented interestingly on the casting of Miles Anderson as Orsino (he had been seen recently as the RSC's Peter Pan): 'not the usual lovelorn prince but a grown-up Peter Pan, a character of strange obsessional love for men and women camped permanently outside the gate of a sinister never-never land' (*Plays & Players*, October 1984). Similarly, Zoë Wanamaker as Viola presented an urchin-like figure, no maternal Wendy in disguise. To refine the analogy, one might suggest that the huge wrought-iron one gate represented a closed-off Kensington Gardens, fantasised home of the rich and happy adults of the real world, whom these child-like sexual and social misfits will never meet.

Post hoc, Caird remarked that he hadn't wanted to

> try to give it a sort of generalised feeling of being light and airy and of how we are all going to have a good evening . . . . there is, if you examine the language of the play, an extra-ordinary prevalence of imagery to do with death, plague, pestilence, and hanging.[25]

Although I am not aware of any production of *Twelfth Night* in which the 'plague' of the 1980s, AIDS, is suggested, it is hard not to see in these 1988 comments of Caird's a hindsight about the possible disastrous consequences of the untrammelled desire so frenetically celebrated up to and including 1979. In Michael Billington's opinion, this *Twelfth Night* seemed to be more closely related to *Measure for Measure* or *Hamlet* than to the plays which preceded it:

> Zoë Wanamaker's spirited Viola marks the discovery of Olivia's love with a full-throated cry of panic and is palpably troubled by her own magnetic attractiveness.
>
> Emrys James's Malvolio . . . a finger-wagging tyrant who genuinely deserves putting down . . . whipping himself into a state of erotic fervour and brandishing Olivia's letter to the front stalls in sheer disbelief.
>
> (*Guardian*, 21 April 1983)

Wardle speaks of his final exit as 'no threat of revenge, simply an explosion of intolerable pain'. As in Hands's 1979 production, violence was endemic in the second half of the play – 'the Sir Topas scene is the ugliest I can remember', said Wardle; the duels were 'very extended and very violent', with 'vicious blows to the groin';[26] Sir Toby (John Thaw) was an ugly drunk.

Much the same tone pervaded Bill Alexander's 1987 production: the only major change was in the design, which moved from 1983's darkly romantic *capriccio* by Robin Don to the central square of a realistic Aegean village, the design of Kit Surrey. Alexander justified this by claiming that

> *Twelfth Night* is a very realistic play in the timbre of its dialogue, in the aspects of human behaviour that it's exploring, in the whole feel of it . . . you have to account for behaviour. You have to account for the relationship between love and madness in the play . . . [I did it] by setting the play in a hot country where the heat gets to people, but modifying the mood by using the different times of day.[27]

'There is a predominant sense of a place suitable for holiday madness and sexual escapade', was Michael Coveney's reading of the set (*Financial Times*, 8 July 1987). 'Suitable' it may have appeared, in terms of late twentieth-century holiday culture, but it raised immediate problems of credibility: why should Orsino and Olivia conduct their private lives in the main square of a small village – especially as they were dressed in rich folk-costume which indicated the existence of a social hierarchy (they were clearly not tourists)? Viola and Sebastian, the voyagers, were the only two characters who looked Elizabethan: Viola (Harriet Walter) a very boyish tall crop-haired redhead, with no yearnings towards femininity: 'gruff and gritty', Garry O'Connor in *Plays & Players* (September 1987) called her, and few other reviewers found anything very interesting in her performance of an awkward, melancholy Viola who seemed perpetually on the point of tears. Michael Billington was an exception, but even his praise suggests a fashionably marginalised Viola: 'she is less the cheery opportunist than a shy, sad boy–girl shooting soulful glances at Orsino. Miss Walter admirably suggests the melancholy underlying true ardour' (*Guardian*, 9 July 1987). Here we have another 'universal truth' – which the feisty Violas of earlier days would no doubt hotly deny. This Viola's emotion towards her brother was more evident than that towards Orsino; she wept bitterly in I.2; she and Sebastian were ecstatic mirror-images of each other as the last scene played out its denouements, having found each other like the babes in the wood in an alien country.

Donald Sumpter's Orsino was a balding, bad-tempered, middle-aged village tyrant – more like a bad stepfather to the lost Viola/ Cesario than a potential lover. There was no sexual chemistry between him and Viola, and correspondingly little eroticism in their scenes together, despite his near-nakedness (ascribed to insomnia) in II.4. 'It always amazes me,' said Michael Coveney, 'when contemporary productions miss out, as does this one, on the obvious sexual interplay of the cross-gender comedy'. Alexander, one might infer, found the alienation of his characters more engaging than their sexuality – the 'madness' of his formula privileged over the 'love'. Like Orsino, the melancholy imperious Olivia (Deborah Findlay) seemed not very interested in the boy-ambassador. In fact desire only had a place among the hangers-on of these rather glum gentry: Sir Toby (Roger Allam) was a youngish, good-looking, mellifluous drunk, who was clearly having an affair with Maria. (The cover of *Plays & Players* for August 1987 even showed the handsome Sir Toby attempting to flirt with a grumpy Cesario.) He was also casually brutal, as Caird's Toby had been: the left's image of the upper-class remnant at play. Billington noted that Sir Toby and Maria were 'sexually excited by the cruelty and the torture of Malvolio'. Bill Alexander explained: 'The comedy becomes a meaningless game if it's just a jolly come-uppance for Malvolio: it's not, it's viciously cruel, what they do, and part of cruelty is an excitement at seeing people suffer'.[28] Thus even desire, in this dark production, was corrupted into sadism.

Or into a self-regarding priapism – Malvolio (Antony Sher) was also well under middle-age: a young upstart in the community, costumed, rather oddly, as a Greek Orthodox priest. His display to Olivia was absolutely manic – he flashed not only a yellow codpiece, but long yellow pockets in his gown; his black Greek hat became a phallic yellow clown's cone: his capers, high kicks, and furious energy were typical of the extraordinary physicality audiences have come to expect from Sher in any role ('You can see he is totally enslaved by Olivia [not to mention Olivier]', Michael Billington wickedly but accurately remarked). A 'star' performance, which, for most reviewers, badly skewed the play:

> we end up responding to a performance rather than a char-acter. The Sher-isms are riveting, but rend the fabric of the play by turning Malvolio into a truly tragic character actually driven mad by the machinations of Toby and his callous crew.
> (Allen Robertson, *Time Out*, 15 July 1987)

Billington thought that Alexander saw the play as 'an escapist fantasy into which stark tragedy violently intrudes'; and Sheridan Morley sums up the general impression:

> a kind of holiday romp shot through with dark and scary moments when the sun suddenly goes behind a cloud and it gets unexpectedly chilly: there is no attempt to pretend that, even when all the partners do get sorted out into their correct sexes and couplings, the general happiness will last for much longer than the average summer romance, and we are left alone with Feste singing of the wind and the rain presumably somewhere well away from the offices of the local tourist board.
> (*Punch*, 22 July 1987)

Of the 'dark house' scene – played as a horrific bear-baiting – Garry O'Connor remarked, 'This cruel and juvenile scene is heavily underlined and goes a bit far, yet the actors can hardly be blamed for a current taste for violence as primitive as that in the play-wright's day'. In fact, what emerges from these 'dark' productions of *Twelfth Night* in the 1980s is a sense of the repression of desire, both in the *dramatis personae* and in the audience. Love is difficult (if it exists at all), sex is egoistic greed, laughter is cruel, and any beauty is fraught with melancholy or danger. By displacing the play from an imaginary Illyria to a realistic Aegean community, Bill Alexander offered a metaphor for the conservative and selfish society of the 1980s; but he was also, paradoxically, thereby putting up a barrier against the play's ability to titillate and disturb. He gave both actors and audience a structure which 'explains' – and restricts – the drama's *play*; in much the same way, Caird, by framing the play with a postmodernist appropriation of Renaissance painting, kept its effect within aesthetic limits. In each case the potential disruptive force of the play's protagonist, Viola, was marginalised, as the director signalled his determination to be a moralist for the 1980s.[29]

2

AS YOU LIKE IT
Who's who in the greenwood

Pretty pastoral or exploration of the dark recesses of the psyche? Or damning indictment of a power-hungry urban society? The conventions of pastoral, which Shakespeare drew on so extensively in *As You Like It*, allow for all these interpretive emphases, and more. The play's social framework is clear, but in commentaries it tends to take second place to the fantasy of transformation in the greenwood – self-sufficiency, sudden conversions, and above all, a marvellously fluid sexuality, independent of conventional gender signs and embodied in the image of the free woman in love, Rosalind. Recent critics have stressed the way the powerful fantasy of liberation, particularly sexual liberation, is contained by a reassertion of the patriarchal system, which is always there in the greenwood anyway (in a fantastically benign version) in the exiled Duke's 'court'. Rosalind's last two speeches in the play's narrative are a ritual of voluntary re-entry into the patriarchy:

> (*To the Duke*) To you I give myself, for I am yours.
> (*To Orlando*) To you I give myself, for I am yours.
> . . . I'll have no father, if you be not he.
> I'll have no husband, if you be not he.
>
> (V.4, 114–15, 120–1)

But as Valerie Traub argues, this submission does not take place until after Rosalind has led the play 'into a mode of desire neither heterosexual nor homoerotic, but both heterosexual *and* homoerotic'.[1] Her last line before the teasing epilogue is the provocative reminder to Phoebe: 'Nor e'er wed woman, if you be not she.'

Rosalind's elaborate courtship game with Orlando throws into question not only the regulation and organisation of desire, but also the construction of gender.[2] What *is* the proper behaviour for a

48

young woman in love? 'You have simply misused our sex in your love-prate', says Celia (IV.1, 189); yet Celia herself is of just such a 'coming-on disposition' when occasion finally arises in the person of Oliver – and so too is Phoebe, taking 'Ganymede's' outward signs of masculinity as a licence to desire. *As You Like It* effects, through Rosalind's behaviour, the most thorough deconstruction of patriarchy and its gender roles in the Shakespearean canon; yet it is a carnival licence allowed only in the magic space of the greenwood. At the end, all must return to the real world and its social constraints – though we can read Rosalind's epilogue as a liberating reminder of a world of alternative possibilities: is she/he finally boy or girl?[3] By comparison, *Twelfth Night* seems the more troubled and troubling play, since no exit from Illyria is implied for the characters, despite Feste's reminders to the audience of *their* real world.

Stephen Greenblatt comments that Rosalind belongs to 'a social system that marks out singularity, particularly in women, as prodigious, though the disciplining of singularity is most often represented in Shakespearean comedy as romantic choice, an act of free will, an expression of love.'[4] Greenblatt's second clause has been privileged over the first in the critics' response to Rosalind in performance: she is thought of as *society's* ideal young woman,[5] on the verge of marriage – and when an actress presents Rosalind's 'singularity' as disruptive of social norms, there is often considerable unease in the ranks of critics. The play's history at Stratford over the last forty years reflects most strongly our culture's fascination with this figure of the marriageable daughter; inevitably also it responds to a changing view of the nature of social bonds, in the depiction of the two Dukes' courts, and most notably in the figure of Jaques.

1952–57

The 1952 production by Glen Byam Shaw has all the hallmarks of post-war glamour that are typical of this period.[6] The lovers were the youthful and attractive Margaret Leighton and Laurence Harvey. The sets and costumes by Motley were elaborately pretty – 'the scene is France', the programme tells us – and had the look of tapestries from the court of Louis XIII, though some critics found the foliage 'sub-tropical'. The greensward extended beyond the proscenium arch, and included a fake rock-pool (33 years later the water would be real, a stream across the front of the stage, and much use would be made of it, from narcissism to ritual cleansing). Tellingly, the commonest critical epithet for Motley's greenwood was 'Neverland' – with Margaret Leighton clearly recognisable as Peter Pan; her boyish looks and figure made this a natural association (she played Ariel in the same season at Stratford). In Arden, she was comfortably dressed in a floppy shirt, breeches, and short jacket, and seemed quite at home in her role as commander of various Lost Boys (and girls). She was not reluctant to sit inelegantly on the ground, and many critics commented on her 'sprightliness', her vitality, her 'tomboyish fun and high spirits'. This quality in the performance was perceived by the critic of the *Western Daily Press* (1 May 1952):

> Livened by the sprightly personality of Margaret Leighton, this 'As You Like It' . . . bubbled up to an enchanting make-believe of Spring song. Miss Leighton was a gay deceiver of infectious spirit, boyish and girlish together in swift changing moods that rippled like a babbling brook through the still beauty of Motley's Arden.

Others, however, found all this energy somewhat exhausting, even unladylike:

> Perhaps Miss Leighton's interpretation would be even more satisfying if her apparently inexhaustible vitality were subjected to firmer control. Her gestures sometimes gave the impression of restlessness.
>
> (*Birmingham Post*, 1 May 1952)

> Margaret Leighton had taken her pattern of a boy from an attractive but underfed, over-excitable *gamin*, rather than from the sturdy English adolescent, who can be among the most beautiful of living creatures. She was, it is true, hampered by the clothes designed for Ganymede, for, in an effort to get away from the hackneyed (but becoming) doublet and hose, Motley provided her with an adaptation of the costume affected by girl cyclists on long, dusty tours. This scruffy attire could not obliterate the actress' great beauty, but 'heavenly Rosalind' was almost too well disguised.
>
> (Ruth Ellis, *Stratford Herald*, 2 May 1952)

Clearly there were some members of the audience who didn't care for the image of the modern young woman in her freedom-bestowing pedal-pushers. Another aspect of ladylikeness which Leighton flouted came under the heading of 'reserve' or 'poise'.

Philip Hope-Wallace thought that she 'ha[d] not the aristocratic sense of comedy of the greatest Rosalinds . . . she was obliged to work too hard, in order to save the play, to allow for many of those contrasts of silent happiness which can so well set off the raillery' (*Manchester Guardian*, 30 April 1952). Such vitality and independence might even bring on social disaster:

> If she conceives the part as Shakespeare wrote it, for an Elizabethan boy, her straddle-legged disguise as Ganymede looks right. If she supposes this Princess of Harden [*sic*] to be of courtly breeding, such inelegant posturing is of old-maid inclination.
>
> (Kenneth Pearson, *Manchester Daily Despatch*,
> 30 April 1952)

Perhaps the oddest of these observations from those who have seen the writing on the wall and realise, with fear, that the day of the dutiful, charming daughter is passing came from the critic of the *Sunday Times* (4 May 1952):

> Miss Leighton does not have that bubbling gaiety that Dame Edith Evans brought to the part. She is younger, sadder; she is paler, thinner; dressed as a boy, she is too short in the coat, too long and flimsy, frail and wasted in the leg. What an actress Miss Leighton would be, if only she could be persuaded to transfer her reverence for Stanislavski to steak-and-kidney pie!

It's the foreignness, the un-Englishness of this new image of women that is such a threat to conservative critics: the transatlantic girl bicyclist or androgynous French *gamine* look, lacking feminine curves; intellectual, even. The critics were of Margaret Leighton's parents' generation, and they were not reassured (though often, despite themselves, charmed) by what they saw.

Laurence Harvey's Orlando, on the other hand, was perfectly acceptable: adjectives such as handsome, sturdy, virile, manly and romantic were applied to him, and he was particularly congratulated on his wrestling. He was evidently secure about both his status (despite the play's opening scenes) and his sexuality. Did Leighton's Rosalind, however, perhaps find him a little dull? Ivor Brown reported that 'confronted with the double affection of Rosalind, love of Orlando in his simplicity and of her own wit in its complexity, [she] throws the more emphasis on the latter' (*Observer*, 4 May 1952).

Other aspects of the production brought general approval. Though *The Times* did not care to be shown 'Arden in winter', others welcomed the response to the text's suggestions that it was not always summer in an idealised pastoral greenwood (though the play did in fact move from winter through spring to final summer). Similarly an unusually 'chirpy' Celia (Siobhan McKenna), obviously responding to Leighton's spiritedness, brought enthusiastic comments, particularly as 'Miss McKenna controlled her performance with such tact that the competition was never serious' (*Birmingham Post*, 1 May 1952) – *she* remained a lady. Michael Hordern's Jaques was commended for his 'sad, gentle music' (*Western Daily Press*, 1 May 1952) in a generally admired performance of the conventional melancholic.

Five years later Byam Shaw undertook another production at Stratford, again with Motley as designers; the show was a vehicle for Peggy Ashcroft, then in her forty-ninth year (she had first played Rosalind in 1932 at the Old Vic). The blocking was much the same as in Shaw's earlier production; what was missing, however, was Margaret Leighton's energising sprightliness. Motley's designs did not help matters: still 'French' in general style, the period was moved back to the early sixteenth century; the costumes were heavy, the Forest of Arden was wintry, then very thinly clothed with obviously artificial leaves on Rosalind's arrival. Stage pictures were reminiscent of a Book of Hours, clear and uncluttered to the point of sparseness.

Reactions to Ashcroft's Rosalind were mixed. This star of the English stage was not just a lady, she was a Dame; she had royal approval. 'Triumphant' though many thought her performance to be,

> She could never be an arch young woman, a thigh-slapper. She is an actress whose gaiety is born of truth, and who can speak to us when she is silent . . . . She does not romp and rage . . .
> (J.C.T[rewin], *Birmingham Post*, 3 April 1957)

The fact that she went on on the first night with a throat infection may have exacerbated the general impression of this Rosalind's 'sadness', which 'overflows into almost every line she speaks, the result being that it is barely possible to believe in her love for Orlando' (R.B.M[arriot], *Stage*, 4 April 1957). Rosemary Ann Sisson found her 'gentle and affectionate rather than high-spirited, as befits a girl first in sorrow for her father's banishment, and later

Plate 6 Peggy Ashcroft as Rosalind, Richard Johnson as Orlando, *As You Like It*, 1957, directed by Glen Byam Shaw. Photograph: Tom Holte.

altogether overcome by love' (*Stratford Herald*, 5 May 1957). Plate 6 suggests a distinctly maternal quality in Ashcroft's representation.

Some critics expressed nostalgia for Margaret Leighton's bubbling youthfulness; others, and Dame Peggy herself, looked forward to her Imogen in the same season – 'a character worth at least a pair of Rosalinds', said J.C.Trewin in the *Illustrated London News* (13 April 1957). In fact, according to Michael Billington,

> Rosalind . . . has never been one of her favourite Shakespeare parts. It is amusing to find her writing to George Rylands in the course of rehearsal: 'Rosalind is a wonderful girl but I wish she didn't talk *quite* so much.'[7]

This sounds like the judgment of a 49-year-old woman on the behaviour of the young, and her envy of their irrepressible energy. Byam Shaw's attempt to regain the high ground of conservative theatrical practice by correcting the daring modernity of Leighton's Rosalind – replacing her with a mature 'star' – had missed its mark, receiving faint praise as 'safe, sensible, and good-natured' (*Birmingham Mail*, 3 April 1957). The tide had turned, and what critics wanted to see now was a Rosalind who, as well as displaying the familiar traits of warmth, tenderness, and humour, created the thrill of sexual readiness.

1961–73

Almost thirty years after Vanessa Redgrave's barefoot, denim-capped Rosalind stepped onto the Stratford stage, critics were still recalling her with wonder and delight. Julian Holland of the *Evening News* (5 July 1961) was one of several reviewers who declared themselves 'madly and desperately in love' with Redgrave, who at 24, tall and slim, had no need of heavy stage makeup to give her beauty. Overwhelmed critics attempted to convey the essence of her charismatic performance: it was 'sunny', 'luminous', 'radiant'. *Punch* managed a slightly more telling analysis:

> she is immensely natural, and her gentle mockery is always near the surface, so that even in the extravagance of adoration she is never mawkish. Of course she is an entirely modern Rosalind. She might be any of our daughters, bowled head over heels, and it is a pleasure to watch her.
>
> (Eric Keown, *Punch*, 12 July 1961)

Redgrave's 'modernity' was a matter of her personal style and presence. Her costume (by Richard Negri, as were the sets) was quite remarkably similar to that of Margaret Leighton nine years earlier – floppy shirt and breeches (called 'jeans' by some confused critics, just as Leighton's were), worn with an air of comfort and gaiety. Where Leighton was berated for sitting inelegantly on the ground, Redgrave's naturalness was expressed in her *lying* on the greensward next to Orlando, chatting animatedly, at times grabbing hold of him quite unselfconsciously (plate 7). 'Prone or supine, kneeling or crouching, hugging her knees, or flinging herself backwards before Orlando when in "a more coming-on disposition", she is exquisite,' said Felix Barker, (*Evening News*, 11 January 1962). Some critics thought her 'gawky', but to none of them did this seem a disadvantage; on the contrary,

> Miss Redgrave had the audience in the hollow of her hand. Perhaps it is not playing fair to Shakespeare to turn his Rosalind into a twentieth-century gamin, a fantasticated Bisto kid, a terror of the lower fifth. Miss Redgrave's Rosalind is like all these things. It may be, on the other hand, that 'As You Like It' has had to wait until the 1960s for someone to appreciate that this is what Rosalind is.
>
> (*Birmingham Mail*, 11 January 1962)

'She achieved something rare in acting – she was at once timeless and contemporary': Julian Holland's tribute to Redgrave's quality is typical of the critics' capitulation. No longer are they prescribing ladylike behaviour, describing their own ideal girl: they have been forced to recognise that the part of Rosalind is there to be filled out by an actress who can put into it her own sense of what it is to be a young woman 'fathom deep' in love. But she is also a character thrown on her own resources when exiled by an authoritarian state. It seems entirely appropriate that Redgrave, between the Stratford season and the London revival, became a political activist, for what she was demonstrating on the Stratford stage was literally 'actresses' liberation'.[8]

Michael Elliott's production was a breakthrough on many levels. A minor, but not insignificant, point was that the play had only one interval, rather than the two that were *de rigueur* at the time: going to the theatre was no longer quite so dominated by social considerations – rather, the audience members were expected to concentrate on the play for over an hour and a half before resuming

Plate 7 Vanessa Redgrave as Rosalind, Ian Bannen as Orlando,
As You Like It, 1961, directed by Michael Elliott.
Photograph: Angus McBean.

their social selves. The first half of the play took place in winter, the second in summer (the evocative lighting, by Richard Pilbrow, was much admired). For the first time, also, a 'movement director', Litz Pisk, was credited in the programme; many reviewers found this idea somewhat risible, but henceforward no production of a Shakespearean comedy would be complete without its dances. For both these developments the publication of C.L. Barber's *Shakespeare's Festive Comedy* in 1959 may have been partly responsible; by the later 1960s, Barber's influence was clearly acknowledged in Peter Hall's and other directors' work on the comedies.

Richard Negri's set was another departure from tradition: a single, stylised, huge tree placed on a steepish rising mound. The only changes were in lighting, props, and backcloth. Reviewers complained, not for the last time, about the lack of a forest, but by eschewing picturesqueness Elliott and Negri obliged the audience to concentrate on the characters' relationships and on the symbolic significance of the pastoral. 'At the opening', one critic pointed out, the director 'underlines the tension and violence which is often ignored as a mere prelude to the pastoral sweetness to come . . . the early scenes uncover moments of unexpected force' (*Leamington Spa Courier*, 7 July 1961). Similarly, life in the forest was not, for once, an unalloyed 'golden time': 'The lugubrious tone in which "This life is most jolly" is uttered suggests that most of the banished Duke's followers are thoroughly fed up with picnics and the pastoral life, and will welcome their return to court' (*Daily Telegraph*, 6 January 1962). Jaques was played by Max Adrian, whose wry, rueful, stylish performance emphasised the character's role as cynical commentator on pastoral fantasies; no longer could the actor of Jaques get away with being either slightly daffy or a sonorously venerable court philosopher. Most strikingly, the killing of the deer became a crucial symbolic set-piece which acted as a critique of naive pastoralism and affected the characterisation of the court-in-exile:

> By staging the stalking of the prey, its killing amid bestial cries from men momentarily turned to wolves, Mr Elliott gives point to Jaques' wincing – and suggests a reason for his melancholy, the old nightmare of the horns.
>
> (J.W. Lambert, *Sunday Times*, 9 July 1961)

Thus Elliott brought into question the 'naturally superior' attributes of the male on which a patriarchal social order is based.

This questioning of received ideas about masculinity was also evident in the Orlando of Ian Bannen, who had recently played a neurotic, slouching Hamlet. He at first eschewed the role of romantic hero, taking refuge in a self-burlesquing style. 'He is too complex a character to convey simplicity', said T.C. Worsley (*Financial Times*, 5 July 1961); and J.C. Trewin admitted unself-consciously that Bannen 'has not been my idea of Orlando. He is a lank figure with a weary eye, [looking] like someone from a contemporary novel who has lost his way in the forest' (*Birmingham Post*, 5 July 1961). This modernist consciousness allowed Bannen to explore a possibility in Orlando's character that has been generally ignored – a hint of bisexuality, which, according to Lambert, made him 'respond much more eagerly to the apparent boy than to the dream of the lost girl'. By the time the production moved to London, either Bannen had become more extrovert or the critics had adjusted their spectacles to the contemporary emotional world, for there were no further complaints about miscasting.

The final scene of the play focused on Rosalind, a shining image spotlighted in her white dress, surrounded by flickering torches and the dark night. The irradiating power of the young woman's personality was here most strikingly presented, a challenge to the darkness of the patriarchal system which the young couples are about to re-enter, and to the symbolic winter which inevitably will come again. The adjectives 'sunny', 'radiant', and so forth, describing Redgrave's presence, chimed with Michael Elliott's apparent intention to encourage the audience to receive, however subliminally, a symbolic reading, rather than just another lovely night in the theatre.

'Director's theatre' was underway, and *The Times*'s reviewer was canny enough to comment on it:

> Mr Elliott sees clearly into the double game that Shakespeare was playing. His production reflects both sides of it. We are made to feel both how pleasant it may be for courtiers to seek release from themselves in dreaming of Arcady in Arden, and how preposterous is their dream. Human nature in Arden is still human nature.
>
> (*The Times*, 11 January 1962)

This critic went on to commend Patrick Wymark's Touchstone, 'at the centre of the play . . . the natural gross man who blurts out in every crisis just those undesirable facts, even those touching his own affairs, which it is the whole object of romance to refine away.' In none of the previous productions had Touchstone had such an accolade (Wymark replaced Colin Blakely from the Stratford production), and his role as counterweight to Jaques – deflating the pastoral from a low-life perspective rather than that of the court – is increasingly emphasised hereafter. Elliott's production thus became the first theatrically self-conscious reading of the play, recognising the court-country opposition as a metaphor enabling exploration of the human psyche in its social construction.

In the next production at Stratford, directed by David Jones in 1967, the programme carried a number of quotations from literary critics on the role of Touchstone (and Elizabethan fools in general), and the contrasting figure, Jaques. Touchstone was played by the variety comedian Roy Kinnear. Critics were amazed at how funny Touchstone's tedious jokes could be when 'delivered straight across the footlights like a true clown' (B.A. Young, *Financial Times*, 16 June 1967), that is, acknowledging the theatrical pleasure available in a non-naturalistic reading of the part:

> It is very physical, but this suits well his wickedly accurate verbal timing . . . . He stresses Shakespeare's comic fool, the zany jester, the joker we've often longed for in the long procession of Touchstones with white faces and a secret grief up their motley.
>
> (Gareth Lloyd Evans, *Guardian*, 16 June 1967)

Alan Howard's Jaques more closely resembled this latter type, and developed the characterisation initiated by Max Adrian – 'sour-mouthed, pale and obviously motivated by a cynicism near to hatred' (Doreen Tanner, *Liverpool Post*, 3 October 1967); 'a white-faced, haunted apparition of walking pain, whose view of the world is amply justified by the Darwinian jungle of slaughter and mating he finds around him' (Ronald Bryden, *Observer*, 18 June 1967).

This *As You Like It* was the first Shakespeare production by the young David Jones, and he was keen to show his intellectual credentials; as well as passages from literary critics, the programme contained extracts from Jones's rehearsal notes – 'The forest only helps those who help themselves' – and a page of 'Sightlines', random quotations to help the audience 'read' the production correctly. Yet it struck Irving Wardle as merely 'a middling actors' show', that is, lacking in strong direction; he found in it 'echoes of past productions that take the place of original invention; quantities of awkward moves and a general uncertainty of comic tone' (*The Times*, 16 June 1967). It is possible that casting might have been at the root of the problem: the programme also contained a double-page photographic spread celebrating the fact that the Rosalind, Dorothy Tutin, was playing her tenth role for the RSC. It is hard to avoid the inference that the production was mounted as a star vehicle for Tutin, at that point 36 years old and presumably keen to do 'her' Rosalind on the national stage before she was much older. If this was the case, the intention backfired at several points: uncertain direction, a Rosalind 'in the shadow of Vanessa Redgrave' (Wardle), and a Celia, Janet Suzman, who in youth and vitality was a much more likely successor to Redgrave.

Reviewers were not uncomplimentary about Tutin's Rosalind, but the compliments tended to be on her technique rather than her presence; and her performance emphasised Rosalind's 'femininity' rather than a more modern complex sexuality:

> [Miss Tutin] never allowed her clothes to distract us from her basic femininity. Her gauche walk, the awkward movement of her hands into her trouser pockets, the timorous way in which she bunched a fist, were there to remind us that she was first and foremost a woman in love.
> (Milton Shulman, *Evening Standard*, 16 June 1967)

> Dorothy Tutin plays Rosalind in the disguise scenes with an air of bewildered self-mockery; her comic timing is superb, especially in her deliciously funny attempts to play the man.
> (Doreen Tanner, *Liverpool Post*, 3 October 1967)

Most striking is the extent to which Suzman's Celia is noticed: B.A. Young thought her 'just as gay and hoydenish as her cousin, and never retreating into nonentity as she so easily may', and Wardle found Celia 'an enchanting combination of self-mocking dignity and sheer fun, which redoubles the comic delight of the Rosalind scenes. If Oliver had arrived in the forest as soon as Orlando, Miss Suzman could clearly have conducted an equally brilliant courtship'.

Tutin's costume as Ganymede had a curiously old-fashioned air. Designed by Timothy O'Brien, it comprised boots, breeches, long-sleeved shirt, a fastened jerkin with loose belt, and a straw hat. Nothing except her hands and face was bare, in contrast to Redgrave's bare feet and short-sleeved shirt: the effect was of a buttoned-up, cautious woman in her mid-thirties rather than a very young woman exploring the freedom masculine (or 'unisex') dress could give her. When the inevitable happened and Janet Suzman took over the role in a revival of the production in the following year, her change of style was immediately obvious in her costume. She was barefoot, with an open-neck shirt, the sleeves rolled up, and an unbuttoned jerkin which was removed for some scenes, leaving the shirt loosely tucked into her breeches. Like Redgrave, she wore a soft worker's cap (which happened to be fashionable in the late 1960s). Suzman simply looked like a modern young woman, enjoying the freedom of her body and flirtatious games with an almost identically-dressed Orlando (Michael Williams, whose costume also loosened up between the 1967 and 1968 productions). Among the intelligent young, the production seemed to suggest, gender differences and the power-structures based on them were simply irrelevant.

The *Oxford Mail*'s critic noted the difference between Tutin's and Suzman's performances:

> Miss Tutin played Rosalind as a coy eager sixth-former wilting bashfully from the pangs of calf-love. Miss Suzman plays her – as she played Celia last year – as a young woman of enormous intelligence and sensitivity who falls head over heels in love. And not unnaturally her performance gives a tremendous lift to Michael Williams's warm-hearted, tousle-haired portrayal of Orlando.
>
> (Don Chapman, *Oxford Mail*, 22 May 1968)

A number of critics were happily reminded of Redgrave's performance; a few others found Suzman somewhat over-emphatic (were they still hoping for 'feminine' behaviour – from a young woman in 1968?). But all considered that she lightened a production which, in its revision, had become even darker.

> David Jones never once lets us forget the play's reliance on the disruptive yet sustaining natural world .... This Arden is black and cold; we first see the Duke and his compatriots shivering in sheep-coats, stamping upon the ground in order to forget the discomforts of exile. Jones makes a great deal of the deer-hunting scene which he transforms into a frightening ritual in which the men of Arden stain each other with blood.
>
> (Peter Ansorge, *Plays & Players*, July 1968)

Jones, like Elliott in 1962, but now more emphatically, seized the opportunities offered by the text to explore the values of 'masculinity' embedded in the patriarchy. He was to meet with critical resistance: B.A. Young complained, 'Surely Duke Frederick's orchard was not such an austere mausoleum of black slate last year, or the Forest of Arden such a land of perpetual night? This excessively dim ambience hardly suits such a happy comedy' (*Financial Times*, 22 May 1968). 'While agreeing that the play contrasts the romantic pastoral ideal with the sometimes harsh rural reality', wrote Michael Billington, 'one has to admit that there are reserves of gaiety and lyricism in the play that this production leaves untapped' (*The Times*, 22 May 1968). He went on to comment on Alan Howard's Jaques, a lynchpin of David Jones's directorial concept:

> [Howard] builds up a remarkably complete portrait of a diseased cynic, conceivably suffering from the pox and unable to look anyone squarely in the face. This reading turns the Seven Ages of Man speech, for example, from a mellow poetic recital into an expression of misanthropic disgust, but at times I feel the part can barely support the weight of the interpretation.

Jones's programme note told the audience that Jaques and Rosalind represent 'polar opposites . . . the creative optimistic mind of Rosalind and the destructive pessimistic mind of Jaques . . . . Rosalind's innocence is quite inaccessible to Jaques; Jaques' maimed cynicism is beyond the aid of Rosalind. But the attitudes they represent echo throughout the play' – as they echoed, of course, through the world of the late 1960s, with its rebellious youth and disgruntled elders.

Nineteen-sixty-seven was also the year of a curiosity in the annals of *As You Like It*, the National Theatre's all-male production at the Old Vic. Directed by Clifford Williams (who the previous year had directed the RSC's first sexually-selfconscious *Twelfth Night*), it claimed to be an attempt to recreate the atmosphere of the Elizabethan theatre. The programme carried pictures of 'The Drag Tradition' (hedging its bets for a non-Elizabethan audience), and Williams contributed an essay:

> The examination of the infinite beauty of Man [*sic*] in love – which lies at the very heart of *As You Like It* – takes place in an atmosphere of spiritual purity which transcends sensuality in the search for poetic sexuality. It is for this reason that I

employ a male cast; so that we shall not – entranced by the surface reality – miss the interior truth.

J.C. Trewin was sarcastic about these anti-theatrical pretensions: 'What a relief it is not to be entranced by the surface reality!' (*Illustrated London News*, 14 October 1967). While praising many of the performances, including Ronald Pickup's Rosalind, he found the casting distracting in a twentieth-century context. The National Theatre's theory-based experiment attempted to divorce theatre from its cultural context – the audience of a particular time and place, who have certain 'natural' (i.e., culturally-conditioned) inter-pretations of what they see on stage. What this audience of the late 1960s saw was 'a bard for this season's King's Road silhouette of girlish boyishness' (Ronald Bryden, *Observer*, 8 October 1967), rather than the abstract purity aimed for by Williams – the costumes, by Ralph Koltai, were entirely contemporary, as was the set of perspex tubes and screens.

Some critics made a superhuman effort not to be distracted by the camp associations of the production. Peter Lewis in the *Daily Mail* (4 October 1967) spoke of

> a conception of the play so different, so strange, so visually and aurally hypnotic that the fact that all the girls are really men takes its place as merely one of the elements in a dream-like total experience, which you accept along with the rest.

Shakespeare as Strindberg? But if so, it was Strindberg without the erotic passion, the soul-destroying emotion:

> [Pickup's Rosalind] is completely non-erotic. It begins de-murely with a few well-observed female gestures, and takes on character only during the Ganymede scenes. It is a blank that comes to life under the stress of intense platonic feeling.
>
> (Irving Wardle, *Sunday Times*, 4 October 1967)
>
> Its real effect turns out to be that it puts eroticism, whether ambiguous or straightforward, out of the theatre altogether.
>
> (Harold Hobson, *Sunday Times*, 8 October 1967)

The conclusion, at this distance, must be that the experiment was divided against itself: was its intention to reproduce Elizabethan conditions – a symbolic last stand by the male theatrical estab-lishment to claim a special 'historical' right to Shakespeare? Or did it truly want to speak to a contemporary audience of Jan Kott's fashionable 'thesis that absolute love is absolutely neuter' (Milton Shulman, *Evening Standard*, 4 October 1967), the intellectual version of the late 1960s ideology of polymorphous sexuality? The experiment might have been more convincing had the performers been in Elizabethan dress, or had they allowed homosexual eroticism a place. Of the other women's roles (Charles Kay as a bespectacled Celia, Anthony Hopkins as a Wagnerian Audrey), Irving Wardle said 'the result is entirely comic: and the comic variety seems very much a temperamental reflex of the different actors'. Jeremy Brett's 'very masculine' Orlando, Derek Jacobi's cockney Touchstone ('prettier than any of the girls', said Wardle) were generally admired; as was Robert Stephens's Jaques – 'a white-suited, fastidious, apparently sour old man, fundamentally lonely and kindly, [who] picks his way through the plastic wood with a civilised disdain . . . out of touch with his time' (Frank Marcus, *Plays & Players*, December 1967). Apart from this character-isation, no sense of the play's commentary on contemporary social mores emerges, as indeed it could hardly do, given its determined avoidance of anything sexual.[9]

The RSC's success with a modern-dress approach to *As You Like It* had to wait until 1973, the so-called 'Hair' production directed by Buzz Goodbody and starring Eileen Atkins. Sally Beauman des-cribes Goodbody as

> the most promising young RSC director; she was also the one person within the company who in background and experi-ence bridged the polarities of Seventies theatre. She had been educated at Roedean and Sussex, and had joined the RSC in 1967, aged twenty, as John Barton's personal assistant. Barton had seen and admired a production she directed while at university. Like her fellow male directors she was deeply interested in working on classical texts, and gained experience within the RSC working on both TGR [touring] and large-theatre Shakespeare. She was also a communist and a committed feminist; she had sympathy and connections with alternative theatre work, and in 1971 had helped to start the first feminist theatre company, the Women's Street Theatre Group.[10]

Goodbody's style, in her first major production at Stratford, was relentlessly anti-traditional and defiantly feminist, an attempt to reclaim the play for women after the National's reactionary experiment. The production was contemporary rather than 'timeless'. The design by Christopher Morley echoed Koltai's abstract ideas: a 'forest' of tubing, with some realistic props – armchairs and a somewhat incongruous log. Everyone wore the fashionable gear of 1973: flared jeans, fringed jerkins, silk scarves, headbands and stacked heels for the men (including 'Ganymede'), Laura Ashley-style frills for the women. Critics complained that there was no distinction between court and country, between aristocrats and the local peasantry. To this Goodbody replied that in Arden

> Hardly anyone seems to do any work: the shepherds and shepherdesses . . . are not really country people. I see them as art college students – drop-outs who live in the country and have mummies and daddies in town with large incomes.
>
> (interview, *Birmingham Post*, 9 June 1973)

For Goodbody, the play's comment was on modern society as a whole, rather than on polarisations within it. Both poster and programme indicated that the production would be making points about 'a woman's place' in society. The poster showed a back view of Eileen Atkins in jeans, accompanied by a provocative quotation from Luther: 'Men have broad shoulders and narrow hips, and accordingly they possess intelligence. Women have narrow shoulders and broad hips. Women ought to stay home . . . for they have . . . a wide fundament to sit upon, keep house and bear and raise children.' The programme contained, as well as the usual educational essay on the pastoral, a stage history of the presentation of the forest, and Anne Barton's essay 'A Woman's Place', with illustrative material from Erasmus to Virginia Woolf. The intention of the poster, presumably, was to provoke thought about whether there is any real difference, physical or intellectual, between men and women; to remind us that the play's central character is a young woman who leaves home with her 'sister' and triumphantly makes her way in the world – through a male-dominated wildwood to marriage and a return to the bosom of her father. This final irony (from a feminist point of view) was not in fact explored by the production, which thus rather lost its point: Michael Billington remembers, 'They had great problems with the final scene, because Buzz Goodbody said "I don't believe this". How do you direct something if you don't fundamentally subscribe to that ideal?' (interview with the author, December 1990).

The ideological gap was filled with 'business': one-off gags and easy hits at contemporary fashions:

> a Polonius would have to describe Miss Goodbody's version as farcical-metallurgical-sartorial-stereophonical. In no way does it penetrate to the essence of Shakespeare. The play isn't recognisable as a preworking of *The Tempest*, an alluring picture of a world which (if occasionally cruel) offers new perspectives to the perspicacious, restores values as well as health, couples the young and reconciles the old. Still less does the production make fresh, interesting points about 'a woman's place' in society . . . . A sort of factitious urban glee constantly intrudes, getting in the way of anything sensitive, trenchant or true.
>
> (Benedict Nightingale, *New Statesman*, 22 June 1973)

This critic has his own essentialist view of the play, but he is willing to accept 'fresh, interesting points' – if the production makes them. Ultimately the success of the production (and it was successful with audiences) depended not on a directorial concept, but on Atkins's playing and a general air of contemporary pleasure represented by the rock settings of the songs and a final rain of paper hearts onto the audience – a recreation of the ambience of *Hair* for those who had been too nervous, or too snobbish, to go.

Eileen Atkins was 39 in 1973 – rather old for a representative of modern youth. Goodbody obviously wanted a strong female lead with a distinctly contemporary air – an anti-romantic – and could not find such a figure among younger actresses, who, presumably, would have attempted to emulate the still-potent Rosalind of Vanessa Redgrave, 'a marvellous memory from your reviewer's early adolescence', sighed W. Stephen Gilbert in *Plays & Players* (August 1973) – 'a melting with love which invited the audience to share in it'. Goodbody's gamble, on the whole, paid off:

> fascinating actress though she is, Eileen Atkins is no exponent of springtime romance. With those swivelling eyes and sceptical cadences she expresses the wary defensiveness of someone who has seen too much to have Rosalind's emotional confidence. She is at her best in the Ganymede scenes – jaunty, critical, turning on joke voices and coupling brazen outward assurance with inner confusion.
>
> (Irving Wardle, *The Times*, 13 June 1973)

[Eileen Atkins] makes light of the cliches and finds comedy in places where no-one has found it before. She struts, she rolls her big eyes, she enjoys the ironies which she has lifted from the text.

(David Isaacs, *Coventry Evening Telegraph*, 13 June 1973)

Her evident depression and boredom at her uncle's court marks her out as a woman of more than average capacity for feeling: she proves it when she falls in love. Try as she will, she can't always prevent that bony, spiky face from breaking into a look of extraordinary longing, as if she might suddenly do something unexpected and embarrassing, like clutch Orlando by the bicep or buttock and kiss him. I can't imagine many actresses putting as much covert sexuality into the part.

(Benedict Nightingale, *New Statesman*, 22 June 1973)

It was an uncomplicated heterosexuality, modern and uninhibited:

any hint of sexual equivocation is knocked on the head by Eileen Atkins's minimal attempt to disguise her femininity as Rosalind. Indeed, with her headband, fringed blouse, and crutch-hugging jeans, she seemed even more seductive as Ganymede than before.

(Michael Billington, *Guardian Weekly*, 23 June 1973)

Several critics complained about how hard it is for anyone – male or female – to look romantic in 'drab' jeans. David Suchet's Orlando was distinctly plebeian (he had stepped in for an injured – and much more conventionally good-looking – Bernard Lloyd), though his honesty and directness were admired (plate 8). The unisex contemporary costuming in fact had the effect of 'normalising' the sexualities, and the general behaviour, of the lovers in the audience's perception, since jeans are the one twentieth-century costume which is virtually free of both gender and class specificity.

Much more interesting to the reviewers was Richard Pasco's Jaques, in a crumpled white suit; as Nightingale described him:

half-crazed with old desires and guilts, as contemptuous of himself as of the world: he blinks, twitches, hiccoughs, screws round his shoulders, and half-lopes, half-stumbles across the stage, seizing the Duke by the lapels and scrabbling at his chest. Words like 'p-pleasure' get sneering emphasis, and every speech is likely to end with a tiny, cracked laugh, as if nothing mattered anyway.

Plate 8 Eileen Atkins as Rosalind, David Suchet as Orlando,
As You Like It, 1973, directed by Buzz Goodbody.
Photograph: Zoë Dominic.

According to Robert Cushman, 'In Richard Pasco's hands, Jaques becomes almost the central character of the play – paradoxically, really, since he spends most of his time prowling its periphery, peering at the action with beady distaste through rimless glasses' (*Observer*, 17 June 1973). As in most productions since 1961, Jaques represented the production's built-in critique – here the old cynic watching the young moderns' 'love-in' and reading them all as fools in the forest, who forget the inevitability of the last four ages of man in the illusory euphoria of the Age of Aquarius.

Goodbody's attempts to emphasise the contemporary in the play's relationships and ignore the pastoral conventions (which among other things question the 'proper' behaviour of lovers) delighted audiences but dissatisfied critics, who felt that Shakespeare was being lessened ('*As You Like It* is not about courtship as a developing relationship, but about Courtly Love, which Shakespeare did not invent', argued John Elsom in the *Listener*, 21 June 1973). The effect on the university-educated male hierarchy at Stratford – directors such as Trevor Nunn and Terry Hands – was, one suspects, to make them feel that *As You Like It*'s literary conventions had to be reinstated. Yet the play must entertain a contemporary audience: how was this to be done?

1977–80

Nunn's solution, in his 1977 production, was to create a seventeenth-century operatic extravaganza. Turning a play into a musical had worked extremely well with his *Comedy of Errors*: the artificialities of farce could easily be stopped for a song. But *As You Like It* is a later work than the *Comedy*, and it required a more obviously intellectual approach. Nunn took his cue from the seventeenth-century tradition of masque, which frequently contrasted such things as court and country, or celebrated allegorical figures; there is just such a celebratory masque in Act V of *As You Like It*. Nunn actually began the play with another masque – a ten-minute sung debate between Hymen, Nature and Fortune (words by Ben Jonson, Edmund Spenser, Thomas Carewe, and others, music by Stephen Oliver). At various points throughout the play – not just where Shakespeare specified a song – characters broke into Purcellian recitative or aria. Touchstone and Audrey's mock-wedding was accompanied by a 'Puritan hymn', words by assistant director John Caird, of which this is a fair sample:

O God, in whom we trust
Look on these twain with grace
Who leave their filthy thoughts and lust
To come before thy face.

Sets and costumes, the design of John Napier, were extravagantly French, all frills and bows, with a false proscenium arch and sky-pieces in the manner of baroque theatre. That is, the play was presented by the director as a commentary on the dominance of French culture in England in the mid-seventeenth century – thus solving the dual problems of entertainment and intellectual respectability. But the latter point seems to have gone over the critics' heads. For John Peter, typical of most reviewers but more clear about his reasons,

> As You Like It is quite enjoyable and thoroughly baffling. There was poor old Shakespeare applying all his skill and sophistication to turning the rigid pastoral form into warm human drama; and here comes Trevor Nunn and turns it back into elaborate artifice . . . . Shakespeare meant the Forest of Arden to be a healing and civilising place: so why turn it into a dotty fairyland of toy bridges, painted brooks with round holes for fishing, and daintily gartered shepherds? The final masque is a poetic conclusion towards which the play gently and delicately grows: so why add an opening masque which gives the story a sense of unreality from the start?
>
> (*Sunday Times*, 11 September 1977)

It's a *play*, not an opera or a ballet or a musical called 'Kiss Me Ros', the critics insisted, unanimous for once. Gareth Lloyd Evans commented,

> The frequent recourse to individual and choral singing with music that lacks lyrical resonance tends to generalise and mechanise the human responses of the characters . . . [T]hough there are a number of excellent performances, nobody really connects . . . . [F]or all its virtues . . . it wasn't really a performance of Shakespeare you were seeing.
>
> (*Stratford Herald*, 16 September 1977)

What Lloyd Evans means here by 'Shakespeare' might be read as '*contemporary* Shakespeare': a production which 'connects' (his significant word) with itself and the audience; a production that answers the question, Who is Rosalind and what is this society she flees, then returns to?

Kate Nelligan's Rosalind, resplendent in lace and ruffles, floppy boots, and huge feathered hat, was, in Robert Cushman's words, 'a natural, able with her superb whole-heartedness to rule a scene, but not to govern this stage, this language, and this over-complicated production' (*Observer*, 11 September 1977). The consensus of critical opinion was that although hers was a high-energy performance, full of infectious gaiety, Nelligan was somewhat lacking in complex (modern, ironical) passion – the production did not allow her to explore this possibility. Felix Barker called it a 'Madcap of the Lower Fourth approach' (*Evening News*, 9 September 1977). 'Miss Nelligan' said a delighted John Barber,

> combines a splendid athleticism with a disturbing ardour. At first sight of Orlando, she is disgracefully, shamelessly smitten . . . . But, unrecognised in her boys' clothes, she teases him with so much mischief, laughs at him with so much delight, brims over with so much fun, her whole being becomes a frolic of happiness which it is impossible not to share.
>
> (*Daily Telegraph*, 9 September 1977)

But the ambiguities of the part that critics were beginning to expect in the sexually-exploratory 1970s were missing: 'Kate Nelligan's romping, energetic Rosalind changes not a whit with the donning of male attire, and the sexual subtleties of the trial wooing . . . remain at a pantomime level of meaning', said Gordon Parsons (*Morning Star*, 15 September 1977).

Peter McEnery's performance as Orlando had a similar fresh-faced quality: 'This Orlando is still young enough to have no beard, to rush off spontaneously after new ideas . . . and to play silly games with the teenage kid Ganymede that he meets in the forest' (B.A. Young, *Financial Times*, 8 September 1977). Nunn's directorial concept did not even allow for the now common individual characterisations of Celia, Touchstone, or Jaques. Celia (Judith Paris) was most remarked upon for her ability to skate on the wintry set; Touchstone (Alan David) was costumed as a Watteauesque Pierrot, and had to work hard for his laughs; Jaques (Emrys James), 'in puritan black, laughs a great deal and his final decision to leave the woodland merrymaking and avoid a return to the court shocks, after his having taken a full part in the preceding song-and-dance sequences' (Parsons).

'What then do I miss?' asked Billington:

> The sense that the trip to Arden is a voyage of discovery where
> every man finds his true self; the very pulse and rhythm of this
> comedy, undermined by turning minor figures like Sir Oliver
> Martext into an excuse for another aria; and a basic trust in
> the given material.
>
> (*Guardian*, 10 September 1977)

This last point indexes the final loss of directorial innocence which
is the hallmark of most modern productions. In our postmodern
culture, directors know that there is no such thing as a simple 'trust
in the given material'; it has no intrinsic life, and it must be read in
such a way as to engage an audience which itself reads inter-
textually. Nunn's 'historical' concept could have been more interesting than it was; it needed to go a lot further than the surface
entertainment that he patronisingly offered. A basic trust in the
actors and actresses to do their work, to perform as *adults*,
exploring their roles within the historical framework, might have
produced more challenging results.[11]

Terry Hands, in 1980, continued his personal exploration of the
meaning of 'Shakespeare's festive comedy' for today (his *Twelfth
Night* had opened in 1979), offering a structural contrast between a
wintry and pessimistic opening and spring's optimism in the second
half. But the actors were not swamped by the directorial concept;
instead, they were encouraged to respond to it by flamboyant self-
presentation. The outstanding quality of this production was, in
Irving Wardle's words, that it was

> a performance. From the opening quarrel which erupts over
> the whole downstage area, and the wrestling match where
> Rosalind and Celia join in with hisses and hair-pulling, it is an
> evening of fearlessly extrovert animation by a company who
> have clearly been told never to be afraid of going over the top.
> It is fast, passionate, and tightly controlled . . . the show is
> irresistible. This play is supposed to be about the force of
> fertility and that is what the company deliver direct.[12]
>
> (*The Times*, 5 April 1980)

Billington, with his own quasi-directorial ideas about the play,
thought that it was a bit much:

everyone behaves as if he were in a nineteenth-century Surrey-side melodrama . . . . The problem is that all this wild-eyed frenzy pre-empts the key point: that Cupid was, in Rosalind's words, 'conceived of spleen and born in madness.' If everyone behaves as if he were a bit touched, it undercuts the lovers' especial dementia . . . this is a production that throughout looks stunning and that builds to a climax of real festivity. But the bold, frontal, declaratory style of acting that suited Hands's production of the Histories looks slightly forced in a comedy about inter-relationships.

(*Guardian*, 5 April 1980)

Most critics, however, thought that the up-front physicality of the performers gave greater force to the inter-relationships. For example, Jaques, in his dialogue with 'Ganymede' in IV.1, folded 'him' in his bear-like grasp and presented 'him' with a red rose. This puzzled Sally Aire (and many other critics): 'but I am glad the moment happened, and grateful that a possible new dimension to the play was revealed to me by it' (*Plays & Players*, May 1980). The point was, presumably, that even the cynical Jaques is not immune to desire, and that the multi-gendered Rosalind/Ganymede, for this play, embodies it. By the same token, Sinead Cusack's Celia, a close and loving companion to Rosalind, was 'a sexual competitor for Orlando' (Billington) until she realised she was outrun, though this did not sour her relationship with Rosalind; Cusack remained 'a very obvious and determined and available Celia . . . [sitting] centre stage',[13] a silent commentator on her cousin's excesses.

Susan Fleetwood's Rosalind and John Bowe's Orlando were notably well-matched, and clearly displayed the electric current of physical desire running between them by a vocabulary of kisses, hugs, and romps (see frontispiece).[14] 'This Rosalind', commented Eric Shorter,

is of such a breathless coming-on disposition that as Ganymede . . . she seems to throw to the winds all pretence of being a boy and simply itches to get her hands on her pupil. He in turn . . . steals kisses and embraces in such a way that tends to contradict the plot, but since they are both evidently so many fathoms deep in love that their romantic games seem even sillier than usual, who could really object?

(*Daily Telegraph*, 7 April 1980)

Sally Aire added (and most critics agreed),

> John Bowe's Orlando is totally free of the narcissism all too
> often seen in this role. He is a raw, energetic force, a 'nature's
> gentleman', and on the moral and psychic level is a worthy
> suitor for Rosalind.[15]

Fleetwood's Rosalind produced greater enthusiasm among the
critics than anyone had for twenty years – the bright memory of
Vanessa was at last beginning to be displaced. 'Radiance' is no
longer thought of as Rosalind's intrinsic quality; this one was
rather, said Gareth Lloyd Evans, 'an essentially physical, sexy
young woman whose authority lies not in any mysterious spiritual
femininity (the accustomed emphasis put on the role) but in the
potent example of her own capacity to love' (*Stratford Herald*,
11 April 1980). 'I have not seen Rosalind better played,' said
Sally Aire:

> I don't expect to see her better played for a very long time, if
> ever. Informed by a deep intelligence, this performance ranges
> from the sublimely ingenious to the overtly sexual. There is
> bubbling humour and that human warmth which has always
> been Susan Fleetwood's greatest natural quality as an actress.

Perhaps one might expect this response from a modern female
critic, delighted to see a woman as such a positive, vital, intelligent
centre to a production (certainly it was mine as a member of the
audience); but even the doyen of male critics, J.C. Trewin, gave her
his accolade:

> Let me say, without pausing, that Susan Fleetwood is the most
> persuasive Rosalind I have known in four decades. Fathoms
> deep in love, never arch, she rules her Arden of the spring with
> a gaiety that has nothing of the principal-boy swagger.
>
> (*Birmingham Post*, 7 April 1980)

This production refused to countenance cynicism. Touchstone
and Jaques had a positive role in the play: according to Wardle,

> the love-action is supervised by the two counter-clowns Touch-
> stone and Jaques. As at the National Theatre [where a
> production by John Dexter, with Sara Kestleman and Simon
> Callow, was concurrently showing] a close bond develops
> between these two from the moment when Derek Godfrey,

instead of simply reporting his meeting with a fool in the forest, launches into his own clown routine.

As the reviewer for the *Oxford Mail* commented,

> It is amazing what a difference focusing hard on the young lovers makes to the play. Superbly as Derek Godfrey plays him no longer is there any risk of the melancholy Jaques casting a long dark shadow across the comedy.
>
> (D.A.C., *Oxford Mail*, 8 April 1980)

The play ended with a riotous fertility feast, with huge corn dollies, deer-horn head-dresses, and flowery garlands everywhere. Memories of the court, which in Farrah's design had been a cold and threatening prison (eight metal stakes across the centre of a black-and-white stage), were obliterated in a joyous dance celebrating the healing power of sex. The play inhabited the audience's folk-memory rather than any specific historical period. It was a vision of an England, and an uncomplicated sexuality, that were about to disappear. Hands's directive to the cast had been that *As You Like It* was 'a fairy tale'.[16]

1985–90

Adrian Noble's 1985 production took the perhaps inevitable next step and psychoanalysed the fairytale in a contemporary (modern-dress) reading, set in the country of the modern mind. Here court and country were but flipsides to each other, both metaphors of the prisons/landscapes we construct for ourselves out of our desires and their repressions. Designed by Bob Crowley, the play began in an 'attic' filled with shapes of furniture draped in white material – here Rosalind and Celia had come to escape the oppressive court, but (of course) it pursued them. The move to Arden simply involved the lifting of the covers, with a huge piece of white silk pulled up in the centre of the stage to suggest a tree-trunk, and, eventually, a green silken canopy. 'We wanted something that was genuinely plastic, that would change shape according to what the actors did, according to the moment in the play, because the Forest of Arden in *As You Like It* changes shape, dimension, character, according to the perception of each person.'[17] Over all loomed a huge moon: we were clearly in the realm of the unconscious ('Within the Forest/the Forest within', as the programme directed us). In the Stratford version, much play was made with a large carved looking-glass, through which characters entered and exited, and a clock, which began ticking only when the play was over. In the transfer to London these perhaps over-insistent symbolic props disappeared, and 'key moments of transition [were] reserved for a great luminous port-hole in the back wall, where figures poised for flight or return appear[ed] in silhouette' (Irving Wardle, *The Times*, 18 December 1985).

Instead of the usual educational material on the pastoral, the programme contained poems and prose related to the thematic idea that to enter the 'wood' is to enter a dream or fantasy. It quoted Heinrich Zimmer: 'it is only after . . . a journey in a distant region, in a new land that . . . the inner voice . . . can make itself understood by us.' There were also quotations relating transvestism to the Jungian animus/anima, and the query 'What is love *anyway*?' Juliet Stevenson, the Rosalind, in an interview in *Plays & Players* (May 1985), explained that the play is 'a vital exploration of gender, the male and the female within us all. Rosalind is very released when her masculine aspect is allowed release'. Arden is 'a realm where you can dress up and change your gender, change your way of life'. Bob Crowley's set, she went on to explain, 'is mostly to do with colours, and space, and different moons. These moons get larger and larger as you get into the forest'. Jung's symbolism has probably never had such a thorough outing in the Shakespearean theatre. In another example, the deer-hunt became Celia's dream of defloration:

> Adrian Noble had equated the deer with the virginal Celia, who lay asleep beneath the towering, white, lingam-like mountain of silk that dominated the stage for the forest scenes. Her body had been caught by a snaking, blood-stained trail of cloth, pulled across the stage as she slept . . . and she would awaken to fall in love with Oliver.
>
> (Barry Russell, *Drama*, 3, 1985)

The critics' response was astonished but on the whole quite enthusiastic; some made complimentary comparisons with the effect of Peter Brook's revolutionary *Midsummer Night's Dream* of 1970. John Barber thought that the design 'had the effect of cleansing the text . . . of the greasy fustian of painted scenery and the varnish of old conventions gone stale' – an *As You Like It* for this generation (*Daily Telegraph*, 25 April 1985). Benedict Nightingale's review is typical – resistant but fascinated despite his principles:

I dislike seeing texts strongly slanted by a director .... I dislike being violently and superfluously reminded of a play's contemporary 'relevance' by performers wearing bowlers, braces, tuxedos, donkey-jackets, as happens here .... And yet there are times at Stratford – for instance, when Juliet Stevenson's marvellously bright, buoyant and sexy Rosalind becomes marvellously grave, melancholy and sombre too – when [Noble] achieves a complexity and, yes, a depth I don't recall seeing in any previous production of the play.

(*Listener*, 25 April 1985)

Michael Billington was not so convinced of the success of the production's dealings with the erotic; for him, it was

a highly original reading but one that undercuts the play's sheer Mozartian joy .... [Noble's] chief conceit is to suggest that the court and the forest are not continents apart but simply opposite sides of the same human coin .... I don't mind the absence of real trees .... But Arden is also a place of discovery filled with the 'madness' of love and what I find missing in this production is transforming human ecstasy .... [Hilton McRae and Juliet Stevenson] embody the Jungian animus and anima (hello Jung lovers wherever you are), each having something of the other's sexual nature .... But rarely in their encounters did I feel I was witnessing the marriage of two minds or even two souls.

(*Guardian*, 26 April 1985)

'Better a production with a concept than a bland retread; and Mr Noble's intelligence shines through', he concluded, '[b]ut I would beg him to remember that *As You Like It* is still billed as a comedy.' What Noble may well have intuited, however, is that his working definition of comedy as 'a ceremony or initiation leading towards matrimony'[18] is not necessarily in this age a recipe for joyous laughter or sexual delight. Rather such an 'initiation' might be the opportunity for an examination of power-structures within the community and within the individual psyche (for example, the 'doubling' of the two Dukes' courts indicated two 'aspects of the same person' for each actor).[19]

Juliet Stevenson is an actress ever willing to explore the intellectual issues raised by the character she is playing. She obviously followed Noble's directorial concept with enthusiasm (see her comments in *Plays & Players* above); but she also found herself going beyond Noble to discover a strong feminist reading of the play. For Stevenson,

> what happens to [Orlando] is classically what happens to women in Shakespeare. His love is tested. Rosalind/Ganymede uproots his idea of the wooing process. Not only is Orlando being wooed, not wooing, but his hopelessly romantic notions of wooing are deconstructed in the process.[20]

Further, Stevenson together with Fiona Shaw, who played Celia, considered that an important aspect of the play is the story of the friendship between the two women:

> Armed with this resolve to jettison stereotype, we began work . . . . To liberate Shakespeare's women from the confines of literary and theatrical tradition requires an analysis of the nature and effects of those social structures which define and contain them – the opening of this play sees Rosalind and Celia already contained within a structure that is oppressive and patriarchal, namely the court of Duke Frederick, Celia's father. The modern dress decision served to remind us that such structures are by no means 'ancient history', and that the freedom and self-definition that the two girls are seeking remain prevalent needs for many of their contemporaries today.[21]

This insistence on the contemporary reality of the women's emotional and psychological experience produced a compelling and admirable performance from Stevenson. Irving Wardle's review describes the effect:

> Rosalind begins as a prisoner of a stifling court and discovers her real powers through playing games . . . . She begins as a rather plain downcast girl, very much the house guest of Fiona Shaw's sharp-eyed Celia; then she gets into a white suit and begins to discover herself, first in . . . clown routines with Hilton McRae's Orlando, and then entering deeper waters where neither she, her lover, nor the audience can tell truth from masquerade. I have never seen their later dialogue played with equivalent erotic force; nor seen the mock-marriage take on such sacramental qualities.
>
> (*The Times*, 24 April 1985)

Plate 9 Juliet Stevenson as Rosalind, Hilton McRae as Orlando, Fiona
Shaw as Celia, *As You Like It*, 1985, directed by Adrian Noble.
Photograph: Joe Cocks Studio.

What was evidently lost in this reading of Rosalind was the comic vitality with which actresses have traditionally been able to imbue the role. Stevenson was intense and sincere rather than naturally playful (none of the production pictures shows her laughing or smiling, in strong contrast to the photos of virtually all earlier productions – see, for example, plate 9). Nicholas Shrimpton commented on this quality in her performance:

> Juliet Stevenson's Rosalind is touching in her vulnerable moments but desperately unconfident when she is required to be witty, flirtatious or high-spirited. Possibly she is weighed down by the psychological lumber of the interpretation. More probably this gifted actress is . . . simply not a comedienne.
>
> (*Times Educational Supplement*, 10 May 1985)

Nor need Rosalind be, in such a reading of the play as this; and 'Fortunately', Shrimpton continues, 'the production reminds us that the play has not one but two heroines, and supplies a superb Celia to take up the slack.' Fiona Shaw's Celia brought many appreciative comments, most notably Billington's sense that the production's 'one igniting spark of passion . . . was when Fiona Shaw's Celia (beautifully played as a slightly woozy Mitfordesque deb who turns to mantras and meditation in the forest) exchange[d] instant glances with Bruce Alexander's transformed Oliver.' (*Guardian*, 26 April 1985.) The archival videotape confirms this observation: Celia and Oliver's long, hypnotised stares at each other, ignoring Rosalind's faint, and their comically awkward, mutually absorbed exit, brought a round of applause.

The play's male characters were less complex, except for the directorial concept of doubling the Dukes and their courts (a practice followed by John Caird in the 1989 production). Alan Rickman's Jaques was an arrogant but vulnerable lone intellectual: 'He did not care who married whom, nor who was in power. He had been there and seen it, and cared for it no longer' (Barry Russell, *Drama*, 3, 1985). Hilton McRae's Orlando, according to Michael Ratcliffe, 'is the sole reference to any resolved humanity warming the cerebral chill of the [play's] first half . . . . Into the world of hatchet faces and long overcoats at the start, [he] erupts scruffy, humorous, brave and enormously likeable, if in need of a bath' (*Observer*, 24 April 1985). His wrestling match was a comic epic in the manner of television's rock 'n' roll wrestling, with McRae in a very fetching G-string; at one crucial point he released himself from the grunting Charles by giving him a hearty kiss. 'One might even say', wrote Barry Russell,

> that this Orlando was used as the 'token male'. He took his clothes off, showed us his body, was pretty, long-haired and attractive. He was the romantic dreamer who spent much time in thought, but actually seemed incapable of achieving very much if left to his own devices. Rosalind, by contrast, looked strong and played strong.

So the production achieved its aim of presenting the feminine in the masculine, the masculine in the feminine. But, according to Stevenson, this deconstruction of gender roles presented problems as the play approached its end – a magical, joyous celebration which insists on the characters' return to the patriarchal 'hierarchies of the structured world', which is also the 'real world'. Stevenson and Noble argued about the staging of the ending:

> Having spent three hours challenging notions of gender, we couldn't then end with a final stage picture which was clichéd and stereotypical, which threw the whole play away. Adrian did point out to me that, whether I liked it or not, Shakespeare was a monarchist, a reactionary, a bourgeois and a conservative, but I said, 'I think it's irrelevant what Shakespeare was. The fact is the *play* asks the most anarchic questions. It doesn't attempt to resolve them, so why should we?[22]

Eventually, by the time the production came to London, the actors and director had re-worked the ending so that the play continued its challenge to the audience:

> the dance culminated in a moment of still suspension, as the characters took in the Arden they were about to leave, and absorbed the *consequences* of the return to the ordered world. They then exited, through a moon-shaped hole in the backdrop, which both told the story more clearly and laid emphasis on the fantastical nature of the whole event . . . . These changes meant that the issues explored were no longer smothered, at the end, by excesses of 'merry-making', and we no longer felt obliged to abandon ourselves on the stage to some imposed inevitability.[23]

Stevenson hoped that 'the audience would go out of the theatre talking to each other', that the production's serious re-thinking of this comedy would in some way affect the lives of the spectators:

I don't expect audiences to go skipping out of *As You Like It* humming the tunes, because the play isn't about that. It isn't about confirming cosy opinions or settled stereotypes. It isn't about a woman in search of romantic love. The search is for knowledge and for faith, and in that search Rosalind is clamorous.[24]

This clarion call from one of the new generation of feminist classical actresses was, astonishingly, ignored in subsequent RSC productions of the play. Nineteen eighty-nine brought John Caird's new production, and a question from a somewhat weary Michael Billington: is *As You Like It* being done too often? (*Guardian*, 15 September 1989). Stewart McGill found the production 'a major disappointment':

> As the theatre world awaits the announcement of a successor to Terry Hands, the focus of the debate must be on what kind of Shakespeare should this company be doing as we move toward the 1990s .... Caird, his designer Ultz and composer Ilona Sekacz have destroyed the play in a quest for yet another way of reviving Shakespeare for today's audiences. The RSC production is loud, expensive, spectacular and utterly heartless.
>
> (*Plays & Players*, November 1989)

Caird clearly had a 'concept' for the play: an even more radical questioning of the power of the comic paradigm than Noble's. The problem lay in the communicating of these ideas. A case in point is the opening scene, as striking a directorial imposition as Nunn's operatic masque in 1977. The audience entered the theatre to find a 1930s cocktails-and-tango party going on on stage. The effect was overwhelmingly funereal, not to say sinister. These were the bored, idle, and corrupt rich; no-one smiled; the men grimly challenged each other in toreador postures; Duke Frederick's heavies eyed the auditorium; and no-one danced with Rosalind. Yet for the two male critics quoted above, 'The aim, I take it, is to build up a party atmosphere' (McGill) ; 'Why, if Duke Frederick's court is an incipient tyranny, is everyone having such a good time?' (Billington). Billington incorrectly describes the event as a 'tea-dance' – apparently unaware that people don't wear black and diamonds, and dance with cold formality, at a *tea*-dance. The brutalist mood continued with a wrestling match in which Orlando appeared to be badly injured, spitting blood, and which he finally won by fighting dirty. The Duke's henchmen pulled guns on him when he revealed whose son he was: this 'court' was the home of a tough, loveless gangster, whose conversion is never remotely likely.

The 'forest' was created by the same henchmen (with a change into brown overcoats; the Dukes too were doubled, by the actor Clifford Rose) simply pulling up the black boards of the floor, to reveal a small patch of wintry ground, which was gradually enlarged, as the forest ethos took over. All this provided a strong moral contrast between court and country – or rather, as Caird was clearly reflecting the ethical concerns of the 1980s, between the City and those who try to escape its circle of power – while at the same time indicating, as Noble did, that the two are inextricably linked. It was, however, the image of Arden which most worried the critics – an alien, vaguely sinister world in the play's first half, all piles of planks and swirling mist, and in the second half, a pool surrounded by surrealistic bullrushes; no trees (again). Its inhabitants, most notably Silvius and Phoebe, behaved very oddly indeed, pursuing their courtships in underwear (eventually, in the 'summertime', the court in exile was also reduced to boxer shorts). The audience was clearly invited to take a patronising view of the absurd behaviour of these pastoral types ineptly aping their betters (by contrast, an admired aspect of Noble's production was that the yokels were treated with respect as people, not caricatures). As Irving Wardle commented, 'they, no less than the courtiers, are giving a per- formance . . . the forest has no claims to reality' (*The Times*, 15 September 1989) – as opposed to the all-too-grim reality of the court.

The programme was little help: it carried a number of Blake's *Songs of Innocence and Experience* which reflected the production's ambivalence about the relation between the loveless adult world and 'the echoing green', but it was hard to tell what value was placed upon the green world. Perhaps the portrayal of Rosalind as a bored young sophisticate released into her true self, a tomboyish schoolgirl, was meant to present an image of Blakean energy which might transform the oppressive social world. Certainly Sophie Thompson's performance offered an excess of manic vitality. But if this was Caird's intention, it was somewhat skewed in performance by Thompson's comic genius. She used the role of Rosalind to create a highly inventive and amusing study of the tomboy schoolgirl in love. For Michael Coveney this was enough:

a performer of blazing comic personality, powerful voice, dimpled, darting radiance and quixotic charm .... Sophie Thompson joins an exalted company of tomorrow's Denches and Smiths in a performance that ripples with invention, bubbles with high spirits and delights at every turn.

(*Financial Times*, 15 September 1989)

Others were less enchanted:

Sophie Thompson's Rosalind emerges as a simpering St Trinian's schoolgirl, dressed in shorts, gym shoes, straw hat and a satchel. Eschewing any hint of androgynous appeal Miss Thompson runs a gamut from bawling declamation to the doleful quaver, whose nasal stresses are reminiscent of Maggie Smith.

(Nicholas de Jongh, *Guardian*, 13 April 1990)

As one might expect from such a characterisation the production was short on sexual excitement, a lack which disappointed de Jongh:

there is small hint of sexual pathos, flirtatious mockery or erotic tension in her larkish, gamey performance when set against Jerome Flynn's morose Orlando, a youth whom you almost feel would prefer to be otherwise engaged.

Hugo Williams of the *Sunday Correspondent* (17 September 1989) offered a more generous judgement – which also reminded theatre-goers of the ephemerality of the art they support, dependent on performers and performances:

As usual, the play's success depends on Rosalind, with a little help from Touchstone. It is almost thirty years since Vanessa Redgrave's Rosalind, and yet one goes on comparing succeeding Rosalinds to her lanky principal boy. Sophie Thompson could not be more different: short, knock-kneed, Chaplinesque, it is a knockabout characterisation which takes some getting used to because of its lack of physical allure, but which finally triumphs by radical conviction and wholeness .... Though never 'luminous', she is finally loveable.

As, one might add, small children or clowns are loveable. Thompson's Rosalind and Mark Williams's red-nosed Touchstone provided between them many laughs; but it might be argued that this directorial emphasis suggests a curious desperation: does 'comedy' now only mean a brilliantly-performed joke? Has it, at the end of the twentieth century, lost its power to reconcile and renew? Ultz's design for Arden had created a surrealist dream-world – Wonderland, or a return to the Neverland of the 1950s. Now, however, it is a dream-escape from an extremely unpleasant contemporary real world. Perhaps the biggest clue to the production's perspective is given by the poster advertising the show. Rosalind and/or the greenwood are nowhere to be seen; instead, Charles the wrestler throws Orlando, in front of a grim-faced male courtier. The sources of power and energy are not to be found in Rosalind or the greenwood, but in the world of macho games ruled by the men in suits (these games were grimly parodied in the deer-killing, whose primitivism disgusted the cold dandy Jaques). The same pessimism underlay the uncomfortably jokey 'business' surrounding the Epilogue: Orlando stepped forward to speak it, had a fit of stage-fright, and Rosalind came to his rescue – she was not *in herself* an authoritative figure, just a Blakean 'happy child'. One wondered how these children of the greenwood would survive on the outside, lacking even the empowerment of sexual desire.[25]

3

THE TAMING OF THE SHREW
Avoiding the feminist challenge

It is worth questioning whether *The Taming of the Shrew* would still be in the dramatic repertoire if it did not have the magic name 'Shakespeare' attached to it. The story implied by its title is more thoroughly rooted in a medieval and Elizabethan way of thinking about women and their relation to the patriarchy than any other of Shakespeare's plays (excluding the histories). Yet as soon as one begins to consider the question the answer seems obvious: *The Shrew* has remained consistently popular because it reinforces a profoundly-held belief of its audiences. In the four hundred years since Shakespeare wrote the play the patriarchal system has remained entrenched in our society, changing a little superficially, but in no way relinquishing its power. The play enacts the defeat of the threat of a woman's revolt: it does so in comic form, and often with apparent good humour – thus it offers the audience the chance to revel in and reinforce their misogyny while at the same time feeling good. It ends happily, so all must be right with the world. Yet, looked at with sober late-twentieth-century eyes, this is a story in which one human being starves and brainwashes another, with the full approval of the community. Cruelty can be funny – it is the basis of the 'practical joke' – as long as one is on the dominant side, and no lasting damage is done to the victim. *The Taming of the Shrew* argues that the cruel treatment is for the victim's good, to enable her to become a compliant member of patriarchal society. Whether we in the late twentieth century are convinced of this depends on the way the play's world is depicted, and particularly on how Kate's astonishing last speech is spoken and received, both by her on-stage audience and by the audience in the theatre. Ann Thompson points out in her thoughtful introduction to the New Cambridge edition of the play,

Of course not all modern Katherinas have been bitter, but it has often seemed the case that a straightforward and apparently sincere delivery of the final speech has provoked as much topical thoughtfulness in reviewers (and presumably audiences) as the more subversive mode . . . . Obviously the interpretation of this speech can lie as much in the mind of the reviewer as in the intention of the director or the performance of the actress . . . .

Productions of the play have frequently attracted whatever thoughts were in the air on the perennially topical subjects of violence and sexual politics, and this tendency can hardly fail to increase in our own time.[1]

Thompson may be over-optimistic in this last point: the evidence offered by the history of the play at Stratford in recent years suggests that it is all too easy to evade its social and political aspects.

The Taming of the Shrew was enormously popular at Stratford before the Second World War; it was constantly in the repertoire, and as a 'boisterous farce' it was always acceptable fare.[2] On the eve of the war, the emigré *enfant terrible* of Stratford in the 1930s, Theodore Komisarjevsky, produced a *Shrew* which was, by all accounts, *too* farcical: a 'burlesque' (there was never any reverence for traditional Shakespeare in Komisarjevsky's work), in which elements of the *commedia dell'arte* were mingled with Restoration frills, and the rough romance of Katharina and Petruchio for once failed to touch the audience's heart. Perhaps Komisarjevsky was by this highly artificial style distancing himself from a story which in human terms he found unacceptable. Certainly what one finds in most post-war productions is an uneasy mixture of his over-the-top farce and a native English sentimentality, which would appear to be an attempt to woo the audience into not feeling worried by Kate and Petruchio's unpleasant story.

Frequently directors will further divert attention from the implications of the story by using the Christopher Sly material not only from Shakespeare's Induction but from the anonymous contemporary *Taming of a Shrew* (1594): the intention being to frame the story in a 'realistic' representation of the drunken tinker, the rich household, and the travelling players. *The Shrew* thus becomes a crude entertainment put on for a lowbrow audience.[3] The play has its own energy, however (moreover Sly disappears from the Shakespearean text after I.1 – the 'frame' is incomplete): the story of

Katharina and Petruchio is witty and well-characterised, and involves the audience in complex and problematic ways. And it would seem to be virtually impossible to remain at a Brechtian distance from a text which offers such opportunities for full-blooded performance.

1948–61

Michael Benthall's 1948 production set the tone of what was to follow in the next 25 years: the play is essentially a self-referential piece – it is about *theatre* – in which any sort of theatrical trick is justified, as long as it is entertaining. In this reading it is essential that the Induction be played, and that Christopher Sly be kept as on-stage audience throughout. *The Shrew* is put on for his benefit: the fact that the respectable middle-class theatre audience was thereby equated with a drunken, stupid vagrant was something which seemed rarely to bother directors, though critics at times found it problematic.

Benthall argued in a publicity release that the play is

> farce, a romp designed to make people laugh – perhaps written as a sop to the groundlings after a long season of histories . . . . Any theatrical business is permissible to bring the play to life, but it is important in 'The Shrew' that the focus of interest should be kept on the wooing of Petruchio and Katharina, and this I have aimed at doing.
>
> (*Warwick Advertiser*, 7 May 1948)

Benthall's aim was not as accurate in this as he hoped: most reviewers found the aiming of custard-pies much more central – *Punch*, for example (19 May 1948): 'The air hums with beer-bottles, flower-pots, disintegrating plates and the dull slosh of custard-pie roosting on the human face. Baptista gets up his strength on fish-and-chips out of the Padua Gazette'.

Benthall's 'actors' were a Victorian troupe of strolling players – a comfortable evocation of the English pantomime tradition, who dressed themselves in whatever costumes came to hand from their wicker hampers: they

> varied from Trelawny of the Wells to supper with the Borgias . . . an eighteenth-century Gremio, a Tranio who looks like Escamillo, an Hortensio who might have wandered straight

from playing Simple Simon in pantomime and a Grumio who is an obvious Sancho Panza to this Quixote of a shrew tamer.
(*Birmingham Mail*, 8 May 1948)

Continuing the theatrical metaphor, Petruchio and Kate (Anthony Quayle and Diana Wynyard) were played as drop-ins from the production of *Annie Get Your Gun* which was currently showing at the London Coliseum: he in fringed shirt, neckerchief, and tight trousers (and an ear-ring), and she in long skirt, boots and a tight T-shirt – and a whip (plate 10). A hint of cross-dressing in both roles: neither representation corresponded with contemporary images of the 'masculine' and the 'feminine'. In fact, Benthall had wanted Robert Helpmann to play Kate, but the idea was quickly squashed by the Stratford establishment.[4] Thus the power of the market stymied what might have been an early challenge to entrenched gender ideas: certainly it would have foregrounded the role-playing aspect of gender in a production in which *every* role was consciously presented as 'theatrical'. Despite this failure in dramatic adventurousness, Beauman also records that 'Peter Brook remembered [the production] years afterwards as marvellously funny, daring, and inventive'.[5]

Quayle's persona was 'easy, conversational . . . an indulgent conqueror' (*Coventry Standard*, 15 April 1948); some found him quietly masterful, others saw more of the rip-roaring cowboy. His most striking moment was another theatrical trick: he caught Kate with a lassoo before carrying her off over his shoulder. Wynyard's Kate, with her flashing eyes and long flowing red hair, was universally admired: 'Diana Wynyard endows Katharina with a fierce, smouldering spirit and a predatory prowl, both of which are extremely effective' (*Birmingham Post*, 8 May 1948). It would appear that Wynyard played a more modern Kate than audiences were used to (though they were probably prepared for it by the image of gun-toting Annie Oakley): according to several witnesses, she gave a gargantuan final wink to the audience as she finished her speech of submission. Even a conservative female reviewer, who thought that the play would appeal to post-war 'ex-feminist women, burdened by more than they bargained for in jobs and responsibility', was forced to conclude that 'she is not conquered. She joins forces enthusiastically with a kindred spirit' (Ruth Ellis, *Stratford Herald*, 14 May 1948). The reviewer of the *Birmingham Gazette* (8 May 1948) hoped in vain for 'a little more gentleness in the final scenes'.

Plate 10 Diana Wynyard as Katharina, *The Taming of the Shrew*, 1948, directed by Michael Benthall. Photograph: Angus McBean.

However powerful the Kate, she cannot control the whole *Taming of the Shrew*: that is the prerogative of the director, who is usually male. Fiona Shaw was to say, forty years later, of a production which appeared to offer a radically new reading,

> The Kate I played in *The Shrew* was a direct product of the rehearsal process. I was conscious of wanting to radiate the sense of terribly clouded confusion that overwhelms you when you are the only woman around. That was Kate's position, and it was mine: she in that mad marriage, me in rehearsal. Men, together, sometimes speak a funny language. You don't know what's happening, and you get so confused that you can no longer see. You become one frown. I get like that sometimes; so did my Kate.[6]

Benthall and most of the directors who followed him at Stratford knew that the play worked as a farce, that with the addition of sufficient slapstick business it could be made into a good show which would please an undiscriminating audience. A few critics questioned this procedure, though none could suggest what reading might take its place:

> In the rough and tumble Shakespeare's play gets trodden upon rather severely. Words cease to count in this welter of action .... There was plenty of laughter in the Theatre tonight, but one felt that it was at Mr Benthall's 'gags' rather than at Shakespeare's humour.
>
> (*Birmingham Post*, 8 May 1948)

Perhaps this reviewer had not stopped to ask (as Benthall may have) just what was so funny about 'Shakespeare's humour', in this play a dubious concept to the modern observer. But reviewers are often nostalgia-addicts: the *Birmingham Mail* similarly regretted the loss of 'the familiar magic of Shakespeare's story'; and even *Punch* found 'the total effect is ... boring. There is no comic focus, no emphasis to give shape to the comedy, and very little peace to enjoy its poetry'.

George Devine, in the next Stratford production in 1953, made some effort to find both a focus and 'poetry'. He added in material from the 1594 *Taming of a Shrew*, so that the whole play, set solidly in an Elizabethan country house by Vivienne Kernot, became Christopher Sly's dream. Yvonne Mitchell, the Katharina, recalled,

The play was played in Elizabethan costume, and Bianca and I dressed as boys for the arrival of the players in the opening scene, which was great fun, and to me it was exciting that I was playing a boy who played a girl. At the end of the play, George Devine, the producer, devised the going-away of the players, to a distant sad trumpet-call, and we were once more the boys, tired after their exertions, slowly leaving the lord's house where we had been playing.[7]

This ending, like the whole production, had 'an undeniable charm and grace', said Cecil Wilson of the *Daily Mail* (10 June 1953) Antonia White, the novelist, commented that

Devine manages to give what is little more than a rather brutal farce a lyrical overtone . . . . The lighting is admirable; so mellow that at times, with the subdued colour harmonies of the dresses, one seems to be looking at a living Giorgione. At the end, when the bright figures fade like a dream and Sly wakes from his fuddled dream, there is a moment of pure magic.

(*Spectator*, 12 June 1953)

To present the play as an idealised past viewed through the frame of aesthetically pleasing pictorial composition is, like playing the piece as 'rumbustious farce', simply a way of deadening its power to offend. Moreover, as Graham Holderness points out apropos Barton's 1960 production, the aesthetic pleasure offered is coercively conservative, 'a crystallisation of that nostalgically-regretted organic past' which is itself a literary myth:[8] the idea that there was once a time when everyone accepted their place in the Great Chain of Being under God the Father and his representative on earth, the monarch.

Devine's 'lyrical' intention was assisted by his casting of Katharina and Petruchio, the physically lightweight Yvonne Mitchell and Marius Goring – both of whom were more noted for their performances in serious plays than in comedy.[9] Their performance together was generally found refreshing: the 'line' they took was that Kate and Petruchio fall in love at first sight, and spend the rest of the play getting to know each other. The 'leading players', said Ruth Ellis, 'have brought tenderness into parts often merely farcically rumbustious.' Thus Mitchell's Katharina was

a little spitfire of a girl, isolated at home by the genial stupidity of her father, and the mewing smugness of a coy sister. Petruchio is her chance of escape, which she takes, with some lively attempts to prove some independence, but no real reluctance. In surrender she is so whole-hearted, so cheerfully serene and gay, that a particularly happy marriage never seems to be in doubt.

(*Stratford Herald*, 12 June 1953)

Ellis also noted a 'moving moment . . . when Katherina addresses part of her long final speech to her father, holding his hand, looking down at him to promise a new daughter in her penitence for her past naughtiness'. 'More Kate the sensitive than Kate the curst, suggest-ing] a dark-eyed fawn rather than a clawing virago', thought Ivor Brown (*Sunday Observer*, 14 June 1953), though other critics noted the 'tolerant amusement' and 'playfulness' with which she endured her taming (W.A. Darlington, *Daily Telegraph*, 10 June 1953; John Barber, *Daily Express*, 10 June 1953). It is interesting to contrast these observations of Yvonne Mitchell's Kate with her own memories:

> The opening scenes of *The Shrew* I never enjoyed as much as the rest. At Kate's first entrance everyone says what a termagant she is, yet she has as yet done or said nothing to warrant it. I felt I would have liked to throw something at somebody to start myself off into a flaming temper. Later in the play she proves her mettle, and I enjoyed it enormously. My niece, aged six, came to see a matinée performance, her first time in any theatre, and in one scene where I viciously bit Marius's hand, I heard her call out, 'She bited him! She bited him!'[10]

Out of the mouths of babes! This is not the last time we will encounter a conflict between the actress's perception of her role and the public's, mediated as the latter is by assumptions about the normal parameters of feminine behaviour.

Marius Goring made up for his lightweight physical presence by a great deal of swaggering, substituting 'gay bravura for ferocity', said Brown. It was a performance showing some sensitivity, which most critics found a relief:

> Mr Goring is none of your whip-cracking bullies . . . . Instead, he allows romance to gallop on a riotous tongue. He is a fellow of temperament, high humour, and rolling speech. Occasionally he suffers a fleeting qualm, but when triumph finally crowns endeavour he welcomes it with the ecstasy of

the artist whose inspiration is realised. His invitation 'Kiss me, Kate', is as much a sigh of relief as an expression of conquest.

(*Birmingham Post*, 11 June 1953)

Goring's Petruchio seems to have anticipated by some thirty-four years the interpretation of the role by Brian Cox in Jonathan Miller's RSC production; according to the *The Times* (10 June 1953), he

> suggests a Petruchio who perceives the good nature of the girl he has undertaken to woo for her money and is resolved to bring it to life by his own methods, which are admittedly eccentric but carried out without a particle of ill-humour.

This 'therapeutic' interpretation is suggested also in Ruth Ellis's analysis of Kate's home situation, quoted earlier. However, Devine was unable to carry this line of psychological realism through into the other characters and situations of the play. The audience, largely composed of 'American and Empire tourists', must have the 'simple fun' that they expect from *The Shrew*, noted Paul Holt (*Daily Herald*, 10 June 1953). Cole Porter's *Kiss Me, Kate*, with its high good humour, energetic dance score, and relatively uncomplicated romance, had opened with great success in London in 1951, and had stamped its image on the play in the popular mind. Did its success invade Devine's thinking about the play?

> It is one of those busy, breathless productions in which nearly everyone seems to say more than Shakespeare wrote . . . . No character makes an ordinary exit when there is a chance of leaping over the balcony; none contents himself with a mere fall when a somersault would do; and the extravagance of the dresses matches the exuberance of the acting.

(Cecil Wilson, *Daily Mail*, 10 June 1953)

John Barber's complaint was more subtle: perceiving a story in which 'the joke is harsh and not polite', he objected to 'the actors danc[ing] it as a mincing frolic. They giggled, they rolled their eyes, they pouted and pulled quaint faces. They tried so hard to be funny, I hardly laughed once' (*Daily Express*, 10 June 1953).

There is clearly a discrepancy between the critics' sense of the play's possible significations, and what they were seeing – and the audience was enjoying – on stage. There is a further ambivalence discernible between the lyrical playing of Katharina and Petruchio

nt in Devine's production, and the broad
formance. The issue of the moral status of
onfronted: is the play merely a rough
omething which speaks to souls more

was revived in June 1954, cast changes
ics' job: the youthful Keith Michell and
roles of Petruchio and Kate, and played
tly: both were described as fiery, gallant,
intelligent, amusing, strong and spirited. *Plays & Players* (July
1954) wrote,

> Savagely splendid in her rage, Barbara Jefford bursts on the
> scene as the most untamable of shrews. Anger blazing from
> her every tone and gesture, this Katharina calls for a Petruchio
> of exceptional ruthlessness and virility. Keith Michell brings
> just these qualities to the part, battling his way through
> Katharina's defences like an eloquent Errol Flynn. His rough
> charm and swashbuckling impetuosity would have swept any
> ordinary young woman into his arms in a matter of minutes.

The critic of the *Wolverhampton Express and Star* (2 June 1954)
identified the *extra*-ordinary quality of Jefford's modern, angry
Kate: she 'had a mind of her own – which was out-of-joint with the
times. Today she would be a successful woman Parliamentary
candidate'. This realistic contemporary edge to Jefford's playing was
finally negated, however, by the reimposition of the dream-frame,
leaving viewers unsure of the production's meaning: 'the confusion
of the tinker's mind as it wrestles with Pirandellian complexities
spreads to our own', said the *The Times* critic (2 June 1954).

Peter Hall's first season at Stratford in 1960 included, as an example
of the development of Shakespearean comedy, *The Taming of the
Shrew* – 'farcical rather than comical, though still more human than
most farces', Hall's note for the programme read. It teamed the
surprise casting of the 52-year-old Dame Peggy Ashcroft and the 28-
year-old Peter O'Toole with a director new to professional work,
the Cambridge don John Barton. What was to become Barton's
hallmark, a detailed realism, informed the production (though the
more experienced Hall was called in at the last moment to get the
show ready for first night). The set, designed by Alix Stone for the
new Stratford revolve, showed a Renaissance proscenium arch with

a small apron; behind the arch the two-storied exterior and interior of a Breughelesque sixteenth-century inn. The 1594 Christopher Sly material was included, and at times expanded by the director's hand: Sly (the Irish actor Jack MacGowran) was a very active audience-member, 'running up and down stairs and tak[ing] up half-a-dozen different vantage points . . . his frequent exchange of glances and nods with the players keeps him in the picture right through the play' (Eric Johns, *Stage*, 23 June 1960). Barton emphasised the status of the play-within-the-play by having a prompter at times assist the 'players', and by allowing 'fleeting glimpses of various members of the troupe crowded in a little back room every time the stage revolves from the yard to the interior of the Inn.' For the *The Times* reviewer (22 June 1960) the production offered 'in lavishly comic detail a gently amusing antiquarian spectacle . . . [and] the curious thing is that this spectacle has the effect of taming farce by introducing into it overtones of comedy.' Once again, and for the same reasons, a defused play, 'gently amusing', *tamed*.

The casting of Ashcroft also had the effect of slanting the play towards high comedy. She did not look her age – perhaps mid-thirties, rather; much the same as O'Toole. Most critics thought that she was playing against the grain of her natural gentility, but they nevertheless found the performance curiously moving and convincing. She 'had to fight to be a termagant', said J.C. Trewin (*Birmingham Post*, 23 June 1960). 'She never manages to find a withering tongue to lash out the lines . . . but once she stoops to be conquered she melts our hearts with the underlying pathos of the lines' (Johns). Milton Shulman remarked that she 'is not a slapstick shrew. She plays the part for sympathy rather than laughs' (*Evening Standard*, 22 June 1960); 'she is indeed a woebegone figure at the height of her ordeal', added the *The Times*. Following through this line of emotional realism in her portrayal of Kate, Ashcroft offered a final speech of submission that, while knowingly humouring Petruchio, was also blissful, radiant with content. Kenneth Tynan's analysis of her performance indicates its psychological depths, but also points to the production's ultimate moral evasiveness:

> we have a sulky, loutish girl who has developed into a school bully and a family scold in order to spite Bianca, the pretty younger sister who has displaced her as her father's favourite daughter. Her fury is the product of neglect; Petruchio's

violence, however extreme, is at least attentive. He cares, though he *cares cruelly*, and to this she responds, cautiously blossoming until she becomes what he wants her to be. The process is surprisingly touching, and Dame Peggy plays the last scene ... with an eager, sensible radiance *that almost prompts one to regret the triumph of the suffragette movement*.

(*Observer*, 26 June 1960 [my emphases])

Peter O'Toole played a dashingly extrovert Petruchio; according to Milton Shulman,

the most aggressive, virile, dominating Petruchio in years. Any woman who stood in his way would be blown apart by a puff or a sneeze. It is a marvellously comic performance which will put heart into even the most brow-beaten husband in the audience. Against such a whirlwind of masculine ego even so sturdy an actress as Peggy Ashcroft can but yield and surrender. There is no doubt that women's suffrage suffers a considerable beating in the completeness of her capitulation.

The extraordinarily complacent anti-feminism of these two influential reviewers (in the *Observer* and the *Evening Standard* respectively) leads one to think that they must have observed the Amazons approaching at a distance. Certainly O'Toole's Petruchio presented the most wonderful heroic fantasy-figure for these poor threatened males:

he seems to be centre stage even when he is half-hidden in the wings. As with Olivier, even his silences excite, for there is no telling how his next line will be delivered, with what whiplash roar, or whisper he will assail the ear.

(Felix Barker, *Evening News*, 22 June 1960)

Charismatic, sublimely confident, totally in control (so much so that he remained comfortably squatting on nothing when Katharina pulled a stool out from under him): what could the audience do but admit he was a lord of the universe, and what woman, especially an ageing spinster, would not 'naturally' succumb to him?

When the production was revived in September 1961 at the Aldwych, the principals were Derek Godfrey (aged 37) and Vanessa Redgrave (aged 24). The age imbalance, which had led the audience subconsciously to pity and feel for Dame Peggy's Kate, was now righted. The *The Times* (14 September 1961) reported with relief that the play was unproblematic, despite its nastiness for readers:

> Actors have found that they are able wordlessly to indicate in both the scold and the bully a touch of dissimulation which makes all the difference. They have fallen headlong in love with each other at the very first encounter.
>
> Miss Vanessa Redgrave and Mr Derek Godfrey . . . are delightfully at ease with the comparatively new fashion. They make it clear from the start that we should be foolish to bother ourselves with social and ethical considerations . . . . It is not Kate's spirit that needs to be broken, only her pride . . . . Miss Redgrave is all youthfulness . . . . when it is her turn to be tormented she shows the tough resilience of youth . . . . Miss Redgrave shows good judgment and great charm in marking the stages at which her pride gives way before her shy but rapidly growing desire to let Petruchio know that he has won the game.

Only one slight doubt remained in this reviewer's mind: 'does she sufficiently coat her final surrender with irony? The farce should surely end in a negotiated, not an imposed, peace'. As Caryl Brahms remarked, 'there is more than swing and swagger in Katharina'; the very youthful Redgrave missed the role's irony, that 'recognises that there is a twist about the taming of the Shrew – that the hand extended to do Petruchio ease at one moment is capable of swinging up and catching him one across the ear, the next' (*Plays & Players*, November 1961). Male reviewers, however, were swept off their feet by Redgrave's grace, charm, and sweetness: she was simply '*playing* at being a bad-tempered girl', said Richard Findlater (*Financial Times*, 14 September 1961). She won the *Evening Standard*'s 1961 award for best actress for this performance.

Derek Godfrey was commended for a more restrained performance than O'Toole's: Findlater admired the 'subtle and irresistible effect' of 'that brand of self-amused irony' which was his trademark: 'He is enjoying the joke . . . because its fundamental brutality is camouflaged by the conspiracy of sympathy between this Petruchio and his Kate'. Also contributory to this effect were the broadly slapstick performances of the other 'players' before Christopher Sly: there were easy laughs in abundance, which meant that no-one need pause to question the central characters' exercise in sexual politics.

With Trevor Nunn's 1967 production *The Taming of the Shrew* arrived at intellectual respectability, at least as far as the programme was concerned: in this solid compendium of notes and essays Nunn signalled that he had looked anew at the play and its implications for a modern audience. There was a double page headed 'What does a woman want?', with quotations from various male chauvinists from the sixteenth to the twentieth century, and from two twentieth-century feminists of the 'first wave' of post-war feminism, Simone de Beauvoir and the journalist Marjorie Proops. Another double page tackled the subject of strolling players and acting in general. Here Nunn quoted from his own rehearsal notes:

> Where then is the reality of *The Shrew*? Is it in the Royal Shakespeare Theatre, or in the Warwickshire that is presented within it, or in the play that is presented within that, or in the deceptions those actors acting actors, acting parts, then openly perpetrate on each other, or is it in the more subtle deceptions of self knowledge within these characters? When is anybody acting or posing, what do we accept, and what reject, where is the basis of truth in this ever diminishing or ever expanding fantasy? It's a theme that Shakespeare never leaves . . . . It is only embryonic in *The Shrew*, but it is excitingly and un-deniably there.

Naturally this approach meant that the expanded Sly material of 1594 was once again included. The set was a wintry Warwickshire ale-house (designed by Christopher Morley): the play, noted Nunn, 'in its language and characters is rooted in Warwickshire, in England, in Elizabethan domesticity . . . . It is derived from the Medieval mummer plays and ballads. Its background is brutal and instinctual male domination'. The players, including a quartet of musicians, extemporised a set for 'The Shrew' out of the ale-house's furniture; they juggled and tumbled, and played to the on-stage audience; they 'doubled' in minor roles, and on occasion held up the show, *commedia*-fashion, to consult about the plot. For W.A. Darlington, this emphatic framing of 'The Shrew' was a frustrating dramatic experience:

> We are therefore never allowed for one moment to think of the main play's characters as real people. They are puppets in a crudely designed farce, crudely yet capably acted by a

strolling troupe who lose no opportunity of introducing bits of clowning into their parts, sometimes at the expense of their impersonations.

(*Daily Telegraph*, 6 April 1967)

Others found this distancing of the main tale reassuring: for Ronald Bryden it 'establish[ed] the play's nature as a tavern-tale from Bocaccio, strayed worlds away from its origins, told to divert a beery snugful of yokels on a wintry Warwickshire night' (*Observer*, 9 April 1967). R.B. Marriott in *The Stage* (13 April 1967) admired Nunn's 'marvellously created' impression of 'a genuine breed of vagabond players'.

Where, however, did this leave Nunn's other ideological concerns, as signalled in the programme? Or was it enough simply to indicate the director's awareness of fashionable feminist issues in the programme and then get on with the entertainment? It was a popular show, greatly enjoyed by its audiences: Roy Kinnear's fat, wheezing fall-guy Baptista was particularly admired for its comic impact – 'throughout he gives his celebrated impersonation of a gallant, though quaking, jelly. Shakespeare might have enjoyed this', thought J.C. Trewin (*Birmingham Post*, 6 April 1967). Petruchio and Katharina were played by the youthful Michael Williams and Janet Suzman. It was his first star part; Suzman had already made an impression with Portia, Celia, Ophelia and Rosalind for the company. They made a cheerful, energetic, unproblematic couple: 'it is love at first sight again', reported the *Birmingham Mail* (6 April 1967): 'in fact in the long silence at the first meeting, before war breaks out, the couple seem awe-struck with each other.'[11] Typical of their relationship, and of Williams's good-humoured 'taming', was the treatment of the 'sun and moon' scene: Petruchio was clearly teasing her; finally, 'Kate laughs hysterically for two minutes, lies down at full length on the ground, and agrees "It is the blessed sun!"'[12] Production photos show several shots of the two laughing together. Harold Hobson, who did not like the general 'proletarian' tone of the production, found, as others did, a touching humanity in the relationship:

> Throughout the production [their] dawning tenderness gradually increased; Miss Suzman endured Petruchio's tricks with a weary and affectionate patience, and Mr Williams showed that even the brashest exterior may hide a heart bursting with misgivings. The submission scene, thus led up to, had a

profound effect. At Katharina's obedience a great stillness fell upon the stage audience; these louts and layabouts were moved to a bemused silence, and so were we.

(*Sunday Times*, 9 April 1967)

Suzman's Katharina was never venomous: 'She's not so much a hell-cat as a petulant girl over-indulgently brought up by her father' (Felix Barker, *Evening News*, 6 April 1967). Gareth Lloyd Evans found her, interestingly, 'a superbly *virile* Katharina whose shrewishness is but a cloak for waiting love' (*Guardian*, 6 April 1967). In both these assessments, the answer to Katharina's problems can be found in a man – father or lover. Despite Lloyd Evans's suggestive adjective, there is no questioning the patriarchal system that regulates women's individuality; in fact it is read as positively benign. Michael Billington was moved to see 'a Baptista overcome with emotion at the change that has been wrought in his daughter' (*Plays & Players*, October 1967). Janet Suzman is a strong-looking woman who performs with great energy, and Williams matched this as a cheerful unaggressive 'Marlboro man', unshaven, in buckskin shirt and ten-gallon hat – though all the other costuming was realistically Elizabethan, including 'wickedly assertive codpieces' for the men, Barker noted. This was clearly, though comically, 'a man's country', not far removed, for all the programme's intellectual pretensions, from the straightforward fantasyland of Benthall's production thirty years earlier.

More of much the same was offered by Clifford Williams's production in 1973. Again the programme offered various double pages of intellectual fare: 'the debate on the treatment of women', including Germaine Greer's justification of *The Taming of the Shrew* from *The Female Eunuch*:

The submission of a woman like Kate is genuine and exciting because she has something to lay down, her virgin pride and individuality . . . . Kate's speech at the close of the play is the greatest defence of Christian monogamy ever written. It rests upon the role of a husband as protector and friend, and it is valid because Kate has a man who is capable of being both, for Petruchio is both gentle and strong (it is a vile distortion of the play to have him strike her ever) . . . . There is no romanticism in Shakespeare's view of marriage. He recognised it as a difficult state of life, requiring discipline, sexual energy, mutual respect, and great forbearance.

Once again the extra Sly material was used (though the hunting party and its lord were cut), and the tinker remained on stage throughout the production, enjoying it hugely; once again the audience was shown the action in an Elizabethan inn. Michael Billington reported (*Guardian*, 26 September 1973):

All the production's special effects are created within full view of the audience . . . . But, having created a splendid framework, Mr Williams fills it with a strenuous, slapstick production that drains the play of its emotional reality and substitutes instead a kind of Norman Wisdom benefit show.

For both Harold Hobson and Irving Wardle the elimination of the controlling lord was one of the most significant aspects of the production. Wardle felt that it 'obliterate[d] the sense of class cruelty, and . . . emphasise[d] the theatrical artificiality of the occasion' (*The Times*, 26 September 1973) – this allowed Williams to 'treat the whole thing as a joke unconnected with life outside' (class-cruelty is worrying and real, cruelty to women apparently not). Hobson considered that this 'offensive' play had been given a *raison d'être* by Williams's historical framework: the lords have been changed into strolling players who have fled from London because of the Plague: 'Those who have been buffeted (and frightened) by life will see no harm in buffeting others. In such circumstances a vicious play becomes right and proper' (*Sunday Times*, 30 September 1973).

What was presented was not, however, a noticeably vicious play, but rather an anodyne, slapstick entertainment, as Billington indicated. The 'riot of prop-ridden capering', said Russell Davies in the *Observer* (30 September 1973), 'might well serve as a young person's guide to the resources of inventive low comedy, so thoroughly did it explore and demonstrate the possibilities of plywood furniture, huge cream cakes, outsize cardboard hands and plastic vegetables'. The plastic vegetables were particularly resented by reviewers, for they appeared in the 'starvation scene', and deprived Kate's suffering of any dramatic truth:

since the food here is all ludicrous pantomime grub (we even get a carrot floating down on a parachute and the audience pelting the stage with prop vegetables) the scene loses any sense of dramatic reality. With the best will in the world I suspect Mr Williams has tried to take the offensiveness out of the play; the trouble is he has removed much of its point at the same time.

Thus Billington (op. cit.); but the complaint was general. In the midst of this melée of funny business Alan Bates and Susan Fleetwood were attempting to play Petruchio and Katharina. There was a general feeling that this pairing did not provide the right chemistry: Bates was all ironic, swaggering courtesy, somewhat offhand; 'the actor at all times keeps a safe Brechtian distance from the role' (Eric Shorter, *Daily Telegraph*, 26 September 1973). Fleetwood, playing in a quite different style, puzzled some critics: her Kate 'seems at first strangely out of tune with the relentless good humour of the others – desperate and sad rather than fiercely scornful . . . soon submissive' (Christopher Hudson, *Evening Standard*, 26 September 1973). 'I felt sorry for Susan Fleetwood', said Russell Davies, 'wading through the debris towards a rather interesting sub-hysterical interpretation of Kate, perpetually on the verge of simultaneous tears and laughter' (*Observer*, 30 September 1973). Wardle (op. cit.) identified the basic problem:

> When one is informed so firmly that 'it is only a play' it is hard to get much fun out of the fight . . . who are these people, and what do they think of each other? At one moment Miss Fleetwood is casting rapt glances at her implacable lover; at the next she treats him with indifferent disdain (her performance is very short on anger) . . . . She does blossom radiantly at the end but it is without any help from him.

And, it is clear, without any help from the director, who by imposing the theatrical framework so insistently, and refusing to legitimise Fleetwood's performance within the production, abrogated his responsibility to explore the play's human problems.

Later in the same year Charles Marowitz's horrific re-working of the play premiered in London; thereafter, no-one could conscientiously claim the play for 'fun'. Beth Hayes reported in *Plays & Players* (December 1973):

> the dark, stark set at the Open Space tells us at once that we are no longer in sun-soaked Padua where Petruchio's tricks and ploys are all part of Shakespearean sit-com, but rather we are in a cruel world where masculine victory in the sex-war is part and parcel of a broader canvas of property-stroke-domination, whereby men must rule and women must obey.

> . . . Made mad by Petruchio's brutality, [Kate] is raped, to return in chains to her father's house. Demented, she delivers Kate's famous speech exhorting all women to love, serve and obey their husbands.

Marowitz's adaptation also contained scenes from a twentieth-century courtship, in which the young woman domineers over the man, though not by physical means. 'Marowitz shows us that both sexes have their bullies and blackmailers, and that nothing much changes despite the passage of time, or the reversal of roles' (Hayes). Hayes questioned the relevance of these scenes to the play's basic effect; similarly, my own memories of the production remain those of the physical torture and madness of Kate, which placed the play firmly in the emerging feminist context of the 1970s. A production which ignored this context would hardly seem conceivable after 1973.

1978-87

For Michael Bogdanov, who directed the *The Taming of the Shrew* at Stratford in a modern-dress production in 1978, Shakespeare is undoubtedly a feminist:

> all the plays I direct analyse that matter; analyse the roles of women from that ideological point of view . . . . Shakespeare shows women totally abused – like animals – bartered to the highest bidder . . . . There is no question of it, his sympathy is with the women, and his purpose, to expose the cruelty of a society that allows these things to happen.[13]

This was the production which began with a genuine *coup de théâtre*, as Jonathan Pryce, playing an updated and ad libbed Sly, drunkenly abused an usherette (Paola Dionisotti, the production's Katharina), then climbed onto the stage and destroyed the traditional Italian proscenium-arch set for the play that the audience thought they had come to see. At early performances, a number of people left the auditorium, or attempted to call the police or the front of house manager, so shocked were they by the apparent reality of what was happening. Thus Bogdanov made his first point: that male violence and the desire to dominate are a *present* problem, not something which 'used to happen' in a safely sanitised past. The opening 'act of theatre was self-reflexive,' he explained, but leaving the nerve ends raw and tingling, ready for the violent experience to come. The violence of my production was meant to engage the audience on an emotional level, to the extent of asking an audience to stand up and be counted. To ask what you really believe, are you really sitting comfortably in your seats, or is there something else that theatre makes you do? Makes you angry, makes you fear, challenges you, and finally makes you want to do something to change the world.[14]

Pryce's Sly metamorphosed into Petruchio – two faces of the same male chauvinist pig – and was not seen again until a double appeared on a catwalk to watch the final scene. Bogdanov, having used the theatrical framework to create a sense of present reality, then had no further use for it (nor did Shakespeare, in the Folio text which was now played): if 'The Shrew' is Sly's dream, it is a frighteningly powerful dream in which we are all involved. 'I believe', said Bogdanov,

he set out to write a play about a wish-fulfilment dream of a male for a revenge on a female. I think that emerges very clearly from the 'Induction', which is the key to the whole play. Sly, the drunken tinker, is thrown out of the pub by the hostess, falls asleep, and dreams a dream of revenge and power; not only power over women, but class power through wealth. The first image that comes to him in his dream is the huntsman who bets on the dog in exactly the same way, and with the same amounts of money, as the women are bet on at the end of the play. It is a cruel oppressive world where nothing will ever really change.[15]

The production was undoubtedly violent, and not only on Petruchio's part (he pinioned Kate's wrists, he hurled her to the ground (plate 11)). Katharina and Bianca fought like cats, rolling on the floor – demonstrating what Gareth Lloyd Evans called 'the characteristically 1970s' unfeminine aspects of both Katherina and Bianca, the one hard-jawed, steel-lipped, dull-eyed, and whose every word is a militant confrontation, the other unattractively characterless' (*Stratford Herald*, 12 May 1978). Dionisotti's Kate was certainly not the 'neglected beauty' commonly portrayed: Bogdanov was looking for a mould-breaking image. But her plainness did not give her any compensating strength; despite her

Plate 11 Paola Dionisotti as Katharina, Jonathan Pryce as Petruchio, *The Taming of the Shrew*, 1978, directed by Michael Bogdanov. Photograph: Laurence Burns.

slapping Petruchio's face on his 'Kiss me, Kate' in II.1 – no love at first sight here – she was thoroughly cowed by the bullying scenes of Act IV. Michael Billington found himself questioning

> whether there is any reason to revive a play that seems totally offensive to our age and our society. My own feeling is that it should be put back firmly and squarely on the shelf.
> . . . Bogdanov, like any intelligent man, clearly finds The Shrew a barbaric and disgusting play. Instead of softening its harsh edges like most recent directors, he has chosen to emphasise its moral and physical ugliness . . . . I found [the production's] sheer brutality almost unbearable.
>
> (*Guardian*, 5 May 1978)

And Benedict Nightingale pinpointed the production's despairing contemporary vision – no revolution of the oppressed is possible here:

> Padua, it seems, is that sort of place, a competitive, grasping, cynical, and really rather horrible city. A city in which well-fed men slouch indolently over their port, baying 'hear, hear' when one of their number extracts a particularly ignominious confession of inferiority from his woman. A city where the sound of the hunting-horn echoes symbolically over the walls. A city in which a man as unscrupulous and deadly as Jonathan Pryce's Petruchio is all too sure to thrive.
>
> (*New Statesman*, 5 May 1978)

Astonishingly, few other critics had the same response. Most found it still an amusing farce; for B.A. Young, it was positively 'a joyous evening' (*Financial Times*, 5 May 1978) – a nice contrast here between the response of the financial establishment's news-paper and the Left's (in the *New Statesman*). Other reviews detail with delight the new business enabled by the modern setting: Petruchio's arrival on a motorbike, Baptista's exploding calculator, a brass band playing snatches of *Kiss Me, Kate*, a pantomime horse for the wedding. Had Bogdanov lost his nerve, or had he misjudged his audience's ability to see the deadly reality underlying these games? It would seem that entrenched social attitudes – the 'taming of a shrew' is *of course* funny – were largely undisturbed by Bogdanov's attempted radicalism, and the fault must partly lie in his allowing the comic business to overtake his radical reading.

A woman reviewer, Jane Ellison in the *Evening Standard* (5 May 1978), saw clearly the production's intentions:

> it is she [Katharina] who wins the final, joyless victory, spitting out her famous speech of submission with such indomitable scorn that he flinches and turns away as she licks his foot like a dog.
>
> Winding horns and the dismal cry of hounds reverberate through this hard and brilliant production . . . . Modern attitudes dictate sympathy for Katharina's 'shrewishness', fully justified in this atmosphere of commodity dealing, and her sour refusal to be sold to the highest bidder is seen as frustration and rebellion rather than a 'devilish spirit'. By contrast, it is Petruchio who repels us with his inhumanity, passionate for his quarry's wealth, dispassionate towards suffering. With frightening speed he switches fron hysterical bouts of clowning to dark, brutish rages which gives his boast to 'kill a wife with kindness,' a psychopathic horror. Jonathan Pryce plays Petruchio with a deadly and glittering arrogance which holds us fascinated.

When the production was revived at the Aldwych (after a tour around the country), both Ellison and Billington slightly revised their opinions, indicating an ambivalence centred on Pryce's portrayal of Petruchio. For Billington,

> I now see what Mr Bogdanov was driving at: a complete reversal of the roles within the play . . . . [T]his production is entirely about the taming of Petruchio . . . what we see in the final scene is the ultimate humiliation of Petruchio by a mature, witty and ironic Kate.
>
> (*Guardian*, 30 April 1979)

Billington felt that Pryce's self-indulgent clowning 'could do with a touch of directorial discipline'; and Ellison offered a gloss on this observation:

> Playing the audience like an old music-hall pro, Pryce gives a performance of dazzling riskiness which he pulls off triumphantly . . . the comedy now seems heightened . . . . Petruchio has lost the psychopathic violence which dominated his performance at Stratford, so that we are left reeling, with Paola Dionisotti's Katharina, by his manic energy.

Only the ending is feminist, said Ellison: 'For the rest of the evening we are on Petruchio's side, bawling with laughter at Katharina's humiliation and rejoicing in his attempts to subdue her as if feminism was an unknown word' (*Evening Standard*, 2 May 1979). So it seems that a radical experiment collapsed before the old theatrical urge to entertain the punters, and that Pryce's 'star' qualities insisted that – whatever the enlightened reading of the play – it was about Petruchio, not Kate. Comic or vicious, Pryce was essentially dangerous as the driving force of this enacted narrative. Graham Holderness points out that 'the kinds of theatrical excitement generated by such representations' of physical violence are 'likely to impose little moral or intellectual restraint on the release of emotions of which the director's politico-moral perspective would scarcely approve';[16] the gut reaction to the charismatic display of aggressive power can all too easily become the approval of the *fascisti*. The rowdy charm of an O'Toole or the gentle strength of Brian Cox (in the 1987 production) are simply different versions of the same problem. A narrative which legitimises male supremacy in the audience's eyes can only be deconstructed, I would argue, by a much more independent Kate than any RSC main-stage production has yet allowed.

It is symptomatic of this insidious male suprematism that Paola Dionisotti, interviewed some ten years after the production, seems to have conceded the position:

> I wanted the play to be about Kate and about a woman instinctively fighting sexism. But I don't really think that's what the play is about. It's not the story of Kate: it's the story of Petruchio. He gets the soliloquies, he gets the moments of change. All the crucial moments of the story for Kate, she's off stage.[17]

This last point is not in fact true: the wooing, the wedding, the scenes at Petruchio's house and on the road to Padua, and the final scene, are all 'crucial moments' for Kate, points at which she could refuse absolutely to submit to male domination. Bogdanov, by putting the play into modern dress, confused the actress: 'I kept finding myself internalising; I kept wondering why I didn't just get up and go', as a modern woman would. But clearly this had not been Bogdanov's concern: what in fact interested him was an anatomy of patriarchal society through the foregrounding of a male who is even more overt and brutal in his acquisitiveness than the monied and 'civilised' Baptista and Lucentio. Dionisotti explains, taking the standard female line of 'understanding' the man: 'Jonathan played Petruchio as that kind of classic man who comes strolling into a society bragging like hell: he is terribly competitive because he has this *need* to be accepted, though he never will be'.[18] Dionisotti gives a long and detailed analysis of her performance of the play's final scene in *Clamorous Voices*, concluding,

> My Kate was kneeling and I reached over to kiss his foot and he gasped, recoiled, jumped back, because somehow he's completely blown it. He's as trapped now by society as she was in the beginning. Somewhere he's an okay guy, but *it's too late*. The last image was of two very lonely people. The lights went down as we left – I following him, the others hardly noticing we'd gone. They'd got down to some hard gambling. They just closed ranks around the green baize table.[19]

Dionisotti's fatalistically ironical reading of the final scene was what the less easily seduced critics saw – those who were not mesmerised by the clowning of Pryce and the other male characters.[20] Perhaps the last word on this production should go to Robert Cushman of the *Observer* (13 May 1979), who recorded his own confusion about its intentions:

> I know I enjoyed the production but I am not sure how to interpret it. I judge from other reviewers that my confusion is shared. I fancy that the director, Michael Bogdanov, is none too clear himself . . . . It is the characterisation that is periodically wrenched out of the true. That too, *at any given moment*, may be true to the text, or a defensible reading of it . . . but the choices here are not always compatible.

Feeling that the ending of the play is equivocal – is Kate 'sincere' or only 'apparently' so? Is Petruchio 'guilty or embarrassed'? – Cushman concludes, 'However you take the moment, it remains an arresting one, that compels you to think about the play and what has gone before . . . . The production is at its strongest in establishing the play's monetary climate . . . . The final banquet is very much a feast of successful men'. And against Michael Billington's doubts as to 'whether this has anything to do with the play that Shakespeare wrote', Cushman argues, 'of the words he wrote and the actions they imply, it is an exact and acute rendering . . . . At his best Mr Bogdanov (like John Barton in his *Merchant of Venice* with its unsympathetic Shylock, now at the Warehouse) has dug out the play's situation and put it on the stage in front of us'.

It remained then for post-Bogdanov directors at Stratford to build on his vision of its 'basic situation', if possible with more clarity and a less frantic desire to keep the audience laughing at what was by now, through the diffusion of generally feminist thinking in the intellectual community, acknowledged to be a problematic and unpleasant play. However, Barry Kyle, the director of the 1982 Stratford production, opted for the older model. In an interview with Jane Ellison, he defended his production:

> Obviously you can't do the play unaware of the rise of feminism. The only way to answer feminist criticism is to see Kate as a wild, wonderful, free woman who is shackled by a barbarian. The feminist mistake is to assert that she is all women. She isn't. She finds her own particular destiny, but her solution is not everybody's.
>
> The taming event, I believe, is about changing the world as she sees it . . . . She is a lovely, proud, desperate spirit and what this Roaring Boy does is to expose her to a few realities, like hunger and cold. He removes the trappings of artifice, and in Shakespeare's later plays this becomes one of his most important themes – that artifice is constantly rejuvenated by natural experience.
>
> (*The Times*, 18 October 1982)

This is of course specious nonsense, an attempt to pretend that the play's patriarchal and sexual politics don't exist, and to replace them with an individualist romanticism with no intellectual structure at all ('lovely, proud, desperate' – she must have a reason for being *desperate*). As far as critics and audiences were concerned, the production offered little by way of insight and a great deal of slapstick entertainment. But most did not find this formula satisfying. Victoria Radin thought it 'a pantomime romp eminently suitable for Japanese tourists and children on their first Shakespeare outing' (*Observer*, 17 October 1982). For Jack Tinker, it seemed that the director

> trusted the text of this notorious tribute to masculine supremacy not an inch . . . . So wonderfully varied and random are the tricks he employs to divert our attention from the cold heart of the play [that the audience doesn't have time to

ponder] why such a wilful woman would give such a slob the time of day by the end of the play . . . . If only Mr Kyle had had the courage to trust his leading players to cope with the text, we might have carried away more than a bagful of cheap laughs.

(*Daily Mail*, 14 October 1982)

As might have been expected, Kyle emphasised the play's theatrical framework by presenting a long, detailed Induction, and having Sly brought back to be awoken just before the final scene. (What status this compromise gives the final scene is unclear.) The Induction was set in wintry Warwickshire:

> Kyle's production opens [well before the house lights go down] in the hall of a meticulously re-created Tudor Inn. To the last detail – even chickens running amok in the stalls – social realism rules and so do the women, running both the household and their menfolk with daunting efficiency.
>
> When a play within a play commences, all this realism evaporates into a chaos of anachronisms.
>
> (Gordon Parsons, *Morning Star*, 18 October 1982)

For example, a surrealist Italian piazza; a 'Generation Game' conveyor belt as Gremio describes the goods he has to offer in exchange for Bianca; the Pedant abseiling down the backcloth; Tranio as an Elizabethan teddy boy, and other suitors in blazers and boaters; the return to Padua on a bicycle built for four. As Sinead Cusack commented,

> I think our production was overwritten with images . . . . We hung on to so much, whereas what we needed to do was to distil the essence of the play and to find its savagery. The invention clouded the production and a lot of the time I felt I was working against the text.[21]

Cusack's Kate was paired with Alun Armstrong's Petruchio. Their relationship was irascible and physically violent (Cusack said she 'pumped iron' in preparation for it): in the wooing scene Katharina swings a punch and falls off the stage, pushes Petruchio into a convenient pool, and kicks him in the crutch on 'Kiss me, Kate'. 'Having successfully coaxed Kate onto his knee he finds himself finishing his compliments in a strangled whisper as she does her level best to snap his windpipe' (Christopher Edwards, *Plays &*

Players, December 1982). In her turn she is swung into the pool by a cunning Petruchio. After the wedding, he slings her over his shoulder and carries her off kicking and screaming (business last used in 1961, when Vanessa Redgrave's Kate showed uninhibited delight). Clearly there *was* 'savagery' here; and, for Irving Wardle, the production was distressing on account of it:

> If the laughs diminish as the evening wears on it is because of the crass insensitivity of the central partnership. This is largely a matter of casting. Petruchio is the ruthlessly grinning Alun Armstrong, Katharina the vulnerable Sinead Cusack. Locking those two up together is like pairing Mr Punch with the Bride of Lammermoor .... Miss Cusack repeatedly seems to have taken leave of her sanity and then makes lightning recoveries to her old grimacingly imperious self. The effect is more cruel than in any other version I can remember.
>
> (*The Times*, 14 October 1982)

Others found Armstrong 'charmless' and 'loutish'; B.A. Young thought that Petruchio's 'simulated bullying and selfishness . . . belonged to his normal life' (*Financial Times*, 14 October 1982). But there was one striking moment to Armstrong's performance. He spoke the soliloquy in IV.1, 'My falcon now is sharp', with a live, hooded falcon on his wrist; as he finished the speech, he unhooded her and raised her up towards the flies: 'The point is clear', said Michael Billington: 'by "taming" Kate he has released her true, unfettered spirit. This does not justify Petruchio's tactics; but it at least gives him a more humane strategy and lends the production a heart and soul' (*Guardian*, 13 October 1982). What it also does is legitimise Petruchio's view of Kate, presenting it as an interpretive metaphor for the whole play. Sinead Cusack herself found the metaphor compelling, and did not question its implications in terms of the power hierarchy: 'What I felt strongly was that the falcon would be free: it was liberating her to a role that she was going to enjoy playing'.[22] She appeared for her marriage dressed in funereal black with strong 'falcon' suggestions in the trimmings (plate 12), and sulked during the deprivation scenes, but then began to join in the 'game' with Petruchio. In the 'sun or moon' scene she got the giggles, and fell on the floor laughing helplessly (business repeated from the 1967 'good-humoured' production) – and even Armstrong laughed. In the final scene, dressed in radiant white, she sat on the floor to speak to him, almost privately:

At the end of the play I was determined that Kate and Petruchio were rebels and would remain rebels for ever, so her speech was not predictable. Having invited her to speak, he couldn't know what form her rebellion was going to take. He was very shaky indeed in the scene, not knowing what was coming. This so-called 'submission' speech isn't a submission speech at all: it's a speech about how her spirit has been allowed to soar free. She is not attached to him. He hasn't laid down the rules for her, she has made her own rules, and what he's managed to do is allow her to have her own vision. It *happens* that her vision coincides with his. There's a privately shared joke in that speech. And irony. And some blackness. The play is dark, savage sometimes. But I enjoyed the last speech. They're going to go on to a very interesting marriage.[23]

As long as Kate keeps up her weight-training, one might add. The speech, as Jill Burrows noted, is among other things a 'provocative sexual game' – 'However we may feel about [it], in performance an audience positively drools for it' (*Times Educational Supplement*, 22 October 1982). It did provide an image of the sexual desire that was significantly absent from the rest of the production. At the end, said Stanley Wells,

> suddenly we realise that not merely has she learnt, she has found a way to teach. And Petruchio responds, with surprised emotion and pride turning to a consummatory passion which gives a new but not cheap intensity to 'Come, Kate, we'll to bed'. Barry Kyle's production achieves subtlety in its last moments.
>
> (*Times Literary Supplement*, 22 October 1982)

Kyle's romantic individualism also made a final appearance: Petruchio gave Kate the money he had won on the wager; she threw it in the air, and they embraced again, as Elizabethan (not Italian, not modern) dancers filled the front of the stage to gracious music. This nostalgic note (which had no logic in the terms of the production) was the final indicator of the conservatism of Kyle's production.

In early 1987 Adrian Noble's RSC production of *Kiss Me, Kate* had opened to great acclaim; it went on to an extended run in London.

Plate 12 Sinead Cusack as Katharina, *The Taming of the Shrew*, 1982, directed by Barry Kyle. Photograph: Donald Cooper.

Porter and Spewack's show is witty and fast-moving, and uses the conceit of the play-within-a-play considerably more effectively than the original Sly material does. It is also very much more egalitarian in its exploration of sexual and gender relations, dispensing entirely with physical cruelty and apportioning the 'mental torture' equally between the two principals. If the Kate still has to sing her submission, Lily, the performer of Kate, has a wickedly funny feminist anthem, 'I Hate Men'. Perhaps the RSC directorate was trying to hedge its bets this year in providing one guaranteed funny and politically modern *Shrew*, since in September Jonathan Miller was to make a long overdue debut at Stratford, with his third production of *The Taming of the Shrew* (his first was at Chichester, with Anthony Hopkins and Joan Plowright, his second for BBC television, with John Cleese as Petruchio and Sarah Badel as Kate). Miller, doctor, social historian and polymath, has very clear ideas about the play, which he has explored increasingly in these three productions: 'it is not a romp or a riot, but a serious and often comic look at the Elizabethan requirements of family life. It has nothing to do with women's lib – either for or against.'[24] The programme provided a text-book background to the production, with extracts from social historians on the sixteenth and seventeenth-century ideas of the family and marriage, and on modern psychology's view of the causes of female self-aggression and low self-image. The whole is prefaced with a quotation from L.P. Hartley: 'The past is another country; they do things differently there', a line which Miller repeated to his Kate, Fiona Shaw, when she questioned the play's sexual politics (*Drama*, 4, 1987). Eliminating the theatrical Induction, and setting the play naturalistically in a sixteenth-century community, Miller anatomised 'a society where domestic relationships are based wholly on power: sexual, financial, or simple physical strength . . . . [He] firmly anchors the play in a departed world whose rigid values exclude any concession to female equality' (Irving Wardle, *The Times*, 10 September 1987).[25]

But the production was not simple antiquarianism: Miller was interested in how, according to modern psychological theory, human beings would have reacted under these social conditions. Thus the production had a curious time-warp quality, especially as regards the portrayal of Kate, who suffered from recognisably modern neuroses although dressed in Renaissance costume. Fiona Shaw, continued Wardle, played Kate from the first as an unwanted child. She may knock Bianca about, but she also takes it out on herself – snipping locks from her hair, digging her nails into her palms and cultivating a bent posture that expresses agonies of self-contempt. With Petruchio she at last meets someone who wants her.

It was that old standby, love at first sight, given a new subtlety by Brian Cox's delivery of his opening speech to her – offhand, formulaic, and with his back to her, until he idly turned on 'thy beauty' and was thunderstruck. Cox then set about playing the 'amateur shrink in an attempt to uncover a loving Kate beneath a multitude of defences' (Jane Edwards, *Time Out*, 16 September 1987). His Petruchio, outwardly unattractive, rough-hewn and swaggering though never coarse, surprised audiences by displaying 'quite unexpected resources of softness, innocence and wisdom' (Andrew Rissik, *Independent*, 10 September 1987). Mesmerised by Petruchio from the moment he first pays her attention, Fiona Shaw's shy, awkward Katharina seemed to recognise that he is her only hope of rescue from herself: she was patently shocked at the effect of her blow on him in II.1, and patently bowled over by his long, gentle kiss which closed the scene. The therapy continued: 'Petruchio fascinates and repels her because he is so different, because she recognises in him an intelligence and largeness of imagination equal to her own' (Rissik). 'Even the appalling scenes in Petruchio's house', wrote Michael Billington, 'here become bearable: they are like the final stages of a drastic surgery with Kate emerging as one "new-risen from a dream"' (*Guardian*, 10 September 1987). Their mutual treatment of the final speech is typical of the production: spoken, as Billington said, 'with the cool gravity of a grateful patient', it was delivered as the two of them sat side by side, looking at each other. Finally, she offered her hand (nowhere near his foot): Cox, 'deeply moved by her strength, affection and magnanimity' (Eric Shorter, *Daily Telegraph*, 10 September 1987), clasped it in friendship, then kissed it; then they mutually embraced in a long, passionate kiss. Several reviewers recorded with astonishment a spontaneous burst of applause which followed Kate's speech of submission: Eric Shorter commented with acuity,

Miss Shaw draws applause not, presumably, for the speech's sentiments, but rather for the sentimental state into which her acting (and Mr Cox's) has put the audience. We feel that this marriage will work, better than the sneering Bianca's anyhow.

Kate has not been driven, or starved, into submission. She has simply learned to play marital politics.

Fiona Shaw's reading of the part of Katharina – after playing it for a year – is distinctly different from Miller's. It is political rather than psychological; as a modern feminist actress, she consciously opposes her politics to his (though his are disguised as an ideologically-neutral, 'scientific' reading of history). She sees Kate as not a 'child', not a 'quiet, sullen delinquent', but 'a woman who's raging . . . . My Kate was very unhappy. She radiates unhappiness' – not just because she's an 'unloved child', but because she's 'the voice of pain in the community', the voice of those who are bought and sold, the marginalised and silenced women in the patriarchy.[26] Choosing to go with Petruchio after the wedding, rather than stay with her father, she then enters Petruchio's absurdist world: 'She who has been characterised by violence now has to observe what violence really is', – what she may have let herself in for in the reality of Elizabethan (or any) marriage. 'It's a wicked, terrible play because she's got to render herself up before she gains herself. In losing her life she wins it. What a dilemma. What a gamble.' The play is about 'someone on the brink . . . who found a way of saying "yes" without being compromised. At the end of the play, Kate wins. She can say anything now and she's still Kate'. For Shaw, Kate in her final speech is saying, '"I acknowledge the system. I don't think we can change this" – which is a terrible indictment of a system of patriarchy that is so strong it is unchangeable *even for its own good*. To say "I see . . . our strength is weak" in front of men is terribly strong.'[27] This is a view of Miller's production that Miller himself refused to see, or didn't need to see – the 'women's lib' angle, the voice of the 'patient' in his therapeutic and recuperative project. Undoubtedly Fiona Shaw's reading of Katharina gave her a dignity and intelligence that Miller's simplistic 'unloved child' would have lacked – though the perceptions of the critics, as we have seen, were on the whole very much within the parameters set by Miller in his public pronouncements.

Miller's production did give huge satisfaction to both critics and audiences, not only because of the intelligent, complex performances of Fiona Shaw and Brian Cox, but because he treated the whole play as a document in social history, an anatomy of an acquisitive masculine society, which had recognisably the same impulses as our own, though a different social structure. 'Far from skating over passages that might seem obscure or dull, Miller brings the sub-plot to Dickensian life', said Eric Shorter, and Michael Coveney pointed out 'an almost electric sensitivity to master/servant relationships that runs the play straight on to Beaumarchais and Marivaux' (*Financial Times*, 10 September 1987). There was plenty of comic acting, but it was not slapstick: the audience's laughter on the archival videotape is gentle, as it were sharing in the play's wry revelations, rather than the usual raucous hilarity which greets this play's elaborate business. Andrew Rissik summarised Miller's persuasive achievement:

> Miller has looked penetratingly at Shakespeare's text, seeing that his views of marital harmony are surprisingly close to his views on political stability. Happiness is hard-won, and has much to do with accepting the limitations as well as the advantages of the role which society allots to you. His superb supporting cast presents that society, with all its pettiness and snobbery, in marvellously clear relief. What we get, triumphantly, from Fiona Shaw and Brian Cox is a sense of the freedom and understanding which can redeem the social ritual.
>
> (*Independent*, 10 September 1987)

But however 'poetic' the two performers managed to make the final relationship, Miller's Renaissance world and its modern parallels envisaged no disruption of the patriarchy and its configurations (man as husband/psychotherapist/master of the woman). As with Bogdanov's reading, it would have required some – not necessarily large, but radical – change in the performances of his charismatic actors in order ultimately to open up the text, rather than close it off as an individual case-study. This is a change which clearly the various actresses who have played Kate since the early 1970s are more than ready for, and so are their audiences – despite the temptations of comfortable sentiment and easy laughter. All that is now required is a radically feminist director – perhaps even a woman.[28]

4

MEASURE FOR MEASURE
Sex and power in a patriarchal society

'Then Isabel live chaste, and brother die:/ More than our brother is our chastity' (*Measure for Measure*, II.4). This resounding couplet is a moment of enormous difficulty for the modern actress of Isabella, and for the audiences who are watching her. Is she a heroine, a prig, a hysteric, impossibly naive, or fiercely feminist? The play has been regarded as problematic since well before the term 'problem play' was invented in the early twentieth century. In the eighteenth and nineteenth centuries its subject matter was considered indecent (Anna Jameson wrote a whole chapter on Isabella in her *Characteristics of Women* (1836) without once specifying the nature of the bargain Angelo is offering her). After a mid-twentieth century period of mild interest in the play as an allegory of God's mysterious but ultimately benevolent ways, it was perceived as increasingly relevant in the era of sexual liberation which began in the 1960s: sexuality, or its repression, was seen as the key to all the characters. Recent critical interest has shifted to the analysis of power structures in society; the relations between Isabella, the Duke, and his deputy, have become paradigmatic of the relation between the individual and authority.

Measure for Measure is, however, technically a comedy. It demonstrates the social disruptions of carnival in its low-life scenes; it centres on a redemptive female figure; and it ends with marriages. It even includes a song, 'Take, O take those lips away' (IV.1), which allows for the same somewhat satirical commentary on romantic despair as does 'Come away, death' in *Twelfth Night*. It is set, like *Much Ado*, in a 'real place', Vienna, which with its brothels and its provosts, its respectable people and its low life, must have felt very like contemporary London to its Jacobean audience. This realism combines with the theme of sexual licentiousness to produce a play-text which unrelentingly questions the optimism of comic form – from within, as it were: *Measure for Measure* deconstructs comedy.

For instance, the low-life scenes might be performed, as Kathleen McLuskie points out, so as to 'deny the lively energy of the pimps and the bawds, foregrounding their exploitation of female sexuality':[1] so much for the licence of carnival. Isabella may represent a figure of female redemptive power – but if she wears a full nun's habit she begins to look more like a pornographic fantasy in this carnival context. Though she has (or is forced to discover in herself) the verbal facility of the Shakespearean comic heroine, her words cannot direct the course of the play's plot: her eloquence only serves to inflame Angelo, and it is the Duke, not she, who finesses the play's 'comic' resolution. As for that resolution, here the happy parade of 'eight that must take hands' of *As You Like It* is a glum procession of the forced marriages of Angelo and Mariana, Lucio and his punk; even Claudio and his Juliet, parents of a new child, are, one assumes, marked for life by the traumatic events of the play. And, famously, Isabella makes no reply to the Duke's repeated offer of marriage. The last scene of the play is an extended demonstration of the Duke's absolute power, now visibly resumed, but never in fact abrogated. As he has done throughout the play, he teases to the point of agony the other major characters, including Isabella. When he obliges her to confirm her 'feminine' status (saint, mistress, servant) by kneeling to ask pardon for Angelo, it seems unequivocally sadistic behaviour from one human being to another.[2]

These elements make the play particularly interesting to audiences and performers in the latter half of the twentieth century. In the history of post-war productions at Stratford, we can see various attempts to explain – to allegorise or humanise – the character of the Duke; to engage some sympathy for Angelo (muted in recent years, with the community's growing awareness of the facts about sexual harassment); and, in Isabella, to examine the possibilities for female power in an entrenched patriarchy.

1946–62

In 1946 there was a bright, simple, comfortably comic production of *Measure for Measure* directed by the American Frank McMullen, who had been invited to Stratford as a gesture of appreciation for American support during the war. Produced under conditions of austerity (using stock costumes), it was unremarkable except for the

Lucio of the young Paul Scofield, who gave the character 'such dry, ironic significance that the indiscreet young fantastic and the somewhat touchily romantic duke seemed in the *dénouement* to have shared the story together' (*The Times*, 26 August 1946). Revived in 1947 with some cast changes, it gave Beatrix Lehmann as Isabella another Shakespearean role in this season (see chapter 1 for discussion of her Viola). As the critics obviously expected from the president of Actors' Equity, it was a performance of feminist and worldly authority. The *Birmingham Gazette* (12 April 1947) said, 'She is hard, even calculating, and we get the impression that here is a woman – chaste or not, as you will – who knows her world and her men'. The *Birmingham Post* (12 April 1947) spoke of her 'intense intelligence and assurance', her 'pos[ing] a cold detachment against Angelo's smouldering plea' (the previous year's Isabella, Ruth Lodge, was sweet and tearful and did not impress the critics). Unfortunately neither the Angelo nor the Duke presented a real challenge to this Isabella; the production remained what *Punch* called 'a kind of ethical fantasy' (September 1946).

Peter Brook's mould-breaking production of 1950 set the play in a world of Hogarthian pimps, bawds, and criminals; torture instruments were visible in the prison scenes, in which the *Punch* reviewer (22 March 1950) noted 'the grotesque arms that claw through the gratings and the awful faces that peer dimly from the shadows'. Brook stated later in *The Empty Space* that the play embodied his ideas of Holy and Rough Theatre:

> This is the disgusting, stinking world of medieval Vienna. The darkness of this world is absolutely necessary to the meaning of the play: Isabella's plea for grace has far more meaning in this Dostoevskian setting than it would in lyrical comedy's never-never land. When this play is prettily staged it is meaningless – it demands an absolutely convincing roughness and dirt.[3]

Against this dark background Brook placed two figures of light, Isabella and the Duke, and a figure of tormented human consciousness, John Gielgud's Angelo. The play became his story: that of the bureaucrat who discovers his human waywardness and who at the end sobs aloud with remorse and relief as Isabella pleads for his life. 'The repentance that comes with discovery is profoundly moving in its intensity, so that the last great scene has something of the awe that Shakespeare seems always to have felt in the presence of man confronting truth' (Ruth Ellis, *Stratford Herald*, 17 March 1950). The play is not a problem, that is, as long as we can identify with Angelo and his 'representative humanity'. The fact that he roughly manhandled Barbara Jefford's Isabella in II.4 (as is clear from the promptbook)[4] seems not to have been a matter for concern among the critics. The 19-year-old Jefford played a young, innocent, warm-hearted Isabella,[5] wearing a vaguely medieval form-fitting dress, with a light (non-conventual) veil which allowed two kiss-curls to be seen – a subject evidently ripe for sexual harassment. She was protected from any concern the audience might have for her by her very ardour and innocence, and by the always benevolent presence of the Duke, who was played by Harry Andrews as a figure of quiet strength and straightforward virility (plate 13): 'He rules over this play deftly, surely, strikingly' (*News Review*, 16 March 1950). Only Richard Findlater questioned his 'sense of purpose: [he] seems too amiable to conduct such a rigorous and dangerous experiment' (*Tribune*, 17 March 1950).

The production embodied Brook's version of the play textually as well as dramatically. Herbert Weil Jr, in an article of 1972, made a devastating analysis of Brook's cuts to the text, particularly as they affected the image of the Duke. 'Gone are a group of lines that suggest the Duke is either confused or conniving' at various points in the text. The scene with Lucio (III.2) was shorn of its final speeches 'so that Lucio will seem only a malicious and selfish gossip and – it seems – so that no lines will reflect unfavourably on the Duke.'[6] Brook's Duke, that is to say, was unsullied by his contact with the 'Rough' world: a holy and charismatic ruler whose actions no right-thinking person would question. Even his proposal to Isabella was unproblematic: the lines 'and for your lovely sake/ Give me your hand, and say you will be mine', were cut, leaving only his lines in the final speech, 'Dear Isabel,/ I have a motion much imports your good . . . ' – a rather more gracious, less autocratic offer, which this Isabella was happy to accept, seeming to have no regrets about leaving her religious vocation. But then, she had never, to the critics' relief, been 'strident'; she had avoided 'unbecoming self-righteousness' (*Plymouth Western Morning News*, 11 March 1950).

> When she came to the perilous words she turned, from speaking full to the audience, to hide her face passionately against the wall behind her, as if herself ashamed that her intellect could find no more adequate expression of her heart's certainty.[7]

Plate 13 Maxine Audley as Mariana, Barbara Jefford as Isabella, Harry Andrews as the Duke,

Findlater thought her 'Cordelia, rather than Isabella, with a sweet and passionate pathos rather than an implacable, hard virginity, a gentle sister, not a good hater. Her chastity is negative abstinence, not a positive principle'. He felt that Jefford was in fact 'too womanly', missing out on the character's masochistic aspects that make her a 'female Angelo'.

Brook was evidently looking for a different image of the power of the feminine, one that is epitomised in his famous instruction to Barbara Jefford in the last scene: to hold the pause before she knelt for Angelo's life 'until she felt the audience could take it no longer'.[8] It was usually about thirty-five seconds: 'Then hesitantly, still silent, Isabella moved across the stage and knelt before the Duke. Her words came quiet and level'.[9] This Isabella's power, that is, was in her silence followed by her decorous speech, rather than in the 'strident' speeches of the scenes with Angelo. By this piece of business Brook made the play's gender politics potentially very clear, yet by presenting also a strong, kindly Duke, he reinforced a conservative view of the acceptable 'manly' behaviour of those who govern us for our good.

Anthony Quayle's production in 1956 made some effort to correct this over-generous view of the Duke, while at the same time building on Brook's insights as to the symbiotic relation between authority and low-life carnival. According to Harold Matthews,

> So long as the dilemma of Isabella is the theme, the play is unsatisfactory and distasteful, but make the Duke's caprices the theme and things, though preposterous enough, are not so bad. It would seem that the Duke was jealous of Angelo and used his high place to humiliate him utterly . . . . The staggering presumption of the Duke is well brought out in this production. Mr Anthony Nicholls presents him as a dandy, a daisy, an arrogant egoist taking his right to play with human lives and tell extravagant lies for granted, a gilded dragon-fly darting zigzag over the social cesspool. He is grand in attire and bearing on all occasions. Even as a friar he does not hide his kiss-curls and his cross is too fanciful to be the emblem of anything but his own vanity. His voice is resonant and he fires his phrases with military rapidity. All ideas of the forgiving father are banished. This Duke lacks spirituality and the warmth of compassion and exhibits the crass geniality of conceit.
>
> (*Theatre World*, September 1956)

This charismatic authority-figure managed to pull the wool over most critics' eyes, however: Rosemary Ann Sisson even saw 'some quality of Christ, bringing the New Testament of mercy and forgiveness in place of the harsh Old Testament rule of measure for measure'. There was general agreement that the Duke was the undoubted centre of the play; it was his 'look of joy and triumph' as Isabella knelt for Angelo's life that was the last scene's climactic moment (*Stratford Herald*, 17 August 1956).

No ewe-lamb, Margaret Johnston's Isabella might well have threatened ultimately to refuse authority's benevolent command. The 38-year-old Johnston,[10] wearing a full nun's habit, 'played Isabella with a cold flame, raging against a materialistic world, torn between a naive reticence and a passion for purity' (*Oxford Mail*, 15 August 1956). She was

> no maiden hiding her bashfulness in a nun's habit, but a woman of character and integrity virtually crucified by the intolerable strain to which her dedicated loyalty is subjected . . . . [S]he makes her passionate abuse of [Angelo's] cowardice the expression only of her own moral agony.
>
> (*The Times*, 15 April 1956)

Kenneth Young found even this amount of maturity and self-esteem disturbing to his concept of female decorum:

> Margaret Johnston's Isabella is from the beginning too much the shrewish, maiden-auntish defender of her chastity; and the mystic medieval ideal of chastity never emerges at all. In the scene where Emlyn Williams's Angelo, looking like a black Renaissance cardinal, forces himself upon her, she gives forth crude animal roars and moans.
>
> (*Daily Telegraph*, 15 August 1956)

(Should she squeak? Should she put up with it in silence?) The reviewer for the *Stage* (16 August 1956) was also quite forthright about Johnston's failure to conform to his ideal of the feminine: she

> is steady, virtuous and utterly contemptuous of any effect her physical attractions might have on men . . . . [W]hile one may admire her powerful moral principles, morality is not the most enduring quality one looks for in a woman: one feels one would like her better with a little frailty, a little warmth of even 'irregular' emotion . . . . [H]er bitter spittings-out are remembered better than her anguish of mind.

Rosemary Ann Sisson agreed, evoking the ideal of the 'silent woman', but despite her reactionary gender-politics, Sisson evidently admired what she saw:

> As Isabella Margaret Johnston speaks to fine effect all the great speeches, but does not do, perhaps, all that might be done to soften the harshness of the part. Isabella must be, like Cordelia, possessed of a shining, wordless tenderness if we are to love her (as we must, or the play suffers), and this does not, I think, emerge. But the debates with Angelo and Claudio are full of emotion and intelligence, and the last sue for mercy is a great one.
>
> (Stratford Herald, 17 August 1956)

The fact that Isabella is not written as a 'shining, wordless' part, but might rather be thought of as Shakespeare's redressing of his failure to give Kate the Shrew language wherewith to protest at her treatment (see Fiona Shaw's comment in chapter 3, note 26), is something that most critics were yet to become aware of, blinkered as they were by assumptions about what constituted an image of female heroism. But there was sufficient originality in Johnston's playing to disturb the comic paradigm: the *New Statesman* reviewer felt that 'her acceptance of the Duke at the end becomes a purely perfunctory and quite arbitrary effect of winding up' (25 August 1956). Perfunctory, too, was the acting of Emlyn Williams as Angelo (he had been playing the role on and off for over twenty years): Kenneth Tynan thought that overall 'his aspect suggests incipient nausea, a queasy stomach rather than a troubled soul' (*Observer*, 19 August 1956). With a half-hearted Angelo, a complacent Duke, and a passionate Isabella who, said the veteran Trewin, 'gets us to hear anew' (*Illustrated London News*, 25 August 1956), it would seem that the play's centre of interest was moving inevitably towards the woman. But progress was to be slow.

Casting a very young-looking Judi Dench as Isabella, and keeping her throughout the play in secular costume (a Holbein dress with considerable *décolletage*), allowed John Blatchley in 1962 to avoid the issues raised by the image of Margaret Johnston's thirtyish nun. Dench was making her Stratford debut (she had been Zeffirelli's Juliet at the Old Vic in 1960): she presented 'a young woman inexperienced, lacking in guidance', said the The Times (11 April 1962); 'an urgent, desperate girl with the ring of truth in every phrase' (J.C. Trewin, *Birmingham Post*, 11 April 1962). A number of critics, noting her *ingénue* quality and short stature, thought that she was too 'kittenish' for the role: Dennis Barker 'could not wholly believe that this Isabella would worry that much about being deflowered' (*Wolverhampton Express and Star*, 11 April 1962). Lurking behind these observations is the conviction that Angelo can hardly be blamed for falling prey to the temptations of such a sexy little thing – a familiar no-win situation for women: if they say 'no' with critical force, they're unnatural (Johnston was a 'repressed spinster' to several reviewers); if they exhibit sexual allure, even unconsciously, then men can't be responsible for their actions. To do him justice (presuming the critic for this august journal is male), the anonymous reviewer for the *The Times* (11 April 1962) found her 'already formidable as a member of secular society . . . . It is Isabella's initiation into the battle of life and she proves to be a very tough and courageous fighter'. A glimmering awareness of the power hierarchies of organised society, reflected in the dramatic performances of that society, is beginning to shape this reviewer's perspective.

J.C. Trewin thought 'the Duke . . . ha[d] found a most enviable Duchess' (no question of her acceptance of his offer). Tom Fleming's Duke was an uncomplicated ruler of a rather grey and austere Vienna, in which the low-life figures were 'diminish[ed] into nasty-minded children' (Harold Hobson, *Sunday Times*, 15 April 1962). Edmund Gardiner described Fleming's traditional paternalism, with 'all the attributes sentimental churchgoers equate with the God–Man: the physical dignity, manly mannerisms, facial compassion', and a fine, authoritative voice (*Stratford Herald*, 13 April 1962). The production's only real effort at originality was in Marius Goring's Angelo, a hysterical neurotic given to self-flagellation and fainting. For his second interview with Isabella he was wearing a nightshirt and dressing-gown, but he offered little sexual threat. 'When he throws himself at Isabella his action is not so much one of sensuality as of almost hysterical despair. He falls writhing at her feet' (*The Times*). Harold Hobson commented,

> He stands in frozen fear, on the platform of justice, or in the secrecy of his candle-concupiscent chamber. He is ever in the midst of appalled silences. It is impossible to conceive that anyone is at his mercy . . . . From the beginning his nerve has gone.

Perhaps his prophetic soul had sensed the advent of an army of assertive women.

1970–4

After an eight-year gap in productions of *Measure for Measure*, a younger Angelo, Ian Richardson, was steel-nerved and icily savage towards Estelle Kohler's fierce and youthful Isabella in John Barton's 1970 production (plate 14). In strong contrast, the Duke, played by Sebastian Shaw, was a late-middle-aged, bookish, bumbling ruler, saddened but not surprised when Isabella reacted with utter dismay to his proposal. Barton's production was revolutionary in this treatment of the Duke, and of the play's end: Kohler stood alone, looking out at the audience, as the other characters departed. Barton's intention was to be faithful to the ambiguity of Shake-speare's text in providing an 'open-ended' final image: Isabella is left 'wondering, puzzled about what she should do'.[11] The silent body language spoke differently to different members of the audience, however, depending on their own perceptions of the play's sexual politics. The *Birmingham Mail* (2 April 1970) thought she remained 'a frigid enigma' after her 'unglamorous, uncompromising' per-formance; others thought her simply emotionally isolated. D.A.N. Jones perceived a defeated feminist, 'silent rage written all over her high forehead and stubborn chin. She is to be a chattel after all – and all has not ended well' (*Listener*, 9 April 1970). My own perception, from that time just before the 1970s' huge expansion in feminist consciousness,[12] was of the loneliness of this young woman in a world ruled by men. I remember also sending an excited postcard to a friend with whom I'd studied the play: the production hit me with the force of a revelation – Isabella was *right* in refusing Angelo: she was no longer just a locus of literary-critical 'moral ambiguity'. As a living woman, in her plain white dress, with her long hair flowing freely down her back, she was a figure of personal integrity in a sordid world. (Reviewers in fact complained that Barton's 'under-world' was far too clean and cheery, and rather sparsely populated – it was a time of RSC financial constraint – but for someone who had never seen the play it was enough simply to see the whores, pimps, and criminals embodied on the stage.)

The impression of sordidness and of a genuine threat of violation towards Isabella was greatly increased by Ian Richardson's per-formance as Angelo. The first-night reviewers saw Richardson 'butt Isabella with his groin' onto his desk (Wardle, *The Times*, 2 April 1970), but they were much more aware of Angelo's narcissism, his breaking down in tears, for instance, in the soliloquy at the end of

Plate 14 Estelle Kohler as Isabella, Ian Richardson as Angelo, *Measure for Measure*, 1970,

II.2. As the production progressed both actors delved further into the psychological sub-text. As Richardson reports,

> It became very fascinating because about two months after it opened, censorship was withdrawn and it meant that it was possible to do certain things on the stage. So I asked the director, John Barton, if Estelle and I could re-examine what we did in the scene following the proposition scene. He agreed, and we did rather a lot. I physically abused her and pressed my hands firmly up her skirts. I also felt that Angelo's sexuality was rather sinister, so I asked Estelle if we could do some business where I pulled her hair.[13]

Kohler enthusiastically co-operated with Richardson in exploring this 'obscure vein of sado-masochism' in their relationship (Ronald Bryden, *Observer*, 5 April 1970). Their scenes together were charged with an erotic force, each egging the other on with plea and refusal. At one point, 'begging for her brother's life, she extended her arms as if to embrace Angelo, only to adopt a praying posture' (*Leicester Mercury*, 2 April 1970). At another, Isabella manoeuvred herself into a position of strength behind Angelo's desk, playing the dominant mistress. Yet no critic blamed her for this use of her sexuality: rather, her combination of passion with fierce intelligence sparked the audience's sympathy: 'Why should she surrender her body, as if it were trivial, to save one man from another man's punishment?' asked D.A.N. Jones, moved to a new and feminist perception of the play. More than one reviewer thought Kohler's young but independent Isabella 'unusually strong'. However she stood in regard to the still-dominant patriarchy at the end of the play, it was clear she had no truck with the benevolent but bumbling paternalism of the Duke's public mask.

Representation of the Duke as an unambiguous god-like figure was clearly no longer acceptable. Going to the other extreme, Keith Hack, directing a challenging new *Measure for Measure* in 1974, had the Duke in a golden wig return in Act V on a ramp satirically labelled 'Deus Ex Machina'. The whole play was performed in Brechtian style, as though by a group of discontented actors in a seedy Victorian stock company, with Barrie Ingham's Duke as the actor-manager and company 'heavy man' (his first appearance in the play prompted comparisons with Bela Lugosi's Dracula). Hack, who had come to Stratford from the Glasgow Citizens' Theatre, saw the play as a 'fable of social oppression' (Irving Wardle, *The Times*, 5 September 1974), in which the Duke was even more corrupt than Angelo, using his power for his own perverted pleasure. The programme included a photo-montage of figures of male authority: Hitler, Mussolini, Nixon, Stalin, the Pope, Willi Brandt – and Richard III; also a note by Edward Bond to the director which endorses Lucio's view of the play's world: 'he tells the truth about the Duke. That is, he describes the Duke as another Angelo, a public fraud . . . . It's not just the ending of the play that's a charade, the whole political set-up is'.

Peter Thomson described the symbolic setting by Maria Björnson:

On the right of the stage stood a figure of Christ the king in baroque decay, surrounded by festoons of jewellery and a huge red curtain that was no longer fine . . . a splendid relic, the emblem of a stock company that had seen better days. Stage left was bare, and the acting area was surrounded at the back by a wire grid and downstage of the proscenium by unadorned scaffolding. Through the grid, extras and on-lookers would gaze at the encaged action. The resultant ambiguity was intentional. Who was in the cage – onlookers or actors (or audience)? . . . In Keith Hack's Vienna, a garishly perverted sexuality was in league with an established church; and the chief ally of the corruption was the Duke.[14]

Critical response to this production was predictably mixed. Peter Ansorge, in *Plays & Players* (October 1974) admired it for its 'theatrical rather than textual power – the image usurping the word . . . a genuinely dangerous quality about the images, a feeling for what the underbelly of Jacobean life *might* have resembled during a particularly plague-ridden or repressive period in its history'. The fact that this imagery also had strong echoes of Brecht's Mahagonny brought the production uncomfortably close to home. Michael Billington found it too despairingly critical of bourgeois liberalism for his taste:

Any connection between this farrago and Shakespeare's ambiguous, morally complex study of the interdependence of good and evil is purely coincidental . . . it doesn't allow of any psychological growth . . . the production has no visible roots in human reality . . . the play is seen simply as a phantas-magoric charade in which nothing finally matters.

(*Guardian*, 5 September 1974)

Billington evidently regretted the loss of psychological interest in the Duke and Angelo – the one a figure of melodramatic evil, the other (Michael Pennington) 'a lounging sensualist, complete with bulging codpiece from the start' (Hilary Spurling, *Observer*, 8 September 1974). What remained, though of less interest to most male critics, was Francesca Annis's Isabella – not only the figure of the oppressed in this decadent male world (even Mistress Overdone was played by a huge male actor, who did a public strip to become Francisca the nun), but also a complex representation of a woman who is in opposition to every aspect of the society she lives in. Hilary Spurling saw the other two remaining female roles as adding to this critique – 'Debbie Bowen and Gay Hamilton, who barely speak as Juliet and Mariana but none the less combine with Isabella in an image of fragility and strength which runs through this production like a thread of pure, pale gold'.

Annis was universally praised for a finely sensitive and passionate performance, though few critics could see what it had to do with Hack's production. Dressed in sober but elegant Jacobean costume, Annis was clearly related to the desperate female protagonists of early seventeenth-century sensation-drama: another Duchess of Malfi, perhaps. She was visibly horrified and disgusted by both Angelo's and the Duke's propositions, but, ultimately, could not escape: 'The play ends with the Duke burying her unwilling body in the folds of his voluminous furs' (Jack Tinker, *Daily Mail*, 5 September 1974). Spurling saw him 'plucking the shrinking Isabella from the altar steps with a horrid flourish which plainly shows that a single night of shame with Angelo would have been a kinder fate than marriage to this satanic rapist'. For Peter Ansorge (op. cit.), continuing the analogy with Jacobean horror plays,

> The emotional centre of the production is reached as Isabella runs at Angelo shrieking, 'Seeming! Seeming!' as an agonised, helpless accusation against the corruption of *both* Dukes . . . . It's an enthralling moment, as are her clashes with Malcolm Tierney's Claudio, charting Isabella's slow withdrawal into complete horror and implied madness.

Keith Hack did not return to Stratford after 1974: his vision of Shakespeare's relevance to issues that are 'clearly central to the prevailing moral climate' (Wardle) was too harsh for an audience and a critical establishment that desired control rather than confrontation.

1978–87

Barry Kyle's 1978 production provided a solid, clear, and un-exploratory reading which recuperated the play into the tradition of comedy. The underworld remained conventionally sordid, sombre rather than carnivalesque in Christopher Morley's all-purpose black box with many doors; the whores were pox-ridden; but Barnardine was transformed 'from the usual dissolute ruin into a sort of Aryan Caliban, the stark-naked but not undignified victim of other people's oppression' (Benedict Nightingale, *New Statesman*, 7 July 1978). He had genuine comic power:

> When it comes to the scene where Barnardine refuses to be executed just to suit the Duke . . . [t]he only thing the Duke hasn't thought of in his splendid plan is that anybody might say no. So when he thinks he's found the perfect solution to all the problems, there's this fellow that won't play . . . . There's a lot of comedy in the Duke and I think the play changes direction very rapidly in the second half.[15]

Michael Pennington's Duke and Paola Dionisotti's Isabella patently enjoyed their plotting together, giggling as they mapped their plan out with straw at Mariana's bucolic retreat. There was a good deal of chummy kissing and hugging between them from III.1 onwards. The Duke was young and good-looking, mischievous and generous, quite definitely the romantic lead – he knelt to make his proposal at the end, and Isabella responded by enthusiastically pulling him up to her. Pennington described this ending, however, as 'not the traditional romantic one': 'it is a secure relationship brought about through joint endeavour and so, by the end of the play, they are the only two people competent to govern'.[16]

One problem with this 'soft' reading of the play is that the Angelo–Isabella scenes can lose their potential force:

> Jonathan Pryce is a neurotic little civil servant, always twitchy and awkward, while Isabella, an overdone portrait by Paola Dionisotti, is an irritating evangelical spinster, and their big confrontation scene is played as comedy.
>
> (Helen Reid, *Western Daily Press*, 28 June 1978)

Pryce, reported Irving Wardle, 'respond[ed] to the onset of lust as an amused observer . . . never fully surrendering to it' (*The Times*, 28 June 1978). Other critics queried the casting of Dionisotti, dowdy-looking in her voluminous nun's habit, and failing to project any spark of sexual liveliness. It is interesting to contrast the cool critical response to her performance with Dionisotti's own sense of the role; there was obviously some disagreement with Kyle:

> When Barry Kyle first approached me about Isabella he had a very specific view of the part, which he thought I would be able to fulfil, related to somebody who was rather uptight. I have a thin bony face and a small mouth so I could slip into that model for him very easily.
>
> He saw Isabella as somebody who was very repressed, who didn't acknowledge a lot of things about herself, and who was maybe quite old, 'old' meaning forty. She was someone who had *longed* to go into a convent. (That would automatically make her an extremist. We were all pretty busy being promiscuous in 1978. There wasn't an awful lot of sympathy around for chastity.)[17]

Although she softened this portrait by adding in the 'giggliness' of the nuns she had known in her childhood, she agreed that Isabella was fearful of sex, and claimed that she could only relate to Pennington's Duke by constructing him as

> the experienced man of the church. And since I was quite new to the church, he became my unquestioned authority figure . . . . I had to resign my will to him completely. I was being taken on a journey away from anything I was centred on *by him*. Which is why I finished the scene kissing him. That's what it had come to: he was my magic uncle. He could make things right.[18]

Dionisotti consequently had trouble reconciling her sense of 'betrayal' by the Duke in the last act with the director's desire for a happy ending: 'It struck me at the end that Isabella is deeply weary' – but she was not permitted to show this. In fact, if we set Michael Pennington's sense of what he was doing with his part against Paola Dionisotti's, it becomes clear that he and the director had in a sense conspired – simply not questioning the 'natural' decisions of two men working together – to present the play as the Duke's story, an upbeat tale of personal discovery that never stops to question the ethics of his behaviour:

> we felt that there must be this journey for the Duke and that through his encounters with Lucio, Pompey, the jailors, the

whores and, above all, Isabella he comes to learn something about true government, about justice, about the entire system by which he has governed and lived. He now has to question all that. By the end of the play he has come to a sense of a method of justice which is humanistic and Christian, but not biblical; practical and unsentimental, but not cruel; and he has also coached Isabella towards such a system, Isabella who also has been lost in her own way.[19]

What this Isabella has learnt, though, might be thought of as the dispiriting art of compromise, or acquiescence to the *force majeure* which declares that men's experience is important and meaningful, women's merely the product of hysteria and ignorance about the real world. Roger Warren's enthusiastic report of the production's last scene reveals its patriarchal Christian conservatism:

On a pure white carpet at the very front of the stage, the resolution seemed able to merge the symbolic and realistic aspects into single, highly-charged moments. Claudio, his face bandaged and in a shroud-like prison smock, returned pale and shaken . . . with the additional suggestion that he had come from the grave . . . . The tension was enormous, the sequence intensely moving, with magical echoes and yet the work of man. It was *natural* that Isabella should respond to her friar/Duke/preserver and that he should propose to her.[20]

For Daniel Massey's Duke, in Adrian Noble's 1983 production, the play was also 'a journey', but the difference from Kyle's concept was that the journey was equally one of self-discovery for Juliet Stevenson's Isabella – the play became genuinely humanist rather than overdeterminedly Christian. It is the only production, in my experience, in which it becomes clear during the course of the play that this extraordinary couple have fallen in love. Daniel Massey describes the critical scene (which I recall as astonishing yet utterly convincing):

We found moments . . . scattered through the play, where we could build a growing awareness of each other. Isabella becomes so excited about the scheme of the bed trick with Mariana in Act 3 that she plants an impulsive kiss on the Duke's cheek. There is more than a vestige of the adventure caper about the whole moated grange sequence which proved wonderfully useful, and at IV.3.142 where he must, in the short term, steel himself to put her through an awful emotional struggle, he plants a kiss upon her forehead. This is interrupted by the arrival of Lucio. They spring apart, and, in a long look across the stage at each other, during Lucio's bitter-sweet speech, much seemed to be accomplished.[21]

What this interpretive decision does is to provide Isabella with a consistent emotional development, not to frustrate it, as Kyle's production did by first encouraging a sense of companionship between the two and then denying it. The final scene became a test of their relationship, in which undoubtedly the Duke had a socially-endorsed advantage, but he also knew that in Isabella he had met his match. Stevenson explained, 'He's got no faith any longer. But he has a need to have that faith restored. So he puts her through fire to have his faith confirmed. Not once, but again and again and again'.[22] For Massey,

> the struggle to bring Isabella to her knees was quite literally exhausting. Juliet was wonderful here. In essence, of course, it was a battle of wills. Significantly, he is tougher and harsher with Isabella. Instinctively he knows that he must push her to the limit. He knows her well now, her passion, her stubbornness, above all her sense of justice. I remember that when she finally sank to her knees, I gave in to an almost trance-like state.[23]

If Massey recognised something of Petruchio here in his Duke, testing his unruly but loving partner, he also had the contemporary good sense to play against his public image: the proposal, he said, often got a laugh for its 'chutzpah . . . . It is nothing more nor less than autocratic licence', the Duke re-establishing his public authority with a newly acquired self-confidence due to his interaction with the world. Isabella, kneeling on the floor with Claudio, simply stared at first, then returned her attention to her brother. Eventually she turned again to look at the Duke, rising from the floor on his 'Dear Isabel'. He kissed her hand, she stroked his face; they kissed fondly, then the Duke broke away, looking like a gleeful small boy who has won a prize he knows he doesn't deserve.

Juliet Stevenson was determined that her Isabella 'should be looked at not as a frigid hysteric with a big problem about sex, but that we should kick off by exploring the *positive* reasons for

entering a convent' – which she characterised as 'to create a channel
through which good is introduced into the world' through a life of
prayer and meditation. 'The Isabella I played', she said, 'was clued
in to her sexuality from the first' : what she was defending was not
so much her decision for celibacy as her commitment to *chastity*, to
personal bodily integrity – a distinction few if any earlier Isabellas
had been able to make clear. She played the role not habited as a
nun, but in a sober but elegant black dress, with her shoulder-length
hair hanging free:

> I didn't want the audience to be looking at a nun all night. I
> wanted to break down what they would invariably have
> associated with that image. I wanted to say to them, 'Look at
> this person. *Listen* to this person. Don't judge her from the
> image. Listen afresh.'[24]

Noble set the play in late eighteenth-century Vienna; with Ilona
Sekacz's nightmarish echoes of Mozart's music it seemed to inhabit
the same world of egoism, sexual licence and the threat of ultimate
damnation as *Don Giovanni*. The audience saw the Duke, at the
beginning of the play, narcissistically admiring his image in a large
mirror; but on becoming the Friar he frequently surprised himself
with unknown potential: sudden eloquence, street-wise thinking,
and a much more direct relation with the people than he had ever
had, imprisoned in his formal role.

David Schofield's Angelo was a thin, pale-faced, black-clad public
servant: no match for either Isabella or the Duke, around whom the
play really revolved. The scenes between Isabella and Angelo
sparked only as a battle of intelligences and a jockeying for power:
'In pleading for her brother's life she takes such command of the
stage that she ends up sitting in Angelo's chair' (Irving Wardle, *The
Times*, 5 October 1983). It was the combination of passion and
intelligence in Stevenson's performance that had most critics convinced she was the best Isabella they had ever seen: relieved that
they no longer had to deal with a woman who found the thought of
sex revolting, they welcomed the transformation of the role into
'romantic heroine: maybe the first such heroine this play has ever
had' (Robert Cushman, *Observer*, 9 October 1983); 'a girl whose
inflexible chastity in no way warps her natural spirits' (Wardle).
Andrew Rissik, profiling *Drama*'s Best Actress of 1983, recognised
in Stevenson the qualities that would make her pre-eminent among
actresses of her generation in a few years' time:

a performance of extraordinary range, intensity and feeling that strips the role of its traditional Freudian impedimenta and presents it, new-minted, with unprecedented passion and calm. This Isabella seizes the centre of the stage with effortless command and compels us to remake the play around her. Her dilemma is an absolutely central and tragic one ... The achievement of the performance is that it turns Isabella into a major dramatic protagonist like Antigone, a woman who says 'no' not because of fear or inhibition or downright frigidity but because, in a world whose standards are demonstrably corrupt, she believes 'no' to be a test of moral courage and the only right answer. For once, the specifics of the character's sexuality are not the real issue.

(*Drama*, 1, 1984)

Stevenson's Isabella was the embodiment of late twentieth-century feminism come of age and accepted into mainstream thinking; her performance enabled audiences to see that a woman's claim for control of her own body is reasonable and normal, and that such autonomy can be a positive force in society. In this production, just as comedy always promises, the world is a happier place because Isabella and the Duke have met and loved. But this was a romantic transformation of two extraordinary people – the ruler who questions his own divine right and the morally passionate feminist. It represented the triumph of a momentary utopian vision, aptly set in the Vienna of the Enlightenment.

Nicholas Hytner's 1987 production – his first for the RSC – challenged this optimism, with a design (by Mark Thompson) which set the play in a bleak modern city with fascist overtones (Dogberry turned out to be little Corporal Hitler from Bavaria). The low-life scenes were sordid and lacked any signs of pleasure; the jail was a realistic modern one, with strip-searches, slopping-out, drug-trading. Hytner said in an interview in the *Birmingham Post* (7 November 1987),

From the point of view of the sexual revolution of the early 1970s it was very clear that several characters had sexual hang-ups, that the duke was a quasi-fascist and that the people who had a lot of sex were the heroes. It's not about that now. I think it's become a completely different play. That's why you can never aim for a definitive production of a Shakespeare play.

Giles Gordon described his perception of the production's relevance to the late 1980s:

> The civil scenes are dominated by a gigantic gilt safe, symbolising that money rules . . . . *Measure for Measure* is definitely for now and, as Hytner's production aptly suggests, we should regard these corrupt characters on the make, privately or publicly, with considerable scepticism.
>
> (*Standard*, 12 November 1987)

Michael Coveney thought it 'a powerful reading that casts a contemporary financial and moral collapse in the burnt-out mould of inter-War Europe' (*Financial Times*, 13 November 1987), and admired Hytner's advance on Jonathan Miller's 1975 setting of the play in Freudian Vienna: 'the arc of the play here extends to the modern legacy' of the 1980s. John Peter was pleased to welcome this 'dark, gripping, mercurial production [which] reveals it, at long last, as a political play . . . a profound political parable about morality, legality and justice' (*Sunday Times*, 15 November 1987).

In such a setting no romantic individualist 'journeys' were undertaken, no self-transforming discoveries were made. Roger Allam as the Duke and Josette Simon as Isabella came together briefly, as they attempted to battle the corruption of their city; there was the by now usual hugging and kissing in the highly emotional IV.3, but these were the acts of mutual comfort of desperately stressed people. The play's end was strikingly bleak: as the Duke uttered his first tentative proposal, Isabella stood aloof, looking silently at him. After the Duke's final announcements, he moved downstage right, leaving Isabella to walk slowly towards the central (distinctly fascist) archway through which could be seen a bright but distant view of the countryside. She turned, looking first towards the small family unit of Claudio, Juliet and the baby amidst the SS-uniformed soldiers, then at the Duke and out to the audience. The image was of a lone but strong Isabella, leaving the 'world of men' to its fate, 'perhaps on her way to the nunnery, having had more than enough of a lecherous opposite sex' (Giles Gordon, *Plays & Players*, February 1988). Here again, it was not a matter of Isabella's revulsion from sex, but rather of her disgust with the whole system of modern government, a patriarchy that has lost the last vestige of credibility for its claims to guide and protect the 'weaker sex'. Irving Wardle was one among many who perceived social dissolution already at work in

Plate 15 Josette Simon as Isabella, Sean Baker as Angelo, *Measure for Measure*, 1987, directed by Nicholas Hytner. Photograph: Clive Barda.

the play's opening scene, which showed the still-young Duke on the verge of a nervous breakdown:

> Nicholas Hytner's production opens with the thunderously amplified crash of a cell door; followed by the sight of the Duke (Roger Allam) trembling with dread as he signs the statute that will shortly put so many Viennese citizens behind bars .... By acknowledging that he is as fallible as everyone else, the production gains a coherence that leaves you wondering how *Measure for Measure* even came to be labelled a problem play .... when [the Duke] finally addresses his quavering proposal to Isabella, she turns scornfully away, seeing her noble protector shrivelling into another compromised male.
>
> (*The Times*, 13 November 1987)

'Approving murmurs from the audience attested the rightness of Miss Simon's response', added Keith Brown in the *Times Literary Supplement* (20 November 1987). Adding fuel to their fire was the treatment of II.4, the second scene between Isabella and Angelo. Sean Baker's Angelo, 'an unsmiling dangerous fanatic from the Celtic fringe' (Gordon), attempted to rape Isabella, ripping her veil off, hitting her to the ground, then straddling her as she sobbed passionately (plate 15). Her 'To whom should I complain?' had a frighteningly contemporary resonance in the context of this overt sexual violence.

Simon's Isabella, in this reading of the play, was not one who needed to discover anything about herself, whether it be repressed sexuality, the possibility of heterosexual romance, or the need for compassionate tolerance of worldly failings. She was an intense, straightforward figure, whose very existence was a critique of the modern world. 'Josette Simon evinces a tangible faith unspoilt by priggishness' (Coveney); 'a burnished icon of impassioned purity', said Wardle, though he thought that 'the penalty is that she emerges as less humanly interesting than the surrounding hypocrites and sensualists'. That depends, of course, on what one finds interesting: I suspect that Hytner's uncompromising morality play for the late twentieth century divided its audience, to a large extent, on gender lines.[25]

5

MUCH ADO ABOUT NOTHING
A kind of merry war

Much Ado About Nothing takes place not in a 'world elsewhere' –
Illyria or Arden – but in Messina, Sicily. From its very opening lines
it insists that the audience recognise on the stage a simulacrum of
the 'real world', with its townsfolk, householders and their families,
servants and visitors – and its gossip. In this *Much Ado* is much
more akin to *Romeo and Juliet* or *Measure for Measure* than it is to
the other 'romantic comedies' with which it usually grouped. This is
not a world in which a girl can disguise herself as a boy and not be
recognised even by her lover; it is, rather, a society structured very
like the Elizabethan one which first witnessed it, in which the
niceties of interpersonal behaviour are directed by accepted rules.
And although those standard tropes of farce, disguisings and tricks,
soon enter the narrative, they are not its principal dramatic interest;
they are merely there to help along the plot which has from the first
held the audience's chief attention – the courtship of Beatrice and
Benedick. The bringing together of two prickly, unconventional
adults in marriage – into conformity with the structures of society
which they have hitherto managed to flout – holds a gleeful
fascination for the audience, as it does for the 'audience' on stage –
all the other members of Leonato's household. None can finally
escape the powerful coercion of our social system: 'The world must
be peopled!' (II.3). Despite Benedick's apparent libertarian bravado
here, what he means and what the play means is a world peopled via
the ceremony of Christian marriage only. The play's triumph is to
make the audience assent to its vision of a community always to be
revitalised from within, by the incorporation of rebellious energy,
not its expulsion. It does this by presenting, in Beatrice and
Benedick's dialogues, such an 'erotic friction' (in Stephen Greenblatt's term) that our profoundest desire is to see that friction come

to its bodily consumption. 'Peace, I will stop your mouth' – the talking only ceases when the lovers' bodies come together in a kiss. (In modern terms, we may read Benedick's 'domineering' action here as a playful and self-conscious taking-on of his social role as 'Benedick the married man'; but we might also remember that in II.1 Beatrice quite unselfconsciously suggests that the roles can be reversed when she says to the newly engaged Hero, 'Speak cousin. Or if you cannot, stop his mouth with a kiss, and let him not speak, neither'.)

The play achieves its conservative victory also by flattering the audience's intelligence, encouraging us to despise the callow foolishness of the conventional Claudio (and to a lesser extent, of Hero) and to identify with the witty, unconventional Benedick and Beatrice. Marriage, it argues, is not just for dull people – in fact, they are lucky to be allowed a second go at finding an appropriate mate. Shakespeare seems particularly interested in the workings of gender in society in *Much Ado*. Claudio's immature behaviour is grounded in his dependence on the hierarchical brotherhood of the military and its ideology of male honour; Hero's helplessness arises from her being the protected daughter of a still-living father, bound to consult and obey him in all matters. Beatrice, by contrast, is, like Rosalind, a 'poor relation', without living parents: one who survives on her wits, intelligence, and the affection and tolerance of her oddities freely given by Leonato's family. The text also suggests that she and Benedick have had some sort of love-relationship in the past ('Marry, once before he won it [her heart] of me, with false dice' (II.1)); that is, that she is no stranger to the vagaries of sexual love and the ways of the social world. But ultimately, for a woman in a solidly-structured patriarchal society such as this one, there are no prospects other than marriage or a barely-tolerated maiden-aunt status. Beatrice's fantasy of spending eternity 'where the bachelors sit, and there live we, as merry as the day is long' (II.1) is recognisably that – a fantasy – in the context of the clearly divided male and female spheres of the society which the play presents. By showing the gaps between ideal and reality in the Hero and Claudio story, Shakespeare deconstructed the gender-ideology of separate spheres; and offered in Beatrice and Benedick an image of the '*merry* war' that may exist between two strong-willed characters resistant to the behavioural restrictions of conventional gender roles. However, once these two acknowledge their sexual attraction, they cannot avoid society's discourse of romantic love and marriage; the best they can do is to meet it with wit, fully conscious of their own absurdity: 'Thou and I are too wise to woo peaceably' (V.2). It is this shared consciousness of the delicious playfulness of language which can always circumvent the dead hand of convention that makes Beatrice and Benedick such an attractive pair: the audience's fantasy of the intelligent, witty, and caring heterosexual couple. The permutations of that image, and of the society which permits it (more or less) to flourish, are typically varied in performance.

1949-61

For many critics John Gielgud's Stratford production of *Much Ado About Nothing*, which premiered in April 1949 and was revived and toured intermittently until 1955, was unsurpassable. Above all, it had 'style', and critics forty years later were still nostalgic for the undemanding, profound pleasure that this production offered both in design and acting. Gielgud, an experienced entrepreneur since before the war, knew what the British public wanted at this point in twentieth-century history – elegance, and a sense of material and spiritual bounty, a sense that the world was indeed a good place and that the social *status quo ante* offered the best possible image of order. He invited the Spanish artist Mariano Andreu to design both the sets and the costumes – signalling, as it were, that the war had been won, and the preservation and continuity of European culture was once again in the right hands. Andreu responded by providing rich and highly elaborate Renaissance designs, reminiscent of Italian painting of the late fifteenth century; one reviewer wrote,

> The scenery opens, shuts, wheels and turns inside out. Gardens become banqueting halls, and by a turn of the hand gaily attired ushers transport us from the pillared exterior of a church porch to the Byzantine reaches of a far-flung nave. These transformations are in excellent taste, but all the same they are slightly distracting.
>
> (*Birmingham Post*, 21 April 1949)

The audience, in fact, greatly enjoyed and applauded the clever scene changes – their pleasure, that is, was not only in illusion but (as Gielgud, with his family's theatrical history stretching back a century, would know) in the amazing transformations of panto-mime. This technical facility added to the air of richness and confidence of the production.

145

As for the costumes, heavy and elaborate though they were, they clearly delighted an audience sick of wartime austerity. The *Birmingham Post* commented, 'Mariano Andreu has celebrated the end of clothes rationing by providing a glittering array of costumes', and the critic of the *Leamington Spa Courier* (23 April 1949) noted the psychological effect of this justified extravagance:

> costumes and decors were not only a joy to those who saw them – they had a subtle but quite definite effect upon the actors, who seemed to catch light and style from their costumes and the garden where they disported themselves.

This air of euphoria characterized the acting of the quartet of lovers. The production did not question the innocence and ardour of youth: Claudio and Hero were played as 'star-crossed children', innocent victims of the wicked Don John. They had 'violent fits of uncontrollable giggles' during the overhearing scenes; Claudio 'wept openly during his accusations of Hero's infidelity . . . . The impression was of impassioned, youthful impetuosity overcome with emotion'.[1] Similarly, the production's view of more adult relationships was uncomplicated: Anthony Quayle was 'engaging and manly' as Benedick, Diana Wynyard 'gay, charming and fiery' as Beatrice (W.A. Darlington, *Daily Telegraph*, 20 April 1949); 'a plain soldier and a mocking maid too much interested in each other to ape the airs of the court', said *The Times* (27 April 1949). Clearly Gielgud's production aimed to reinforce a sense that social (and sexual) relations had returned to normal after the extraordinary conditions of the war. But any description of 'normality' is embedded in the dominant ideology; in this case – still shadowed by the war – that the ideal man is a 'plain soldier' and the ideal woman a 'maid' worth both honourable defence and chivalrous attack in the 'merry war'. In fact, some adventurous critics found Wynyard and Quayle perhaps the tiniest bit dull, lacking in erotic chemistry. 'A warm glow is substituted for the sparkle', said the *Birmingham Post*, and the critic of the *Manchester Guardian Weekly* (28 April 1949) 'had the impression that they had really been married for ages'.

A sense of cosiness and stability underlying the richly elegant style: what more could a war-weary audience want? W.A. Darlington concluded his review by saying, 'I prophesy for it a great popularity', a prophecy amply fulfilled in the next five years, as it ran and ran. Gielgud revamped it for the 1950 season with a new cast, including himself and Peggy Ashcroft, and a new touch to the costumes – extravagant hats, which allowed him, in particular, to lift Benedick from the 'plain man' of Quayle to a fantastical dandy (plate 16): he 'meets Benedick's changing moods in a succession of remarkable hats – blanc-mange mould, floral cartwheel, tarboosh – worn with an air of amused disbelief' (Richard Findlater, *Tribune*, 16 June 1950).

It is this version of the production, this partnership (occasionally varied by Diana Wynyard replacing Ashcroft) which has gone down in theatrical history as a yardstick by which to judge later *Much Ados*. 'This is a perfection of acting', Brian Harvey reported, 'to which a humble and grateful salute can be the critic's only gesture' (*Birmingham Gazette*, 7 June 1950). What were the characteristics of Ashcroft and Gielgud's Beatrice and Benedick which produced such a unanimous effect on their happy auditors? Peter Hall remembers their 'extraordinary display of quick-tongued wit, un-believably fast',[2] which suggests that they had rediscovered the 'erotic friction' of the text. Philip Hope-Wallace noted, at the time, something further about its embodiment by these two performers:

> Mr Gielgud's strong suit remains the distraught, the tragic, or the whimsical rather than cocksure bantering, and Miss Ashcroft's best cards are those of a yielding and womanish pathos without the astringent manner of a natural Beatrice. This involves some playing 'against the grain' and that little obstacle in temperamental affinity which brings out the best in fine artists which would explain the energy of the rallying matches between these devoted enemies.
>
> (*Manchester Guardian*, 9 June 1950)

It appears that these two highly acclaimed actors, whose pre-war partnership (in, for instance, *Romeo and Juliet*) was legendary, in playing roles for which they were not typecast, made visible an edge of vulnerability in their characters, allowed their 'humanness' to be seen. Of Gielgud, it was generally agreed that 'his comedy is the highest of high comedy, urbane and light, essentially of the drawing-room or the arbour' (*New Statesman*, 11 June 1950) – hence, in his unsoldierly Benedick, a self-deprecating 'modesty' noted by *The Times* (7 June 1950), and hence the ironical headgear. Gielgud later said that 'over the years', he 'kept trying to make Benedick into more of a soldier. . . . I decided [the hats] had not much to do with Shakespeare's play, and I gradually discarded them and wore

Plate 16 Peggy Ashcroft as Beatrice, John Gielgud as Benedick,
Much Ado About Nothing, 1950, directed by John Gielgud.
Photograph: Angus McBean.

leather doublets and thigh boots and became less of the courtier'.[3] He retreated, under the pressure of the post-war ideology of gender, into a more conventionally masculine 'soldierly' characterisation. Observe here how conscious the actor is of the semiotics of costume: how a person is dressed is a sign of how closely he or she conforms to gender models.

Ashcroft was also strongly aware of the signals given by costume. Her portrayal of Beatrice demonstrated her intuition that the idea of gender is implicated with that of class; according to Gielgud:

> Diana Wynyard played it much more on the lines I imagine Ellen Terry did – the great lady sweeping about in beautiful clothes. When Peggy started rehearsing she rather jibbed at that and said 'I'm not going to wear those dresses, they're too grand for me.' . . . She wore much simpler dresses and created a cheeky character who means well but seems to drop bricks all the while (perhaps she got it from me). Everybody thinks Beatrice will never marry because she is too free with her tongue and is rather impertinent to people without intending any rudeness.[4]

Richard Findlater found her 'somewhat too anxious and vulnerable' for the 'merry' Beatrice. But he concluded, as did all the critics, that 'her Beatrice is radiant with wit and grace'. It would seem that Ashcroft provided a model by which to judge later Beatrices not because of her 'style' but because she allowed the audience to see an individual Beatrice who could be hurt, rather than a 'lady' protected by her grand costume. Gielgud's early fantasticality (as opposed to his later revivals and to Quayle's 'manliness') by the same token opened the way for a much later exploration of a slightly camp Benedick, a man whose reluctance to marry sprang from an unresolved narcissism. But that was not a line to be explored till thirty years later.

The Stratford production which eventually followed Gielgud's much-loved version was in many superficial respects not unlike it. It certainly had 'style'; it also shared a choreographer with the earlier production, Pauline Grant – the dances, with music by Christopher Whelen, were much remarked on. The whole production had the air of a light opera, an association deliberately made by the director, Douglas Seale, in a publicity note: 'the producer is staging *Much Ado* in the 1850s, in the Italy of Verdi and Rossini, a period in which the play has not been set before and which reflects its

romantic, witty and at times melodramatic situations'. The sets by
Tanya Moisiewitsch and costumes by Motley were 'chocolate-box'
pretty: ten different scenes, accomplished with painted backdrops,
wrought-iron garden furniture and village carts (and an elaborate
church scene which harked back to Irving's atmospheric master-
piece of the 1890s); the women in summer muslins, parasols and flat
hats, the men resplendent in hussar-type uniforms. A few months
earlier *My Fair Lady* had opened its enormously successful career at
Drury Lane; the over-the-top elegance and sheer entertainment
value of this musical must have had an influence on Seale and his
designers (Seale's previous production at Stratford had been a sober
Henry VI). It was as though 'Shakes vs. Shav' was being played
again, this time with music, in an attempt to win the public out for
a good night's entertainment – that public which would not subject
itself to the 'modern drama' of 1958: *Endgame*, *A Taste of Honey*,
A Resounding Tinkle. Richard Johnson's Don John was regularly
hissed by a clearly delighted audience, who felt no real threat to the
comic-opera community presented on stage.

For *Plays & Players*, it was among the year's best productions;
other critics, while enjoying it, had some reservations, largely
arising from an uneasy sense that the play had more to offer than
this production did (the same, of course, could be said for *Pygmalion*
and *My Fair Lady*):

> Already it is more than half-way to being a successful musical
> . . . [with] lots of Palm-Court style music and many gay dance
> routines . . . a dazzling feast for the eye . . . [But] there is a
> point at which costumes and setting become as dangerous to
> an actor as a child or a dog in the cast and that point was
> reached last night . . . . Miss Withers and Mr Redgrave [the
> Beatrice and Benedick] substituted only a charming playful-
> ness for the anticipated courtship.
>
> (*Star*, 28 August 1958)

The critic of the *Spectator* (5 September 1958) thought the
'elaborate, spectacularly irrelevant scenery and costumes' were a
sign of 'a fear of the text'. For Googie Withers, however, whose
performance as Beatrice gave great pleasure, there was no question
that elaborate staging was an advantage: 'people came to the theatre
to see the play and to be enchanted. Otherwise, they could merely
listen to a lecture', she said at a forum in Stratford (*Stratford*

Herald, 5 September 1958). Her Beatrice was a triumph of the old school of thought about *Much Ado*:

> [she] sails magnificently through the play with all her comedy guns firing – and reaching their mark .... She is no shrew, but a woman of fine spirit and keen intelligence who will make marriage a splendid adventure instead of merely 'dwindling into a wife' . . . a performance that glows, sparkles, and makes every man in the audience a surrendered Benedick.
>
> (*Stage*, 28 August 1958)

This critic is reading Withers's Beatrice with the help of a later dramatic model, Congreve's Millamant, as one who is essentially of her society (the cynosure of a male gaze) rather than on the margin of it. But there was no equivalent Restoration toughness or worldly cunning in Michael Redgrave's good-natured, easy-going Benedick, 'quick to renounce his bachelor's creed and go[ing] almost eagerly to marriage' (*Coventry Evening Telegraph*, 22 August 1958) – though a number of critics noted that Redgrave, a serious Method actor, seemed ill at ease in the Victorian operetta *mise-en-scène*.

The play looked ripe for the 'Peter Hall treatment' under the new regime at Stratford; a darker re-presentation in his ground-breaking series of the middle comedies. But, for reasons presumably commercial, the first *Much Ado* in the newly-honoured Royal Shakespeare Theatre (1961) was backward-looking, offering no advance on the light-operatic charm of Seale's production. Michael Langham, from Stratford, Ontario, had directed a strikingly successful *Merchant of Venice* in 1960 at the Shakespeare Memorial Theatre; for this *Much Ado* he brought with him from Canada a rising young star, Christopher Plummer, as Benedick, and teamed him with the 'lightweight' Hero of the 1958 production, Geraldine McEwan. Once again the production style was that of operetta, and the period setting was nineteenth century. The only notable differences from 1958 were in Desmond Heeley's designs: the costumes were those of Regency England or Second Empire Europe (the men especially resplendent in their military costumes, in which they remained throughout the performance, giving rise to critical jibes about 'chocolate soldiers'); and there was only a single set – a garden *capriccio* with a wrought-iron staircase and balcony attached to nothing. The *Birmingham Mail*'s critic was one of many who felt that the permanent set was 'infuriating . . . [it] spoilt the church scene, looming like some fantastic harvest-festival decoration scheme' (5 April 1961). For no apparent reason the decor suggested early autumn:

> Thunderstorms darkened the blue Messina skies, the guests at Hero's wedding wiped their feet at the cathedral door. Sere and yellow were the vines on the trellis of Leonato's house, chill the ornamental wrought-iron staircase which Desmond Heeley can flog at any time to Tennessee Williams.
>
> (Felix Barker, *Evening News*, 5 April 1961)

This suggestion of a possibly darker reading of the comedy was not carried through in Langham's production. Critics complained of its fussiness, its hurry; 'There is far too much flurry on the stage', said Desmond Pratt (*Yorkshire Post*, 5 April 1961). 'The actresses either screech like agitated hens or giggle like schoolgirls. There is also too much comic business.' However, he added, 'What this production lacks in subtlety, it gains in youth, enormous zest and energy. It has the bounce and flavour of a musical comedy . . . '. All agreed, however, that the production lacked the 'poetry' that they remembered from the Gielgud production. This was partly nostalgic sentimentality for a more gracious age of theatre – 'We, who have seen our Gielguds and our Ashcrofts and our Wynyards playing in the sempiternal sunlight of this almost Mozartian comedy, felt frustrated', sighed Caryl Brahms (*John O'London's*, 13 April 1961). The production had a plebeian air, most notably in the relation of Beatrice and Benedick:

> Miss Geraldine McEwan dispenses almost entirely with the airs and graces of the traditional Beatrice and plays her as a modern young woman who thoroughly enjoys the Elizabethan notion of repartee. There is something a little hoydenish in her enjoyment but she is in her prosaic way very effective.
>
> (*The Times*, 5 April 1961)

'Mr Plummer walked off slapping Miss McEwan's bottom – so much for wit', commented the *New Statesman* (5 April 1961). R.B. Marriott thought that Christopher Plummer was 'more of a watered-down provincial Petruchio than a Benedick in whom we can take real interest' (*Stage*, 6 April 1961); of Geraldine McEwan's Beatrice, Philip Hope-Wallace said 'she can be amusing, but her range seems all too small and her melting into love carries no sort of conviction' (*Guardian*, 6 April 1961). Demonstrating once again the importance of costume, particularly in creating a female character,

McEwan later said, 'I loathed playing Beatrice in a Regency dress. I would like to play her as a Renaissance lady – the full-blooded thing. It's a wonderful complex part; it's got everything' (*Plays & Players*, March 1974). But the director's and designer's 'concept' did not allow the actress to explore the complexity she saw in the role. There was a general disappointment that this Beatrice and Benedick's 'merry war' did not seem to *matter*: 'Mr Langham misses completely the heartbreak that lies within the core of his play's boring heartiness', said Robert Muller. 'Neither Geraldine McEwan nor Christopher Plummer managed to communicate more than its shadow. We lost all the nuances of this superb, erotic fencing match which must end in sweetest reconciliation' (*Daily Mail*, 6 April 1961).

Lacking an exciting Beatrice and Benedick, audience attention may turn to the other pair of lovers, Claudio and Hero, in the hope of finding an emotional thrill. This was provided for many critics by the idealised portrayals given by Barry Warren and Jill Dixon. The sexual politics of the Claudio–Hero story were not yet a matter for concern – neither, for that matter, were Plummer's bottom-slapping exploits – and Marriott, among many, admired

> a striking Claudio, with his fresh true-ringing ardour, his moving display of anger and grief, and his simple but shining gladness when Hero is restored to him. Jill Dixon also impresses, with a charming Hero. These two, in fact, provide the most completely pleasing and satisfying aspects of the production.

Most notably, Don John emerged at last from the melodramatic stereotype which had been his previous dramatic incarnation, in a striking performance by a saturnine, stammering Ian Richardson: 'a surprisingly good Don John, drawing the usually incredible villainy of this character out of a neurosis of romantic self-pity and somehow making it seem plausible' (*The Times*, 5 April 1961). Richardson, a powerful and highly intelligent actor, was obviously encouraged to explore his character in a way that the four lovers, stereotypes of the early 1960s' ideology of gender, were not.

1968

If Langham's production lacked the erotic thrill and the explor-ation of subconscious motivation that audiences were beginning consciously to expect from Shakespearean comedy, Trevor Nunn's 1968 revival went a long way towards supplying the lack. This was after a curiously long gap for such a popular play – perhaps the RSC directorship felt that it had been overexposed in the 1950s, that it was a text exhausted by the popular idea that it was all 'style' (the apogee of the obsession with style was probably Zeffirelli's manic comic-Sicilian production at the National Theatre in 1965).

Set in an early version of designer Christopher Morley's 'great empty box',[5] dimly lit, and with the characters dressed for the most part in mottled reds and oranges, Nunn's production gave at times the impression of a dream, a return to the womb. 'The effect is to enclose and concentrate the action, certainly to darken the mood of the play', said Sheila Bannock (*Stratford Herald*, 17 October 1968). This was a play very much about sexual attraction: the Elizabethan-style costumes allowed the men to swagger in tight breeches and the women to show a great deal of bosom. One of its most striking moments early on was the military masque, danced by the men with clashing swords and huge phallic-nosed red masks.[6] The bawdy lines were given their full value (and more – I still recall Alan Howard's suggestive pause on 'fetch you the length of Prester John's . . . foot'). There was much more physical contact between all the characters than there had been in previous productions, hampered as they were by nineteenth-century costume and notions of style which came down to little more than 'elegant' movement. (Gielgud, objecting to nineteenth-century costuming, had perceptively commented, 'I do not think those fashions can ever suit a play which is so full of Elizabethan sex jokes. The jokes are hardly credible when set in a period in which everybody was ashamed to show so much as an ankle').[7] This physicality was particularly noticeable in the performances of Beatrice and Benedick (Janet Suzman and Alan Howard: plate 17): they stayed close to each other, in smiling and delighted eye-contact, in the early scenes, as though held by invisible threads. In the church scene they began their duet apart, behind separate pews, and finally moved together to hug, kneeling; at the happy conclusion to V.2, 'Benedick lifts Beatrice off bench and holds her in his arms'.[8] This is unequivocally the body language of modern youth (contrast the self-consciously 'modern' behaviour of Plummer and McEwan), and the audience was delighted to recognise it, both at Stratford where the production opened in October 1968, and then at its transfer to the Aldwych in July 1969 after a twelve-week tour in the US: 'it went

Plate 17 Alan Howard as Benedick, Janet Suzman as Beatrice, *Much Ado About Nothing*, 1968, directed by Trevor Nunn. Photograph: Gordon Goode.

very well with an audience containing a lot of young people', reported Philip Hope-Wallace (*Guardian*, 30 July 1969).

The critics were less whole-hearted in their enjoyment than the ordinary members of the audience, and one wonders if their response is that of defensive middle-age against the growing assertiveness of the young, who were seeing the play with the eyes of the 1968 generation. The production had begun rehearsal soon after the student protests of May 1968; its director was the newly-appointed *wunderkind*, 28-year-old Trevor Nunn, and its principal quartet were of a similar age. Nunn's battlecry, which was to find an echo in many theatrical undertakings in the late 1960s and early 1970s (perhaps most notably in *Hair* (1968–73)) rang out proudly: 'what we have to do through the theatre is to lead and make a contact with the audience now through JOY, ENERGY AND AFFIRMATION' (*Daily Mail*, 16 October 1968).

The costumes, one critic reported, were 'Tudor executed in psychedelic chiffon prints, violet and pink, red and orange – the vigorous, exhibitionist colours of youth' (*Leamington Spa Courier*, 21 October 1968). B.A. Young's rather middle-aged carping about the production's style (or lack of it) is typical: 'Miss Suzman seems not altogether to have got over her Katharina in last year's *Shrew*. She wears an untidy straw-coloured wig, and looks, even at Hero's wedding, as if she had just hurriedly got out of bed' (*Financial Times*, 15 October 1968). Similarly, but more tolerantly, John Barber:

> The young players choose a homely English rather than a brilliantly courtly style of behaviour. Alan Howard's Benedick is tousled and charmingly gauche, while Janet Suzman makes a bubbling, almost boisterous Beatrice . . . . In short, a cheerful rather than an inspiring production, with a number of good things and strong on spectacle and horseplay, but without the dancing intelligence of Shakespeare's conception.
>
> (*Daily Telegraph*, 15 October 1968)

The shibboleth of 'Shakespeare's conception' is brought up once again in defence of a conservative performance style. Nunn, however, made it clear in his extensive programme notes that his production had strong claims to intellectual respectability (his own biographical note begins, 'Studied under Dr Leavis at Cambridge'). The programme included quotations from literary critics regarding Beatrice and Benedick; lines from other comedies of courtship – *The Way of the World*, *The Importance of Being Earnest*, *Man and Superman*;

five stanzas from Sir John Davies's *Orchestra*; and Nunn's own scholarly notes on the noting/nothing and semblance/reality tropes. The play, according to Nunn, is a serious comedy of ideas concerning the wholeness and regeneration of the community, most strikingly presented in the youthful Beatrice and Benedick's vitality and non-conformity. Even the Friar (Julian Curry) was young, an embodiment of the new belief in the power and wisdom of youth.

Some reviewers did see the serious intent underlying the production's energetic performance:

> It takes on a warmth and coherence which show up sharply the bogusness of Zeffirelli's attempt at the National Theatre to impose these from outside . . . . The alignment of male against female, townsfolk against military, have the strength of a vanished community life.
>
> (Ronald Bryden, *Observer*, 20 October 1968)

'The production firmly reveals the play's theme of regeneration', said Gareth Lloyd Evans (*Guardian*, 16 October 1968). 'Even Don John' (Terence Hardiman), noted Wardle, 'is finally absorbed into the pattern as a mere carnival monster; and the production prepares for this by showing him earlier as an irresolute tippling malcontent who is led into villainy by Borachio' (*The Times*, 15 October 1968).

In this intellectual scheme Hero and Claudio become rather more than simple foils to the sparring Beatrice and Benedick. A number of critics were struck with Helen Mirren's 'pert teenage Hero', who hinted at a less than pure mind, and by Bernard Lloyd's 'unpleasant' Claudio: 'He is consistently the calculating poseur, who has the good fortune to fall in love with an heiress and is sadistically determined to punish her to the utmost when he believes her to be untrue' (*Evesham Journal*, 16 October 1968). Harold Hobson, who did not much like the production, nevertheless found its lack of elegance 'consistent and defensible':

> it is unlike any 'Much Ado' I have seen before. Mr Nunn builds up his production to the church scene, the emphasis of which he places, not on Beatrice's injunction to Benedick to kill Claudio, but on Claudio's terrible assassination of Hero's character. Bernard Lloyd sets about this with a venom that makes the episode, which is anyway one of the most disgusting in Shakespeare, the penetrating point of the evening.
>
> (*Sunday Times*, 20 October 1968)

Hobson also disliked the unladylike forthrightness of Janet Suzman's Beatrice: 'Where Shakespeare says that Beatrice enters like a lapwing, Miss Suzman's giant leap seems more consonant with Mexico City and the lively buffalo.' But most found her sparky 'bluestocking' (she played several scenes in spectacles) enchanting and delightful, despite her caustic tongue:

> Miss Suzman's Beatrice has evidently been in love with Benedick in the past. A bright girl, scholarly ... she has despaired – like Shakespeare's harsher shrew Kate – of meeting a man of her intellectual level who isn't a sugar-candy courtier.
>
> (Jeremy Kingston, *Punch*, 6 August 1969)

It is interesting to contrast Kingston's comments with Suzman's own feminist recollection and assessment of the role twelve years later:

> I love her defiance. She's *damned* if she's going to admit she loves the man. She's got something so crystalline, so witty, so tough, yet underneath she's soft and vulnerable. She is one of the many women in Shakespeare who shows incredible loyalty and friendship for another woman.[9]

Such terms of evaluation for a female role were simply not part of the vocabulary of the complacently patriarchal critics of the 1960s.

Alan Howard as Benedick impressed most critics with his 'zany' impersonation, thus eschewing, as Jacobi and others were to do after him, the stereotypical masculine misogyny often given to the role. Jeremy Kingston commented that this Benedick was 'honest and engaging, a nice companion, very appealing in his crestfallen expressions and gleefully confident glances at the audience' – in short, a young man who seemed to belong to the contemporary community.

When the production was revived at the Aldwych in 1969 a number of authoritative reviewers found themselves having to revise their opinions; B.A. Young, for instance:

> Beside its Stratford version of last October, this new incarnation of Trevor Nunn's production of *Much Ado* is a revelation. All the aggregation of rococo foolery, and all the superfluous slapstick that concealed the pleasures of Shakespeare's wit in this most witty play, have been ruthlessly clipped away .... A new spirit of intelligence has spread through the whole thing. Janet Suzman's Beatrice ... is witty

and confident, and her lines come sizzling across .... [On 'Kill Claudio':] she does it with a break in her voice [rather than her previous shout] that makes you aware of the terrible nature of her request. And Alan Howard as Benedick, instead of replying with a shouted refusal, pauses for what seems an infinity of time before telling her, firmly but gently, that he cannot.[10]

(*Financial Times*, 30 July 1969)

If there was general agreement that Nunn and his actors were 'trying too hard' in the Stratford performances of what was almost literally a revolutionary new view of the play, it seems that by the time the production arrived in London the actors had become more confident, less aggressive in their presentation; and also that the critics had begun to accept the production on its own terms: Trewin and Wardle were two more who gracefully withdrew their earlier objections and heaped praise on the 'sheer amplitude of life' of this youthful, sexually-aware production (Wardle, *The Times*, 30 July 1969; Trewin, *Birmingham Post*, 30 July 1969).

1971–76

Other readings of *Much Ado About Nothing* emerged in the 1970s, among them a feminist one which suggests that not only *young* women experience sexual desire or are sexually desirable. Ronald Eyre's 1971 revival, which was mounted for the 41-year-old Elizabeth Spriggs partnered by a middle-aged Derek Godfrey, was once again set in the safe world of nineteenth-century decorum. Eyre followed Nunn in providing a programme full of thought-provoking quotations – a page each on 'Adam and Eve' and 'A Woman's World' – but offered no insights of his own, nor did the quotations seem to have much to do with what Michael Billington (*The Times*, 28 May 1971) called 'this amiable lightweight revival ... everything conspires to suggest a leisurely, sunlit, aristocratic society'. The set (by Voytek), an early Victorian conservatory, and the extravagant military costumes and gentlemen's summer country wear set the tone of the production. Much comment was made on the constant business with period-establishing props – cigars, fishing-rods, bird-watching apparatus, painting easels: 'No one is allowed merely to speak for long; he or she must be given something to do: fill a pipe, sign the Visitors' Book, or, frequently, light a cheroot' (*Stage*, 3 June 1971) – or engage in a round of glee-singing ('Sigh No More, Ladies', a charming Victorian pastiche by Carl Davis, was reprinted in the programme for the audience's further pleasure). The contrast between Nunn's military masque of 1968, with its aggressive sexuality, and Eyre's clowning dance by the gentry in masks made of frying-pans and other kitchen implements points up the difference between the two productions:

> although this is a very elegant and even spirited production, it does seem at the moment to lack passion . . . the emotional involvement between Beatrice and Benedick – and indeed, between other characters of the play – is very muted: one does not sense the tug between inclination and instinct, and the comedy, though it is witty, remains rather heartless.
>
> (Sarah Elly Wood, *Stratford Herald*, 4 June 1971)

The period setting, remarked the Birmingham *Sunday Mercury* (30 May 1971), 'constrains the natural airs of the play and identifies too strongly with a period of our history which was not memorable for its easy-going ways or flirtatious habits'. Or an acceptance of women engaging in bawdy banter (in fact much of the bawdy talk was excised, allowing the play to appear even more 'Victorian'); the *Stage* commented:

> Beatrice is made to look too well brought up to speak her mind, or even to speak at all to a man . . . on the brink of each dagger-sharp taunt, [she] hesitates as if wondering if she dare. Then she adds warmth to daring.

Michael Billington nevertheless found the pair's romance touching:

> Elizabeth Spriggs . . . a friendly, bustling spinster, pushing forty, who invents numerous little household tasks to disguise her starved emotional life . . . in the later scenes she quietly suggests Beatrice has acquired a second youthfulness through the transforming power of love.
>
> Derek Godfrey's Benedick undergoes a similar metamorphosis from bovine hearty and born clubman . . . to emotionally mature lover. But in his case the contrast is a shade too explicit.

B.A. Young's opinion was that their performance lacked sexual excitement, and therefore the sense of potential renewal for the community: 'that marriage of theirs is no romantic union. They may become a popular party-going host and hostess; but they're no more likely to raise a family than the host and hostess in *Who's Afraid of Virginia Woolf'* (*Financial Times*, 28 May 1971).

The fact that the production was so deliberately lightweight meant that it also lacked a sense of evil in the Hero–Claudio plot. Billington commented:

> the element of public-school prankishness in all the plotting and counterplotting is really underlined . . . . [However] the operatically villainous plot against Hero seems slightly out of place in this sun-dappled, country-house setting. You feel the worst that could happen here is that someone might get caught cheating at croquet . . . one is left hungering for a much stronger realization of the play's darker, melodramatic constituents.

Eyre's one innovative touch was to give Richard Pasco's Don John a homosexual motivation. The *Birmingham Post* (31 May 1971) reported that Eyre told Pasco 'Don John loves Claudio', and Pasco's performance was by all accounts brilliant. Even the veteran Trewin thought that 'Richard Pasco, more than any man I recall, persuades us of the canker at the heart of that often inexplicable villain, Don John' (*Birmingham Post*, 28 May 1971). *The Observer*'s critic (30 May 1971) noted in him 'a discontent so powerful that it's like a deformity'. The development of the figure of Don John as an outsider, a dramatic critique of the fragility of the community's image of itself, is a notable feature of productions of the last twenty years; more recently, he has even been joined by his brother, Don Pedro, as another who cannot acquiesce in comedy's optimistic vision of the healing power of marriage. Pasco's Don John, however, was not enough by himself to add moral or emotional weight to the production, and audiences left the theatre finally unmoved.

John Barton's famous 'British Raj' 1976 production, still revered by many critics, wrung hearts *and* induced howls of laughter from the audience, owing to three factors: the underlying sadness of Judi Dench's Beatrice, the comic mastery of Donald Sinden's Benedick; and the hilarious antics of the Watch, played as an Indian *Dad's Army*, complete with funny 'babu' accents and Indian body-language ill-adapted to the conventions of the British Army. As a member of the audience I found this clever notion totally offensive – racist and patronising, even though I did find myself smiling at the comic performance of John Woodvine's Dogberry, which certainly put new life into those old jokes which critics almost unceasingly complain are never funny enough. It is significant that Barton had to go back to the early 1950s and 1960s humour of the Goons (Spike Milligan and Peter Sellers) for a source for his comic Watch. The 1970s laughed at Monty Python, a much more inward-looking, self-critical English satire. But Barton was not a young man in 1976 (he was forty-eight); and his production was (again) about a middle-aged Beatrice and Benedick.

Critical opinion was largely complimentary about the production, particularly as it was brought off with such panache by a company of superb actors. Two or three voices were raised in objection, the most percipient Harold Hobson's:

> Mr Barton's premise is that a coloured man is funny merely by being coloured. Ridicule his salaams, comic ways of sitting down, and too precise forms of speech, and you have something that sends audiences into paroxysms of delight. Personally, I found this racial joke offensive, but it clearly filled the theatre with a comforting sense that if the British have lost an Empire they can at least jeer at those who have gained it . . . . John Woodvine enters with enormous zest into his ignoble performance as Dogberry, and the degradation forced on him by Mr Barton is wildly applauded by the frustrated imperialist audience.
>
> (*Sunday Times*, 11 April 1976)

Similarly Benedict Nightingale remarked 'I'm not sure that [Dogberry's] earnest malapropisms were much appreciated by the lady in a sari sitting near me' (*New Statesman*, 16 April 1976), thus reminding his readers that the British audience was no longer as homogeneous as it had been in the 1950s, and that some of those Stratford visitors who come for a taste of Shakespeare might actually not be of Anglo-Saxon origin.

For John Barber of the *Daily Telegraph* (9 April 1976), who did not find the Indianisation offensive, the production offered the audience

> a fantastication on the play that is elaborate, ingenious, inventive and unnecessary . . . . What is missing is the glitter of a sophisticated court, with two sensitive people at centre who conceal their feelings and display their intelligence by waging a merry war of words.

What Barton supplied in place of wit and 'style' was an elaborate realism; his forte, as Michael Billington pointed out, is that he 'has the rare knack among Shakespearean directors of endowing his characters with a complete past history' (*Guardian*, 10 April 1976). The 'Elizabethan' permanent set for the season, constructed of wooden slats, 'with just a piece or two of muslin, becomes a convincing hot, dry and dusty fort' (Peter Whitehouse, *Sunday Mercury* 11 April 1976), in which bored and under-employed officers of Empire and their households fill in their time with idle jokes and petty domestic business (Beatrice, for instance, was seen shelling the peas for dinner, or aimlessly sweeping the dust around the floor). In this context, 'the decision of Claudio (Richard Durden, amiably chinless) to curse Hero at the altar on such slender evidence becomes the mindless reflex action of an officer, gentleman and twit' (*Punch*, 21 April 1976). 'They are a heartless lot, these officers', said B.A. Young: 'they will no doubt be moving to another station shortly; they continue as coldly frivolous after the interrupted wedding as before it, no doubt thinking themselves lucky to have got out of an embarrassing entanglement' (*Financial Times*, 9 April 1976).

Don John's character and motivation were also crystal clear: Ian McDiarmid presented him spindle-shanked, 'curly-haired and studious, obviously sent out to the Army against his will and bitterly resenting it' (Robert Cushman, *Observer*, 11 April 1976). Nightingale thought him 'a reedy milk-sop half-batty with sexual envy. When he calls Hero a "pretty lady", you feel he's verbally goosing her.' He added,

> the setting suits the play's atmosphere, but it does encourage a snooziness of pace – and perhaps also a certain staidness of manner . . . . nor is it easy to believe that one of these Victorian misses, however spirited, would suddenly invite her swain to murder.

In fact Judi Dench's Beatrice was far from 'spirited'. Cherie Lunghi's Hero was much more likely unthinkingly to demand a man's death: she was, said the *Spectator* (17 April 1976),

> far less drearily virginal than usual and the tawdry report of her unchastity is thus, to take a cynical view, a shade more feasible . . . . I can summon no confidence in [Hero and Claudio's] eventual union, which seems headed for a future of languid infidelities at country-house parties back home.

Dench's Beatrice was out of place in this heartless environment. Like Elizabeth Spriggs before her, she played the role as a woman fearing herself to be on the shelf (she was in fact 42 in 1976, though with her blonde gamine looks the Beatrice she presented seemed in her early thirties), and occupying her empty life with a succession of minor domestic tasks. But in contrast to Spriggs's cheerful bustle, Dench was sour and grumpy, in a much less pleasant situation than the nostalgic summer country-house England of Eyre's conception.

Remarking that 'Miss Dench is not, on the face of her, a plausible occupant of any shelf anywhere . . . you could imagine her rejecting suitors, but never failing to attract them', Robert Cushman explained:

> Her strategy is, at first, to damp herself down; her dress is drab and her wit sour rather than sparkling. Her gibes at Benedick are meant to hurt, not to entertain; their first encounter is played, unusually, without spectators.

Noting, as many commentators did, the evidence of 'a previous, scarring involvement between the two protagonists', Cushman describes Dench's emotional exploration of the role: 'Miss Dench pulls this suggestion to the front of the play. We see what is gnawing her . . . . When she melts, the effect is breathtaking . . . . We weep for happiness at Beatrice's conversion.' Peter Whitehouse confirmed Dench's ability to move an audience:

> [she] can turn on one of those needle sharp prickles of wit from a dazzling gaiety (with all the talents and timing of the comedienne) to expose, just for a second, a depth of sadness that makes a theatre full of people hold their breath . . . . So compelling is she that when she eventually gets that kiss of love an uncontrollable 'ahhh' issues from the audience.

Details of Dench's performance indicate the particular stamp she put on the role. In the church scene, she distractedly 'falls to . . . sweeping up the confetti; she must, instinctively, do something. Benedick has to fight hard to reclaim her; has in fact to declare his love to her unyielding back', reported Cushman. 'Miss Dench has prepared in everything she previously does the anguished indignation in which . . . the peremptory demand "Kill Claudio!" is forced from her lips'. And at the end, Young noted, 'in the splendid final dance, she has got stuck with Benedick's sword and stands awkwardly in the middle of the rejoicings'. This final touch is indicative of the profound difference between Judi Dench's Beatrice and Donald Sinden's Benedick. She remained, for all her new-found happiness, an outsider to this conventionally-divided society of flighty young women and macho men; and although Sinden exited with her, on the opposite side of the stage from the rest of the company (thus, says Michael Greenwald, 'deliberately set[ting] themselves apart from the social shallowness of their peers'),[11] the rest of Sinden's performance hardly prepared us for this conclusion.

His Benedick was the regimental eccentric, the butt of the men's jokes, though also comfortably aware of his intellectual superiority. It was a great comic performance, played, said John Barber, 'with his familiar *batterie de cuisine*: the pursed mouth, the stressed sibilants, the pop-eyed indignation, the rotund declamation'. 'I suddenly remembered Mr Sinden's own Malvolio [in Barton's production of 1969]. The devices are the same but they still get the laughs', wrote Peter Whitehouse (Birmingham *Sunday Mercury*, 11 April 1976). Unashamedly playing to the audience, wrote the critic of the *Sunday Telegraph* (11 April 1976), 'Donald Sinden's boisterously histrionic Benedick swims vigorously against the tide of his director's conception, but his detachment, though consistently amusing, undermines the credibility of the later serious passages.' Peter Lewis (*Daily Mail*, 9 April 1976) reported that '"Kill Claudio" brought him an unwanted laugh. He just didn't look capable of challenging a brother officer to a serious duel'; though, to be fair, the *Spectator* thought 'Sinden's stricken, low-toned "Not for the wide world" . . . calculated as perfectly as I have ever heard it done'. The point remains, however, that the two performances by Dench and Sinden are consistently spoken of as distinct in their effects. There was little or no sexual chemistry between them: one felt that Sinden had merely been tricked out of his bachelorhood, not into love; and that Dench's Beatrice was condemned to remain emotionally alone, though she might have a husband. Because of their very different 'masculine' (egoistic) and 'feminine' (affective) acting styles – Sinden playing to the audience, Dench inviting the audience's sympathy with her hidden feelings – they did not body forth the optimistic formula of a recognisably modern marriage offered in Anne Barton's programme essay:

> At the conclusion of *Much Ado About Nothing*, Beatrice and Benedick remain within the flawed society which has fostered them and brought them together. Their relationship, however,

is one that they have created for themselves and it suggests an alternative mode of love to that of the 'model' couple Hero and Claudio: ragged, humorous, a bit undignified, demanding, but also individual and emotionally realised as the other is not.

Barton's production was generally considered very satisfying (always excepting those few critics and members of the audience who disliked its complacent racism); owing to excellent casting and a richly-detailed realistic conception it soon assumed the status of a classic interpretation, which critics still refer to fondly as a yardstick. John Peter's commendation is telling:

> behind all this harmless pantomime there's a first-rate render-ing of the kernel of the play. Like Mr Barton's unforgettable 'Twelfth Night' nine years ago, this is a warm, spacious and perceptive production, its shifting moods cunningly under-scored by the skilful use of music and off-stage noises [includ-ing – of course – a cricket match]. It is a bitter-sweet comedy of middle-aged immaturity.
>
> (*Sunday Times*, 3 July 1977)

If, however, this production were revived today, in a society now acknowledged to be multi-cultural, would the depiction of the foolish Indian servants be considered a 'harmless pantomime'? Can we not read between the lines of Peter's praise that this was, in Hobson's words, essentially a piece of middle-aged nostalgia for an Empire that was past? It is interesting to observe that when Judi Dench herself directed the play in 1988 for the Renaissance Theatre Company she opted for a young and spirited Beatrice and Benedick (Samantha Bond and Kenneth Branagh), though she set the play in the nineteenth-century context of the Napoleonic wars, wanting the recognisably 'masculine' sign of trousers (rather than doublet and hose) for the men.[12] Bond's Beatrice was still very much one who had been previously hurt by Benedick – as, indeed, what Beatrice has not been since Dench's great representation? – but the pro-duction focused on the trials of being young and in love, rather than on the director's loving re-creation of a vanished world.

1982–90

It was five years before Stratford saw another *Much Ado about Nothing*. Terry Hands, who had directed *Twelfth Night* in 1979 and *As You Like It* in 1980, here completed the trilogy of middle comedies with an elegiac Caroline production, as though saying farewell to the old 'Elizabethan' order and the organic community it represented in the mid-twentieth-century literary imagination. The lighting, which was designed by Hands with Clive Morris, was, throughout the play, variations of sunset or evening light thrown onto a huge cyclorama, against which Ralph Koltai's tall trees on perspex screens were beautifully silhouetted. The floor-tiles mirrored the sky, the trees, the few pieces of garden furniture, and the rich satin costumes of the actors. This was not a nostalgic re-creation of lost glory but a very clear indicator that such a narcissistic world had to come to an end – not even Beatrice and Benedick, finally absorbed in each other, could regenerate it for long.

For Michael Billington, the symbolic design concept was impressive, if not as comforting as Barton's naturalism:

> it is clear that we are in a hermetic, self-loving society dazzled by appearance and fashion. It is a brilliantly appropriate image and leads to many solicitous touches: whereas the extrovert Benedick, for instance, plays the scene in which he is gulled in front of the perspex wall, the tricked Beatrice is later seen, lost in wonderment, behind a haze of smoked glass. My only cavil would be that this over-powering design precludes the kind of social detail that can (as in John Barton's Indian Raj production) give a kind of truth to the play's preposterous events.
>
> (*Guardian*, 21 April 1982)

For most critics, and certainly for the enthusiastic audiences, both in England and in America, the production was a triumph. There was general rejoicing that at last Derek Jacobi, a major classical actor now in his prime, had been lured to Stratford. Jacobi has the beauty of voice and elegance of phrasing that remind many people of Gielgud, but he also has a very modern physicality and comic flair, which he used to great effect to present a capering ninny of a Benedick who discovers his masculinity in the course of the play. For Michael Coveney, noting how Benedick is the centre of attention in the play's opening scene, he is this escapist society's 'natural spokesman ... with a dashing but qualified smile and an ostentatiously limp wrist', and, one might add, a much more frilled and

furbelowed costume than the women. This characterisation 'intro-
duces an air of sexual adventure and discovery into Benedick's
progress that is quite new to the part' (*Financial Times*, 21 April
1982). A somewhat more probing perception of Jacobi's Benedick
would note that his 'campness' is one way of dealing with a society
whose conventions he can't take seriously: at the end, in the final
celebratory dance, he sent up its self-satisfaction by playing the
'female' role in an impromptu ballet pas-de-deux, in which Sinead
Cusack's Beatrice cheerfully lifts him – he, however, could not do
the same for her when the roles were reversed.[13]

Jacobi played a late-twentieth-century 'new sensitive man'. He
eschewed martial posturing in the church scene (plate 18), which
was played quickly and with urgency, as though he was as much
concerned about Beatrice's friend Hero as she herself was (the
hysterical laughter with which he greeted 'Kill Claudio' was dropped
quite early in the run). In V.2's relaxed conversation, they stood
together, quietly bantering like old friends, until he turned to ask,
with genuine concern and friendly familiarity, 'And now, how do
you?' His conclusion, 'Man is but a giddy thing' was met with a firm
nod of assent from Beatrice, which gave her, although silenced by
the play and Benedick's kiss, a final feminist utterance. Jacobi's
assessment of the meaning of these two characters for the later
twentieth century fits a recognisable modern paradigm: 'You feel
it's never going to be roses, roses all the way for them, both still have
their extraordinary intellects which will crash against each other,
both are very independent, but they will survive. Their joint sense of
humour is the great saving grace in their relationship'.[14]

Sinead Cusack's Beatrice began the play even more obviously
isolated than Judi Dench's: she circled around the assembled company until she plunged in to offer herself for Benedick's universal
hand-kissing of the ladies; he deliberately ignored her. She played
'Indeed, my lord . . . a double heart for his single one' visibly upset
by the memory, though she recovered herself quickly to rejoice at
Hero and Claudio's engagement. Before the gulling of Benedick, she
was seen wandering alone across the back of the set – and she left
the scene of her own revelation in a slow, private dance, as though
a dream was at last coming true. The fact that Cusack was also
playing Katharina in the same season led many critics to notice the
connection between the two roles: Billington noted that she 'really
is a budding blonde termagant "possessed with a fury" . . . who

Plate 18 Derek Jacobi as Benedick, Sinead Cusack as Beatrice, *Much Ado About Nothing*, 1982, directed by Terry Hands. Photograph: Chris Davies.

through love acquires emotional equilibrium. Instead of the usual Restoration wit, Ms Cusack's intriguing Beatrice is a self-taming shrew'. This is the first record I have found of an experienced critic being 'intrigued' by a performance of Beatrice; we might speculate that it is because Sinead Cusack broke the mould, playing neither the brilliant, confident young woman, nor the desperate almost-middle-aged one, but an emotionally isolated person, using her wit as defence against being hurt. 'Being a woman, and therefore more self-aware and grown-up than men, she knows from the very beginning of the play . . . that she loves Benedick but doesn't dare trust that he reciprocates', commented the *Spectator* (28 May 1983). Cusack describes her own conception of the role:

> When Terry [Hands] cast me as Beatrice, what he saw in me was femininity – that's what he cast, that's what he used in his direction of me. But because of who I am, I showed him other areas of the character. A Beatrice who is very angry. A woman who has been damaged by society . . . . Beatrice has a physical grace which I think is terribly important, so my movements as Beatrice were as fluid as Kate's were jagged.[15]

Young, capable of both anger and hurt, but at ease with her sexuality and her body: this was an image that the young women of the 1980s could identify with. The middle-aged, 'on the shelf' Beatrices of Judi Dench and Elizabeth Spriggs were images from a pre-feminist way of thinking about women in society. Spriggs had even pushed the role towards caricature by using the awkward gait of the comic games-mistress; Dench's social unease in the final dance, and elsewhere, has already been noted.

The play's final image, accompanied by Nigel Hess's unearthly tubular-bells music, showed Beatrice and Benedick alone on stage, cheerfully arguing: a 'Shavian couple', noted the critics. Hands's point, presumably, was that it has always been a relationship based on talking, however defensive at times – contrast the few stilted speeches of Hero and Claudio, in this production no more than a pair of conventional adolescents. As Beatrice and Benedick realised that they were alone, they went into a slow dancing embrace – an affirmation of the importance of mutual affection and support (even more important than sexual fulfiment) when society itself is dis-integrating. It is this human warmth that the play's outcasts missed out on: John Carlisle's Don John was no more an outsider than his brother, played by Derek Godfrey – 'both black-clad siblings take a delight in plotting', wrote Robert Cushman (*Observer*, 25 April 1982). At the end Don Pedro, surrounded by the dancing community, but himself without a partner, put on his black hat and left the stage.

In the late 1980s the RSC at last began to allow more women directors to work on the main stage at Stratford. Di Trevis had had successes with tough modern works at the Glasgow Citizens' and elsewhere, and had worked on satires at Stratford, but her first excursion into 'high' comedy, with *Much Ado* in 1988, was by most critical accounts a disaster. Possibly she was trying too hard to prove her fitness for the august position accorded her; possibly she felt some ambivalence about a play so implicated in patriarchal ideology. Fortunately we have the RSC's archival videotape at the Shakespeare Centre Library to check the critics' impressions against.

The 'look' of the production was the main stumbling-block for the reviewers. Designed by Mark Thompson, it was set in the 1950s, in some tropical haven of the rich, with the British Army not too far away: Malaya, South America, Cyprus presented themselves as possibilities – the last the most likely as the aborted wedding took place in a Greek Orthodox chapel. Most disconcerting was the gimmick of the arrival of the army men at the beginning of the play, dropped from helicopters in their jungle fatigues. Perhaps Trevis was trying to make an opening statement about the parasitism of the idle rich, whose life of gossip and shallow frivolity she then anatomised for the next three hours. If this was the case, she had a resisting audience, who simply refused to think about what they saw: 'The men consistently lack dignity . . . dressed in tropical shorts, bell-hop jackets or dressing-gowns; the women, in a succession of strapless ball-gowns, look foolishly over-dressed rather than glamorous', opined Katherina Duncan-Jones (*Times Literary Supplement*, 28 April 1988). This response was presumably intended; Sheridan Morley thought the 'costumes designed all too clearly to get the laughs they seem unable to find in the text . . . [but] the production has no real point of view' (*International Herald Tribune*, 20 April 1988). (Nostalgic evocation of the Indian Raj is an acceptable 'point of view', but satire of the pink-gin brigade of the last days of the British Empire is apparently not.)

The other visual problem was with the casting of Beatrice and Benedick, Maggie Steed and Clive Merrison. Once again a couple on the verge of middle-age, this Beatrice and Benedick were physically mismatched. Steed is a tall woman, made to look even bigger in the full skirts and high heels of the 1950s (significantly she was in flatties for the intimate conversation of V.2) – a confident socialite inclined to swoop upon people. Clive Merrison was the spindly joker to the company, small, thin and balding, looking ridiculous in the Bombay bloomers and floral shirt he habitually sported. Irving Wardle, whose review was relatively charitable – he thought that 'one aim of the production is to hold out some hope to nature's wallflowers . . . the sexual outsiders' – commented sadly: 'What fails to materialize is any transformation of the lovers. They look as they looked to begin with, a mismatched pair' (*The Times*, 15 April 1988).

The two actors played their roles very much for laughs – and got them, despite the grumpiness of the critics. Merrison got most of his by exasperated shouting – according to Wardle, he 'gives the impression of gnashing his teeth even when in full satirical flow . . . he is apt to explode in her face ("Harpy!") even in company'. Even his declaration of love in the church scene was shouted, as though unwillingly ripped from him; he was only momentarily shocked into quietness by 'Kill Claudio', then the shouting match continued, though the end of the scene was touching in its physical awkwardness – holding hands, they seemed to want to kiss, but couldn't quite work out how to manage it (in the last scene, he simply grabbed her without forethought). One felt, however, that if once he stopped shouting, Merrison's exasperated little man would become the hen-pecked husband of 1950s mythology.

Maggie Steed's Beatrice was a more complex portrayal. She drawled her banter, getting a good deal more humour out of it than previous Beatrices had done for some time. But she was also able to use the depths of her voice to suggest warmth and emotion, as in her emergence from her hiding-place (an ornamental pool) in III.1 – with her dress dripping, she presented a comic figure, but she controlled the audience's response by her speech, low, obviously deeply shaken. 'Kill Claudio' had the same delivery, and got no laugh. While some reviewers found her physical impersonation offputting (Mrs Thatcher and Dame Hilda Bracket were both mentioned as models), others lamented lost possibilities for the actress:

> Maggie Steed is an intelligent actress whose range . . . displays desolate heartbreak, wit and sensuality – the ideal and rarely-found combination for Beatrice. In this production she has to

get her laughs from funny walks, funny hats and hiding in a pond.

In the outburst of grief after her slandered cousin's rejection, Miss Steed fills the theatre with raw passion; and there are signs that, when the lumpen direction can drag itself away from stale gags and corny whimsy, it can generate some tension.

(Martin Hoyle, *Financial Times*, 15 April 1988)

Ralph Fiennes played a very romantic, innocent Claudio, and Julia Ford a spirited and likable Hero. Many critics found them interesting and involving by contrast with the 'caricatures' of Beatrice and Benedick, and Wardle commented, 'There is, perhaps, more substance in the production's feminist angle; as where Hero . . . collapses in church and is immediately surrounded by a flock of sympathetic girls, while the men all retire to nurse their personal grievances'. Was it perhaps Trevis's 'feminist angle', or just a negation of any possibility of finding good in this proto-modern society (contrast this vision of the world after the Second World War with Gielgud's bright optimism), that dictated that everyone in the last scene should be wearing black, as though for a funeral? They did not change out of the clothes worn for Hero's 'memorial', despite the clear instruction in the text to do so ('Come, let us hence, and put on other weeds', says Don Pedro in V.3). Nevertheless the audience laughed and cheered; in their perception, at any rate, love and forgiveness had once more triumphed.

Bill Alexander's 1990 production returned the play to the early seventeenth century, very close to its original period. Set in a topiary garden designed by Kit Surrey, the production established a credible society by careful use of detail in the Barton manner. At the soldiers' arrival, for instance, basins of water and towels were brought for them to wash off after a dusty march. Arrogant lords of creation, they dropped their soiled shirts and jackets on the ground and left them for the servants to pick up.

'The soldiers take off their armour, and ritually wash away the war, but they still maintain their group as comrades, while the young women range behind their "general", Beatrice, as the wary but fascinated other side' (Paul Lapworth, *Stratford Herald*, 20 April 1990). Thus the 'merry war' began again. But the most striking detail in the opening scene was the behaviour of Beatrice (Susan Fleetwood): as the curtain rose she was fencing, cheerfully and affectionately, with Leonato, and she held on to her sword, occasionally feinting at Benedick (Roger Allam) with it, all through I.1. Finally she cast down one of her fencing gloves in front of him; he picked it up and tucked it in his belt, where it remained until he threw it at her on 'I cannot endure my lady Tongue'. (Benedick finally reclaimed it gently from her lap in V.2.) This visual metaphor strongly established two things for the audience: Beatrice's unconventionality – her behaviour anything but ladylike, despite her gorgeous dress; and her passion for Benedick. She could barely take her eyes off him for a second, and the sword-play seemed an almost desperate signal that she wished to engage in sexual encounter with him. In fact the production's foregrounding of the body was a striking characteristic (an emphasis not seen since 1968): beginning with the careless public stripping of the returning soldiers, and concluding with an extravagantly long luxurious kiss between Beatrice and Benedick, which left them both stunned; after a few lines she turned his face to her and kissed him again. In the church scene, also, after an intense, tearful exchange, their hands intertwined convulsively at Benedick's farewell; Beatrice kissed his clasping hands, and then touched his face as though brushing tears from it. The protagonists' physical and emotional need for each other had never been so strikingly presented. Fleetwood commented, 'Beatrice and Benedick are fearful of admitting to their love for each other. Full of defences. The near tragedy is that they almost lose one another and the joy is their voyage of self-discovery and final unity' (RSC publicity release).

'The heart of this production', Paul Lapworth wrote, 'was a powerful projection of real emotion', and he found it also in 'the reality of the behaviour of Don Pedro and Claudio rather than the malevolence of Don John . . . there is a subtler and more disturbing villainy in the so-called "honourable" men, Don Pedro and Claudio'. John Carlisle as a brooding Don Pedro (developing a kinship suggested in his own Don John in the 1982 production), 'create[d] a character where on the page one barely exists':

> This is no princely cipher but an ageing Cavalier shrouded in solitude and hungry for emotional contact. Mr Carlisle enters into the proxy wooing of Hero with suspicious enthusiasm and proposes to Beatrice with direct urgency.
>
> (Michael Billington, *Guardian*, 12 April 1990)

By contrast, the affair between Claudio and Hero was that of callow youth, who did not seem to know much of sexual desire

(Beatrice and Benedick looked in their thirties, both still in their sexual prime). Alex Kingston's Hero was all silly giggles, John McAndrew's Claudio an immature young man who thinks that first Don Pedro (by pulling rank and stealing his girl) and then Hero (by playing the whore) are out to insult and injure him.

The programme carried a solid essay by Lisa Jardine on the 'social conventions of the play . . . recognisably those of early seventeenth-century England', particularly as they concerned 'marriage and courtship', 'reputation and honour'. It also had, as a number of programmes for previous productions had done, extracts from books describing the male camaraderie of military life, and the threat to it posed by emotional involvement with women. Alexander's psychological reading of the play as a text based in social reality allowed its characters' emotions to register directly with the audience: these were not comic or melodramatic types but 'real people' in 'real situations'. Nor was the audience distracted by a directorially-imposed historical period whose relevance might not be immediately obvious – 'There are no suffragettes in it, no carabinieri, no Anglo-Indian colonels. Nobody enters riding a bicycle or exits eating an ice-cream; nobody wears sunglasses or Bermuda shorts', said John Gross with undisguised relief (*Daily Telegraph*, 15 April 1990).

The audience was 'ecstatic', reported Billington, though he himself and several other critics were more 'temperately enthusiastic': he 'never quite felt this Beatrice and Benedick were one of nature's inevitable partnerships'. Others did, however – or at least they recognised a modern, rather than an idealised partnership: John Peter commented,

> Susan Fleetwood presents a brittle but earthy Beatrice: you sense that in her marriage to Benedick she will provide the solid psychological foundations and he will provide the imagination.
>
> How easy it would be to play Benedick as a shallow, witty fop! . . . Allam does not take the easy path. His performance is articulated with delicacy and precision.
>
> (*Sunday Times*, 15 April 1990)

Roger Allam's 'thin-skinned Benedick' (Irving Wardle's phrase), despite his defensive bravado, was a characterisation along the lines established by Jacobi: the course of the play reveals his sensitivity as well as releasing his sexuality from the confines of male bonhomie.

This, for late-twentieth-century audiences, is a profoundly-held fantasy (how often it is the basic material of the television sitcom romance); its complementary image is that of the witty and independent woman (sword-wielding Beatrice) whose libido is high but whose emotions run deep. Thus Beatrice in the eavesdropping scene:

> She has nowhere to hide. She flattens herself against the wall and listens in appalled recognition as Hero and Margaret [*sic*; actually Ursula] take her character to pieces. When she is alone, Fleetwood's emotional resources take over and the comic mask disappears.
>
> (Irving Wardle, *Independent on Sunday*, 15 April 1990)

The audience heard a totally 'new' voice – the voice of profound and passionate feeling – and the lights faded for the interval as Beatrice stood, her hands clasped as if in prayer. The moment prepared us for the extremes of emotion of the church scene; however, some of the older male critics still found Fleetwood's Beatrice a little problematic:

> One cannot see [Allam's Benedick] surviving marriage to someone with Fleetwood's 'wild heart' . . . . [On 'Kill Claudio':] Seconds before, Fleetwood has been exuding a touching tenderness. Now, all is feminist indignation rising to feral rage. In each case the actress is perfectly plausible. She fails to reconcile lover and avenger.
>
> (Benedict Nightingale, *The Times*, 14 April 1990)

'Unfeminine' behaviour?

> It may seem perverse to complain about Susan Fleetwood, since she is probably the most gifted member of the cast. But that doesn't necessarily mean that she is an ideal Beatrice, and I can only say that I found a certain rawness in her acting – I could have done with a little more elegance and poise.
>
> (John Gross, *Sunday Telegraph*, 15 April 1990)

One wonders in what olde-worlde establishment these critics pursue their 'ideals' – certainly not in the modern world, where at least in the arts, the feminist revolution has established images of women which accurately reflect their passion, their anger, their energy – all of which Fleetwood presented, using only the Shakespearean text. Beatrice, said Fleetwood, using a superbly unfeminine set of epithets, is a wonderfully eruptive person, an oddball, like Benedick, they don't quite fit into their society. Beatrice is fascinating, quick-witted, vulnerable, feels deeply and covers it up, has moments of pure joy and wants to fly just for the hell of it. She is delicious and courageous.[16]

The profound hunger for each other exhibited by this Beatrice and Benedick did, ultimately, signal their marginal rather than their central status in their society (in this respect there was no change from Hands's 1982 production). *Their* marriage will succeed, because of who they are, but it is a private bliss, rather than a public ceremony which will regenerate the community, as the extravagant final kiss paradoxically demonstrated. In fact the image of the community was distinctly shaky at the end of the play, despite a superficial air of festivity. Claudio and Hero remained children; or rather, had arrived at a mistrustful adolescence. Social contracts, whether of marriage or male comradeship, had been demonstrated to be hollow: Claudio was petulantly reluctant to take Benedick's hand on 'Come, come, we are friends'.[17] The final dance was performed to a lusty choral reprise of 'Sigh no more, ladies': it was an imposition of communal harmony which Susan Fleetwood thought inappropriate – the song 'says that men will always be unfaithful, and it completely negates what's gone before'.[18] Whether it was a deliberate irony on Alexander's part or an unthinking attempt to provide the traditional up-beat ending to a comedy, it failed finally to convince: the play itself, in this embodiment, was about a society's loss of faith in the conventions it had created and lived by for so long.

CONCLUSION

The quasi-Utopian closure which is thought of as characteristic of Shakespearean comedy is a patterning which is easy enough to derive from the text in the study, but which may, as we have seen, undergo more or less radical questioning when the written text is *retextualised* by actors in a theatre before an audience of their contemporaries. Malvolio's threat may remain a disturbing possibility, Kate's submission may be profoundly depressing. Isabella, after all she has been through, is ambiguously silent as the Duke proposes marriage. Arden is patently not the 'real' world, and even the union of the intelligent and knowing Beatrice and Benedick takes place in a society built on demonstrably hollow foundations. Furthermore there is always the possibility that the production's indulgence in the carnivalesque – through cross-dressing, social topsy-turveydom, or physical playfulness – may not finally be contained by the narrative's movement towards incorporation. Audiences' memories of the pleasures they have experienced in the theatre often remain turbulent, deliciously disturbing, and thus potentially revolutionary.[1]

The uniqueness of Shakespearean comedy is that it operates powerfully on us through the play of a paradox: a conventional (patriarchal) community is revitalised by the incorporation, through the institution of marriage, of the remarkable energies of a charismatic female presence; yet she has spent much of the play flouting patriarchal protocols. The Stratford productions of the 1950s worked hard to convince us that their heroines were 'feminine', 'ladies' at heart; by contrast, actresses of the 1960s and 1970s found it relatively easy to assert their spiritual strength, buoyed up as they were by the progress of feminism on so many fronts. In the decade and more of Thatcherism it was not so easy, and the emergent social structure tended to produce an image of woman as either aggressive bitch or vulnerable outsider.

Perhaps the directorate of the RSC acquiesced too easily in such pessimism; perhaps, as the national theatre of the national bard, it was difficult for it to refuse the role of abstract and brief chronicler of the time.[2] Perhaps, says Fiona Shaw, 'the totality of vision that marks Shakespearean comedy is too threatening – they are explosive and challenging pieces of writing and don't fit easily into the categories of our lives'.[3] To deny them that explosive power is to impoverish the culture, to acquiesce in an official fiction that classical comedy is nothing more than a stylish opiate.

Adrian Noble, who took over the artistic directorship of the RSC at the end of 1990, said in an address to the International Shakespeare Association conference in 1986: 'he is a truly public playwright, by which I mean not only is he accessible but his plays are political in the sense that they reveal models for change'.[4] The biggest model for change is yet to be explored by the RSC – the one which acknowledges and taps into the potential of women that Shakespeare's comedies body forth. Rosalind prefigures this, as writer, director, protagonist, and manager of her own play of women in a man's world. And, despite 'fashion' or decorum, she has the last word. Not yet do women have that voice or that power in the Royal Shakespeare Company, or in society at large.[5] If it is true that neither directors, nor actors, nor audiences, can read the Shakespearean text except through the *spectacle(s)* offered by the age in which they live, nevertheless they can choose an angle of vision, and act according to its revelations. Ultimately, how the RSC and others will read 'Shakespearean comedy' in the 1990s and beyond is dependent on history yet to be enacted.

NOTES

INTRODUCTION

1 Shakespeare himself was aware of the theory of comedy, allowing the academic wit Biron to articulate it in the early *Love's Labours Lost*:

Our wooing doth not end like an old play.
Jack hath not Jill. These ladies' courtesy
Might well have made our sport a comedy.

(V.2, 860–2)

2 The most influential books on Shakespearean comedy since the 1950s have been C.L. Barber, *Shakespeare's Festive Comedy* (Princeton, Princeton University Press, 1959) and Northrop Frye, *A Natural Perspective* (New York, Columbia University Press, 1965). A summary of these and other important critical work can be found in M.M. Mahood, 'Shakespeare's middle comedies: a generation of criticism', *Shakespeare Survey*, 32, 1979, pp. 1–15. The first half of the century is covered by John Russell Brown, 'The interpretation of Shakespeare's comedies: 1900–1953', *Shakespeare Survey*, 8, 1955, pp. 1–13. W.B. Worthen points out that recent criticism's 'relocation of "meaning" from within the text to the ways in which a text can be made to perform has fundamentally altered both the practice and the consequences of literary criticism of the drama, especially in Renaissance studies' (p. 443, 'Deeper meanings and theatrical technique: the rhetoric of performance criticism', *Shakespeare Quarterly*, 40, 4, 1989, pp. 441–55). Stephen Greenblatt's concept of 'the circulation of social energy', in *Shakespearean Negotiations* (Oxford, Clarendon Press, 1988) is an outstanding example relevant to this study: 'Power, charisma, sexual excitement, collective dreams, wonder, desire, anxiety, religious awe, free-floating intensities of experience . . . everything produced by the society can circulate unless it is deliberately excluded from circulation. Under such circumstances, there can be no single method, no overall picture, no exhaustive and definitive cultural poetics' (p. 19). The other important recent development is of course that of feminist criticism, for which see notes 3, 4, 5, 22, 28, and 33.

3 Elaine Showalter, 'Introduction: the rise of gender' in *Speaking of*

Gender (London, Routledge, 1989) offers a good general discussion of the meaning of the term 'gender' in modern criticism: 'the social, cultural, and psychological meaning imposed upon biological sexual identity . . . "gender" has a different meaning than the term "sex", which is the totality of an individual's sexual orientation, preference, and behaviour . . . . Furthermore, gender is not only a question of *difference*, which assumes that the sexes are separate and equal; but of *power*, since in looking at the history of gender relations, we find sexual assymetry, inequality, and male dominance in every known society' (pp. 2–4). Helpful discussions of gender, especially in relation to theatrical performance, can be found in Sue-Ellen Case, *Feminism and Theatre*, London, Macmillan, 1988; Susan Carlson, *Women and Comedy: rewriting the British theatrical tradition*, Ann Arbor, University of Michigan Press, 1991; Valerie Traub, *Desire and Anxiety: circulations of sexuality in Shakespearean drama*, London, Routledge, 1992.

4 Lesley Ferris, *Acting Women: images of women in theatre*, New York, New York University Press, 1989, p. xi.

5 Discussions of this contentious matter from a feminist perspective include Lisa Jardine, *Still Harping on Daughters: women and drama in the age of Shakespeare*, Brighton, Harvester Press, 1983; Phyllis Rackin, 'Androgyny, mimesis, and the marriage of the boy heroine on the English Renaissance stage' (1987), repr. in Showalter, op.cit.; Case, op. cit.; Jean E. Howard, 'Crossdressing, the theatre, and gender struggle in early modern England', *Shakespeare Quarterly*, 39, 4, 1988, pp. 418–40; Traub, op.cit. Lorraine Helms summarizes the various critical positions: 'Cross-casting marks the nexus of character and performer in subtle and shifting ways which historical inquiry cannot recover. The performance of the boy actor could have been eroticized for some spectators, aesthetically distanced for others. It could have been illusionistic at one moment, only to be broken by self-reflexive theatricality at another . . . . It could foreground the social construction of gender by imposing femininity on male bodies and at the same time trivialize women's social roles in puerile caricatures': 'Playing the woman's part', in Sue-Ellen Case (ed.), *Performing Feminisms: feminist critical theory and theatre*, Baltimore, Johns Hopkins University Press, 1990, pp. 196–206 (p. 197).

6 I shall use the term 'actress' throughout this book because (a) it emphasises the physical difference between the two sexes as bodies in performance; and (b) it foregrounds the way conventional theatre represents the culture with its entrenched ideology of two genders. Occasionally, for reasons of euphony or convenience, I use the term 'actors' as a gender-neutral plural to refer in general to male and female performers.

7 'Fiona Shaw talks to Helen Carr', *Women: a cultural review*, 1, 1, 1990, pp. 67–80 (p. 76).

8 Peter Stallybrass and Allon White, *The Politics and Poetics of Transgression*, London, Methuen, 1986, pp. 18, 201.

9 Alan Sinfield, in 'Royal Shakespeare: theatre and the making of ideology', Jonathan Dollimore and Alan Sinfield (eds), *Political Shake-*

speare: new essays in cultural materialism, Manchester, Manchester University Press, 1985, quotes the left-liberal manifestos of RSC directors Hall and Nunn, p. 159. Cf. Terry Hands, interviewed by Christopher J. McCullough, in Graham Holderness (ed.), *The Shakespeare Myth*, Manchester, Manchester University Press, 1988: 'Shakespeare and the theatre in general should be concerned with the real sickness. If they are, they are bound to be questioning whatever political party is in power; and so no theatre can be "establishment", no theatre can be a "national institution" – though it may be a nationally *recognised* theatre. Our particular task must be to question, not to give answers; if we give answers, we become a political operation, which we are not' (p.123).

10 Richard Findlater (*Tribune*, 24 August 1956) commented on 'the enormous institutional popularity of the Shakespeare Memorial Theatre which has been built up since the war . . . charabanc loads of Midlanders who help to pack the theatre in the summer . . . . Such popularity infuriates many people in and out of the business. These full houses, they say, discourage initiative . . . '. *Plus ça change*: the queues and the 'charabancs' are still there, though they are much more international. RST front-of-house staff all have stories of disgruntled visitors who were expecting to see 'museum Shakespeare' in pretty sets and costumes.

11 Peter Hall, Cambridge-trained, became the artistic director of the RSC in 1960; Trevor Nunn, ditto, in 1968; Terry Hands, ex-Birmingham University, worked jointly with Nunn from 1978, and became sole artistic director in 1985; Adrian Noble, who read English at Bristol, took over the reins in 1991.

12 These two *dicta* by Peter Hall are signs of the immense public interest in Shakespeare in the Quatercentenary Year, which saw Shakespeare virtually deified in the official culture. The first (from an article, 'Shakespeare and the modern director') comes from a souvenir album, *The Royal Shakespeare Company* (London, Max Reinhardt, 1964); the second from an interview by Frank Cox, *Plays & Players*, May 1964. See also Alan Sinfield's essay 'Royal Shakespeare: theatre and the making of ideology' in Dollimore and Sinfield, op. cit.

13 Sally Beauman, *The Royal Shakespeare Company: a history of ten decades*, Oxford, Oxford University Press, 1982, p. 269.

14 Ralph Berry, 'The reviewer as historian', *Shakespeare Quarterly*, 36, 5, 1985, pp. 594–7 (p. 595).

15 Judith Cook remarks in the preface to her second version of *Directors' Theatre* (London, Hodder & Stoughton, 1989), 'It is noticeable that while politics and finance were mentioned only in passing by directors in the first book [1974], a large proportion of the people now interviewed feel impelled by the changed climate to comment on both. They are worried about having to raise so much money themselves and concerned that sponsorship may affect their freedom to put on what they want. They find the narrow-mindedness and intolerance of the age very alarming' (p. 8).

16 The report by Sue Dunderdale, 'The status of women in British theatre'

was published in *Drama*, 2, 1984. It concluded, 'the more money and more prestige a theatre has, the less women will be employed in decision making positions and the less women will be on the board . . . the two major national subsidised companies have no female resident artistic or associate directors and no female top administrators. The RSC produced some figures for free-lance directors but these referred to women used, either for no or very little payment, to direct for the 1983 Barbican Festival. A microcosm of the general experience of women being asked to perform the most menial of tasks in any particular power structure'. The 1987 follow-up study, by Caroline Gardner, published by the Women's Playhouse Trust, confirmed that there was no significant change.

17 'Fiona Shaw talks to Helen Carr', op. cit., p. 78.
18 Women's names (for instance, those of Glenda Jackson, Paola Dionisotti, Jane Lapotaire) appear for the first time above those of men on RSC programmes of 1978. The RSC actresses interviewed in Carol Rutter's *Clamorous Voices: Shakespeare's women today*, (London, The Women's Press, 1988) speak with great admiration of these pioneering actresses of the 1970s. Juliet Stevenson says, 'each of us has been influenced by the women's movement in varying ways and to different degrees, and we've allowed that influence to inform our choices on the stage. We haven't sprung from nowhere: there's always been a tradition of actresses in this country who questioned the received ideas about Shakespeare's women and who brought their own sense of female integrity to the roles (Peggy Ashcroft more than any). But those were individuals making personal choices. What has happened in the past ten to fifteen years is that the women's movement has come up alongside, as it were, to provide a conscious framework for these instincts – a framework that has structured those possibilities of re-examination, not just for actresses but for audiences too' (p. xiv).
19 There are also many illuminating comments about the situation of actresses in a male-dominated theatre in Carole Woddis (ed.), *Sheer Bloody Magic: conversations with actresses* (London, Virago, 1991), particularly in the chapters by Jane Lapotaire, Fiona Shaw and Harriet Walter.
20 Rutter, op. cit., p. xxii.
21 Ibid., p. xxiii.
22 Juliet Stevenson asks 'why a director casts an actress in a role when he knows she doesn't share his interpretation of some idea that is central to the play': 'It seems that he wants her power on stage but he doesn't want to inquire too closely into where that power comes from. It springs from the integrity of the actress engaging emotionally and intellectually with the role, so how can a director expect her to play a version of a line she doesn't believe?' (Rutter, op.cit., p. xvi). This comment encapsulates my diversion from the line of criticism initiated by feminist film critics (Mulvey, De Lauretis, Kaplan, *et al.*) and taken up by Sue-Ellen Case: 'In the realm of theatrical production, the gaze is owned by the male: the majority of playwrights, directors and producers are men. This triumvirate determines the nature of the

theatrical gaze, deriving the sign for "woman" from their perspective. In the realm of audience reception, the gaze is encoded with culturally determined components of male sexual desire, perceiving "woman" as a sexual object' (*Feminism and Theatre*, p. 118). What Case does not take sufficient account of is the disruptive possibilities of women's performances (their 'power' in Stevenson's terms) acting on this coercive paradigm. Barbara Freedman, in *Staging the Gaze: postmodernism, psychoanalysis, and Shakespearean comedy* (Ithaca, Cornell University Press, 1991), makes some strong points about the pervasiveness of Lacanian theory in feminist criticism of representation and its limitations as regards theatrical performance. Her discussion of *The Taming of the Shrew* is particularly challenging: 'Both [Lacan and Petruchio] argue that woman does not exist except as a fantasy or theatrical construct and yet both seek to reify a cultural myth of the exchange of women as the basis of civilization' (p. 135).

23 Philippa Kelly, 'Enacting Shakespeare: resistance and reception', *Southern Review* (Adelaide), 24, 3, 1991, pp. 261–77 (p.262).

24 Women theatre critics do exist (and are increasing in number), and they do, quite often, notice interestingly different things in a performance from their male colleagues: see, for example, Hilary Spurling's review of the 1966 *Twelfth Night* in chapter 1. Another nice example comes from the doyenne, Caryl Brahms: 'someone should take [the young Claire Bloom] into any High Street to see how women walk – with weight, purpose, but not with conscious grace' (*Plays & Players*, October 1953).

25 Michael Billington (*Guardian Weekly*, 17 March 1991) is here quoting the senior critic W.A. Darlington – only half-jokingly, I suspect.

26 Cary M. Mazer, 'Shakespeare, the reviewer, and the theatre historian', *Shakespeare Quarterly*, 36, 5, 1985, pp. 648–661 (p. 658).

27 The first paragraph is from Harold Hobson, *Theatre in Britain: a personal view*, Oxford, Phaidon, 1984, p. 18; the second is quoted in Dominic Shellard, 'Harold Hobson and Harold Pinter', *Oxford Magazine*, Second Week, Michaelmas Term, 1990, pp. 10–11 (p. 10).

28 'the materialist position underscores the role of class and history in creating the oppression of women. From a materialist perspective, women's experiences cannot be understood outside of their specific historical context, which includes a specific type of economic organisation and specific developments in national history and political organisation' (Case, op. cit., p. 112).

29 Robert Speaight, 'Truth and relevance in Shakespearean production', in David Bevington and Jay L. Halio (eds), *Shakespeare: pattern of excelling nature*, London, Associated University Presses, 1978, p. 185.

30 'The basically erotic nature of the attraction of actors accounts for the immense importance of casting in dramatic performance': Martin Esslin, *The Field of Drama*, London, Methuen, 1988, p. 60. Michael Billington concurs: 'the actor does enter into a sort of unspoken sexual contract with the audience, and if an actor – male or female – has no sex appeal then they tend to be a rather dull actor. I think there is a kind of public bisexuality which actors often have, the most interesting

ones ... the eye is drawn to them, either because of their sexual attractiveness or because of their sexual ambiguity'. He adds, apropos Shakespeare, 'we have to acknowledge that these plays are company plays, but they also demand magnetic presences' (interview with the author, December 1990).

31 Marco De Marinis points out that acting itself is transgressive: 'in order to attract and direct the spectator's attention, the performance must first manage to surprise or amaze; that is, the performance must put into effect *disruptive or manipulative strategies* which will unsettle the spectator's expectations ... by introducing elements of novelty, improbability, and oddity – in areas where the spectator is habitually certain of her/himself'. The actor does this by '"extra-ordinary" techniques ... based primarily on the transgression of the biological and physical laws governing our "normal" everyday bodily and mental behaviour – the fundamental laws of gravity, inertia, and the rule of least effort': 'Dramaturgy of the spectator', *The Drama Review*, 31, 2, 1987, pp. 100–114 (pp. 109–10).

32 John Harrop, *Acting*, London, Routledge, 1992, pp. 111–12.

33 Greenblatt, op. cit., pp. 86, 88. Catherine Belsey's article 'Disrupting sexual difference: meaning and gender in the comedies' is illuminating on this topic: 'Closure depends on closing off the glimpsed transgression and reinstating a clearly defined sexual difference. But the plays are more than their endings, and the heroines become wives only after they have been shown to be something altogether more singular – because more plural' (in John Drakakis (ed.), *Alternative Shakespeares*, London, Methuen, 1985, pp. 187–8). Valerie Traub in *Desire and Anxiety* explores the topic of sexual plurality at length, concluding, 'The marriages of Viola and Rosalind that purportedly conclude their plays represent the patriarchal closure of heterosexual marriage, but only after the plots embody desires that exceed institutional heterosexuality' (op. cit., p. 145).

1 TWELFTH NIGHT

1 *A Shakespeare Glossary* (C.T. Onions, rev. R.D. Eagleson, Oxford, Oxford University Press, 1986) gives 'That which one desires' and 'Carnal appetite or desire, lust' among the meanings for 'will'.

2 Stephen Greenblatt, *Shakespearean Negotiations*, Oxford, Clarendon Press, 1988, p. 93.

3 Janet Adelman, 'Male bonding in Shakespeare's comedies', in Peter Erickson and Coppelia Kahn (eds), *Shakespeare's 'Rough Magic': Renaissance essays in honor of C.L. Barber*, Newark, University of Delaware Press, 1985, p. 91. She argues that 'the twinship is itself the unfolding in the plot of Viola's disguise; it enacts on the most literal surface of the play the fantasy that one person can be both sexes ... if *Twelfth Night* celebrates marriage and the necessary sorting out into male and female that enables marriage, it also mourns the loss of sexual indeterminacy and works to repair that loss through fantasy ... at the

moment that Viola meets her brother face to face, she splits in effect into male and female components' (pp. 89–91). However, Jean E. Howard argues with rather more political realism, 'The play seems to me to embody a fairly oppressive fable of the containment of gender and class insurgency and the valorization of the "good woman" as the one who has interiorized – whatever her clothing – her essential difference from, and subordinate relations to, the male . . . . The whole thrust of the dramatic narrative is to release this woman from the prison of her masculine attire and return her to her proper and natural position as wife . . . . Despite her masculine attire and the confusion it causes in Illyria, Viola's is a properly feminine subjectivity; and this fact countervails the threat posed by her clothes and removes any possibility that she might aspire to masculine privileges and pre-rogatives'. Olivia, lacking 'a properly gendered subjectivity', is 'the real threat to the hierarchical gender system in this text, Viola being but an *apparent* threat': pp. 431–2, 'Crossdressing, the theatre, and gender struggle' in early modern England, *Shakespeare Quarterly*, 39, 4, 1988, pp. 418–40.

4 The characterisation was not entirely new: the 1939 production directed by Irene Henschel (the first woman to direct at Stratford) 'caused controversy mainly because of the playing of Olivia as a spoilt young heiress rather than the conventionally mature and sympathetic heroine' (Sally Beauman, *The Royal Shakespeare Company: a history of ten decades*, Oxford, Oxford University Press, 1982, p. 159).

5 A.C. Sprague and J.C. Trewin, *Shakespeare's Plays Today*, University of South Carolina Press, 1970, p. 95.

6 John Gielgud, *An Actor and His Time*, Harmondsworth, Penguin, 1981, pp. 142–3.

7 Michael Billington, *Directors' Shakespeare: approaches to 'Twelfth Night'*, London, Nick Hern Books, 1990, p. xvii.

8 The writer appears to be the prolific critic J.C. Trewin. The critics' assessment of this production all indicate that Berry, *Changing Styles in Shakespeare* (London, Allen & Unwin, 1981) is out by a decade in claiming Barton's (1969) as the first production to take the play 'seriously' (p. 109).

9 M. St Clare Byrne, 'The Shakespeare season at the Old Vic, 1957–58, and Stratford-upon-Avon, 1958', *Shakespeare Quarterly*, 9, 4, 1958, pp. 507–30 (p. 526).

10 Billington, op. cit., p. 37.

11 St Clare Byrne, op. cit., p. 526.

12 Diana Rigg, interviewed by Gordon Gow in an article entitled 'Shakespeare Lib' (*Plays & Players*, June 1973), commented, 'I think the really clever thing that Shakespeare posed – and this is something that is not done by contemporary playwrights – is a sexuality which is not based on the extremes of feminism or masculinism that we have nowadays. There are qualities that are shared by both sexes.' This is an early, tentative formulation by an RSC actress of ideas about sexuality and gender that were to become common in the 1970s and 1980s; explored, in fact, in the RSC's next *Twelfth Night*.

13 Promptbook for 1966 RSC production of *Twelfth Night*, Shakespeare

Centre Library. Viola knelt on 'We men may say more . . .'; there was a long pause before 'Sir, shall I to this lady?'.

14 'For me, in the case of *Twelfth Night*, Peter Hall had done what I felt to be a definitive production . . . . But [Nunn] pressed and insisted that I should do it . . . . There would be certain areas where maybe I could find something that hadn't been found before' (John Barton, in Michael Billington, op. cit., p. 61). Compare Terry Hands on the same page: 'When I came to do *Twelfth Night*, I didn't do a production in opposition to John's: what I did do was absorb a lot of John's . . . . But, in one or two areas, I thought, "Now I'm not quite sure that you took the right choice there. I would like to see if I can contribute a little to that area"'. See also note 29, for comments on Hall's return to *Twelfth Night*.

15 Judi Dench in Judith Cook, *Women In Shakespeare*, London, Harrap, 1980, p. 24.

16 Stanley Wells, *Royal Shakespeare*, Manchester, Manchester University Press, 1977, p. 62.

17 Sinden's comment on his playing of this last scene is interesting: 'They are smiling at him, a kindly smile. But the degradation is too great; so, pathetically like a small boy who knows he has lost but cannot leave without an exit line, says to them all "*I'll* be revenged", he pauses and pouts, "on the whole *pack* of you". It is a totally empty threat. The House, Illyria, the World, will shortly be laughing at his predicament. I believe there is but one thing for Malvolio – suicide' (in Philip Brockbank (ed.) *Players of Shakespeare*, Cambridge, Cambridge University Press, 1985, p. 66). One might almost expect a Chekhovian pistol-shot, off. Despite this sombre note, in Cushman's opinion (and mine) Sinden's Malvolio was hugely comic: 'there is more joyousness in Donald Sinden's pride of office than in any of those who oppose him. His first word – a massive, sneering "Yes" – rocked the theatre; not only was it magnificently funny, it was the first laugh of the evening, a cathartic release for the entire audience. The Puritan, it was evident, was our true Lord of Misrule and to him alone could we look for cakes and ale' (*Plays & Players*, October 1969).

18 John Barton, *Playing Shakespeare*, London, Methuen, 1984, pp. 188–90.

19 Lois Potter gives a detailed description of physical contact between Orsino and Viola (including 'running his hand down her body' on 'All is semblative a woman's part', and rolling about on the cushions in act II, scene 4), *Twelfth Night: text and performance*, London, Macmillan, 1985, pp. 57–9.

20 Peter Thomson, 'The smallest season: the Royal Shakespeare Company at Stratford in 1974', *Shakespeare Survey* vol. 28, 1975, pp. 137–48 (p. 140).

21 ibid., p. 146.

22 Terry Hands in Billington, op. cit., p. 2.

23 I am indebted to Dr Beverly Sherry, of the English Department, University of Sydney, for this observation.

24 Zoë Wanamaker, 'Viola in *Twelfth Night*', in Russell Jackson and

Robert Smallwood (eds), *Players of Shakespeare 2*, Cambridge, Cambridge University Press, 1988, pp. 90–1.

25 John Caird in Billington, op. cit., p. 112.

26 Roger Warren, 'Shakespeare in England', *Shakespeare Quarterly*, 34, 4, 1983, pp. 451–7 (pp. 454–5).

27 Bill Alexander in Billington, op. cit., pp. 12–13.

28 ibid, p. 91.

29 In 1991 there was a uniformly disastrous production of *Twelfth Night* at the RST, directed by the comedian Griff Rhys Jones. It looked like a cross between *Patience* and *HMS Pinafore*, and left Sylvestra Le Touzel, as a sailor-lad Viola, absolutely nowhere to go emotionally. As an attempt to 'cheer up' the play after the increasingly dark interpretations discussed, using a non-RSC director, the undertaking smacked of desperation and lacked even basic humour. 'Rarely have I seen a Stratford production so thinly characterised, so poorly acted, so dimly conceived . . . . This production is as sexless as a parish mag', said Michael Billington (*Guardian Weekly*, 5 May 1991). Peter Hall also returned to *Twelfth Night* in 1991 (an independent production at the Playhouse, in London). Billington, who liked it, found echoes of the 'legendary 1960 RSC production: the Caroline costumes, the russet hues, even Eric Porter's Malvolio . . . . What I found as moving as anything, in a visually and aurally beautiful evening, was the distant sound of the waves introduced every time Viola thought of Sebastian as if to imply the way our lives are permeated by memories of human loss' (*Guardian Weekly*, 17 March 1991). For Vera Lustig, on the other hand, 'we are in a museum. Here behind glass are preserved lifelike figures from Caroline England . . . . Viola/Cesario (Maria Miles), in her outsize plumed hat and too-small boots, and looking all of 14 years old, is wooing Olivia, who looks all of 12 and acts even younger' (*Plays & Players*, April 1991). Lustig, speaking from a nineties-style feminist intellectual position, derides 'male fantasies about child-brides, virginal, smooth-cheeked and biddable', and 'Sir Peter's iambic obsessions' – his academic pedantry about verse-speaking. Her sense of Hall's living in the past of theatrical history is summed up in her comment, 'So the tormenting of the maddened, incarcerated Malvolio is not filtered through late-twentieth-century sensibilities. It's simply played for laughs.'

2 *AS YOU LIKE IT*

1 Valerie Traub, *Desire and Anxiety: circulations of sexuality in Shakespearean drama* (London, Routledge, 1992), p. 124. She quotes James Saslow, *Ganymede in the Renaissance* (New Haven, Yale University Press, 1986): 'the very word *ganymede* was used from medieval times well into the seventeenth century to mean an object of homosexual desire' (p. 2). Traub argues that 'the erotics of *As You Like It* . . . are diffuse, non-localized, and inclusive, extending to the audience an invitation to "come play" – as does Rosalind-cum-boy-actor in the

Epilogue. Bypassing a purely scopic [phallic] economy, *As You Like It* possesses provocative affinities with the tactile, contiguous, plural erotics envisioned by Luce Irigaray as more descriptive of female experience' (p. 124).

2 Jean E. Howard offers an illuminating commentary on this matter: 'In my view, the figure of Rosalind dressed as a boy engages in playful masquerade as, in playing Rosalind for Orlando, she acts out the parts scripted for women by her culture. Doing so does not release Rosalind from patriarchy but reveals the constructed nature of patriarchy's representations of the feminine and shows a woman manipulating those representations in her own interest, theatricalizing for her own purposes what is assumed to be innate, teaching her future mate how to get beyond certain ideologies of gender to more enabling ones': 'Cross-dressing, the theatre and gender struggle in early modern England', *Shakespeare Quarterly*, 39, 4, 1988, pp. 418–40 (p. 435).

3 '[W]hen in the Epilogue the character playing Rosalind reminds us that she is played by a boy, the neat convergence of biological sex and culturally constructed gender is once more severed. If a boy can so successfully personate the voice, gait, and manner of a woman, how stable are those boundaries separating one sexual kind from another, and thus how secure are those powers and privileges assigned to the hierarchically superior sex, which depends upon notions of difference to justify its dominance?' (ibid., p. 435). In modern performance by a woman, these ontological confusions are even more present: from what gender position can she possibly be speaking?

4 Stephen Greenblatt, *Shakespearean Negotiations*, Oxford, Clarendon Press, 1988, p. 91.

5 For the history of this cultural appropriation of Rosalind, see Mary Hamer, 'Shakespeare's Rosalind and her public image', *Theatre Research International*, 11, 2, 1986, pp. 105–118: 'In the course of two centuries, as the play from 1741 onwards became ever more firmly established in the popular taste, the presentation of its heroine became fixed in a predictably idealizing mode. Play and heroine acquired a special status in the non-academic imagination. They came to constitute a sort of group fantasy' (p. 107), which, Hamer argues, was reinforced by actresses' 'willingness to display [their] femininity in a particularly appealing and unthreatening way' (p. 115).

6 '*As You Like It* was just the play for the 1950s. Its air of liberation, its informality of style, its delight in "happenings" and eccentricity, above all its "image of life triumphing over chance", which Susanne Langer dubbed the essence of comedy, all chimed in with the mood of the 1951 Festival of Britain': M.M. Mahood, 'Shakespeare's middle comedies: a generation of criticism', *Shakespeare Survey* 32, 1979, p. 8.

7 Michael Billington, *Peggy Ashcroft*, London, Mandarin, 1988, p. 170. Two further reviews quoted by Billington indicate the limitations of Ashcroft's 'feminine' reading of the role: Derek Granger in the *Financial Times*: 'The shades of fancy and wonder which cross her face at the moment of falling in love are as sweetly defined as the light and shower of April weather; and, even in between the lines, her little starts and

hesitations as her heart sways her carry the charming import of a woman becoming *joyfully enslaved'* (my emphasis). Kenneth Tynan found her 'too daughter-of-the-late-colonel-ish' (p. 170).

8 'As I had made a leap as an actress [in Rosalind], I took an irrevocable decision to make a leap into political life as well. Bertrand Russell and members of the Committee of 100 were arrested and charged with incitement to break the law when they spoke at a rally in Hyde Park in September 1961. John Morris, a member and organiser in the Committee, rang me and asked if I would join the Committee to take the place of those who had been arrested. I agreed.' She wrote to her father, the actor Michael Redgrave, explaining her position on unilateral nuclear disarmament: 'I want to act as well and as continuously as possible all my life, no holds barred . . . . But in the present situation I have to realise that there may not *be* another season at Stratford . . . . [M]y awareness of all the life around me, political, personal, natural or theatrical, and my love for that life which is *why* I act after all, had been doubly *increased* since becoming more aware and involved with the present political situation' (*Vanessa Redgrave: an autobiography*, London, Hutchinson, 1991, pp. 95, 96, 99).

Some idea of Redgrave's performance of Rosalind can be gleaned from the Shakespeare Recording Society's record of 1962 (Caedmon Cassette CDL 5210). In the wooing scenes she is passionately involved: the voice is womanly, warm, seductive, seduced, quavering before reverting to brave boyishness. All the 'court' roles are, by modern standards, extremely well-spoken – including Stanley Holloway's Touchstone, today routinely a cockney. Max Adrian's Jaques is a particularly arresting vocal characterisation, elegant yet full of pain.

9 There was in this year another 'Swinging Sixties' production, by Peter Dews for the Birmingham Rep, which transferred to London in the summer of 1967 and was very successful: 'the contemporary version of pastoral is the fancy dress of King's Road and Carnaby Street . . . designed for no real weather or public occasion one can imagine in Britain . . . [rather] an Arcadia of youth, an androgynous, perpetually sunlit Arden of huge paper blossoms' (Ronald Bryden, *Observer*, 18 June 1967).

10 Sally Beauman, *The Royal Shakespeare Company: a history of ten decades*, Oxford, Oxford University Press, 1982, p. 320.

11 The most famous *As You Like It* of 1977 was Peter Stein's at the Schaubühne in Berlin. This was a production in a huge film studio, in which the audience walked 'through a ten-minute woodland labyrinth' to an Arden with 'real trees . . . shrubbery, a sprawling pond, huts, a herbal stall, butterfly displays, an astronomical laboratory and an Elizabethan globe above it all'. The action was played above, below, behind, and in the midst of the audience, and became more and more fanciful, or 'unhistorical', as the play proceeded. Many of Stein's postmodernist ideas seem to have permeated the consciousness of RSC directors of the 1980s (for a full description of the production see *Plays & Players*, December 1977: interestingly, this article does not once mention Rosalind).

12 John Bowe (the Orlando) records, 'Terry's simple solution to lovers' games was circles: histories and tragedies have straight lines, comedies and romances have circles. If you had a map of our footprints in the two major scenes of the second half, you would have a picture of spirals all over the stage': 'Orlando in *As You Like It*', in Philip Brockbank (ed.) *Players of Shakespeare*, Cambridge, Cambridge University Press, 1985, p. 73.

13 Sinead Cusack in Carol Rutter, *Clamorous Voices: Shakespeare's women today*, London, The Women's Press, 1988, p. 115.

14 Susan Fleetwood, interviewed in 1990 as she prepared to open as Beatrice in Bill Alexander's *Much Ado About Nothing* (discussed in chapter 5), recalled 'It was a gift of a production, it was the chemistry of everyone in it that made it so alive and loving. People still come up to me, touch me and say "Oh, I saw your *As You Like It*. Thank you." Emotive about it still, as if it touched something very warm in them. Isn't that marvellous?' (Unidentified cutting [*Daily Telegraph?*], Shakespeare Centre Library).

15 John Bowe thought of his character as 'this energetic but shy young man, suppressed by his eldest brother, Oliver, since his father's death. No bad thing, perhaps, since it meant his life was spent nearer to Nature. Throughout rehearsal and performance I felt more and more that this was of importance to the balance of Rosalind and Orlando's relationship' (in Brockbank, op. cit., p. 68).

16 Bowe in Brockbank, op. cit., p. 67.

17 Noble adds, 'We had not designed that production on the first day of rehearsals. We designed it during rehearsals. And that wasn't a totally successful concept', being very impractical for the actors (Noble interviewed in Ralph Berry, *On Directing Shakespeare*, London, Hamish Hamilton, 1989, p. 163). See also his remarks in '"Well, this is the forest of Arden": an informal address', *Images of Shakespeare*, Habicht *et al* (eds), London, Associated University Presses, 1988.

18 Noble in Habicht *et al.*, op. cit., p. 337.

19 ibid., p. 338.

20 Juliet Stevenson in Rutter, op. cit., p. 105.

21 Fiona Shaw and Juliet Stevenson, 'Celia and Rosalind in *As You Like It*', Russell Jackson and Robert Smallwood (eds), *Players of Shakespeare 2*, Cambridge, Cambridge University Press, 1988, p. 57. Shaw commented elsewhere, 'For that play we were probably more fuelled, as a lot of women were, by the excitement of a new sense of who they were in society. We were exploring – very honestly, not trying to map anything on – the possibility of women's friendships .... We didn't play a received notion of what women's friendships were .... We played it that those two girls betray each other left, right and centre. That's in the text but it does need the colouring of where you are at the time, to see it': 'Fiona Shaw talks to Helen Carr', *Women: a cultural review*, 1, 1, 1990, pp. 67–80 (p. 77).

22 Stevenson in Rutter, op. cit., pp. 119–20.

23 Shaw and Stevenson in Jackson and Smallwood, op. cit., p. 71. The appearance of Hymen also changed: in Stratford 'a flickering silhouette

on a lighted screen, placed upstage, obliging the actors to turn away from the audience to perceive him'; in London 'a mere beam of light whose source was *behind* the audience . . . . in this way, the audience was able to focus not on the god, but on the face of those whose future he is deciding. This afforded each of us the opportunity to play against the "happy ever after" element, if we chose' (p. 70). Despite these developments, Susan Carlson quotes a 1986 letter from Stevenson in which she says, 'for 18 months I played a Rosalind that I never felt I'd been allowed to make truly my own' (*Women and Comedy: rewriting the British theatrical tradition*, Ann Arbor, University of Michigan Press, 1991, p. 66).

24 Stevenson in Rutter, op. cit., p. 121.

25 Fiona Shaw played Rosalind in an Old Vic production by Tim Albery in 1989. It was not well received, owing largely to an awkward design and the interesting suggestion of a lesbian relationship between Rosalind and Celia (which the girls then 'grow out of'). Like the other late 1980s productions, Albery's was dispirited and humourless; as Michael Billington commented, 'it's a play we can't deal with very easily at the moment, for various reasons. Productions . . . are getting more frenetic, darker, gloomier, colder, and unable to embrace two things . . . the marital conclusion . . . and a sort of pastoral vision, because we don't seem to believe in that either' (interview with the author, December 1990).

David Thacker's 1992 RSC production of *As You Like It* did not expand the play's meaning for the audience of the 1990s, and won faint praise as clear but unadventurous: 'Samantha Bond's Rosalind, stronger on languishing than on mischief, settles for a leisurely rhythm that fails to ignite the Orlando scenes. Last year's Cheek By Jowl [all-male] version of the play released an emotional charge nowhere approached in this production' (Irving Wardle, *Independent on Sunday*, 26 April 1992). Benedict Nightingale found Bond 'a kind of androgynous elf or sprite, part Ariel and part Peter Pan' (*The Times*, 24 April 1992). Michael Coveney (*Observer*, 26 April 1992) commented, 'If an audience does not love its Rosalind, and is not heard to be falling in love with her, the play simply fails to catch alight.' He sensed 'a complete indifference to the intellectual and sexual climate of the comedy.'

3 THE TAMING OF THE SHREW

1 Ann Thompson, Introduction to *The Taming of the Shrew*, Cambridge, Cambridge University Press, 1984, p. 24

2 Thompson quotes several inter-war reviews of the play at Stratford: one from 1933 begins, 'That *The Taming* was presented for eight years in succession from 1909 onwards may perhaps be accounted for in some measure as being due to the activities of the vote-hungry viragoes'. Kate's speech of submission is 'a smashing rejoinder to the militant Furies who were making fools of themselves' in their attempts to gain suffrage (ibid., pp. 21–2). This sort of ingrained misogyny will recur, in

more covert forms, in post Second World War reviews; it must have been endemic to much of the middle-class audience at Stratford.

3 Graham Holderness, in his stimulating study of *The Taming of the Shrew* in the *Shakespeare in Performance* series (Manchester, Manchester University Press, 1989), argues that including the 'complete Sly framework' (i.e., from the anonymous *Taming of A Shrew*) would allow for performance 'in the self-reflexive, metadramatic and ironic manner of Brecht's epic theatre. Katherina's final speech of submission, which is in most stage productions explained as a private joke or intimate understanding between Katherina and Petruchio, might well have been delivered on the Elizabethan stage with appropriate detachment, distancing and irony to an audience highly sceptical of such propagandist rhetoric; offered as a challenge and provocation to debate rather than as an attempt at ideological incorporation' (p. 25). As this chapter will show, such ironic distancing from the unpalatable ideology of the role is rarely a performance decision taken by modern actresses (or their directors). Holderness acknowledges this situation on pp. 33–4, pointing to the more common use of the Sly-frame: 'a flexible Sly-frame may ultimately leave the barbaric ideology that the play works on immune from any serious interrogation or subversion'. By the same token, the metatheatrical frame can simply be used as an excuse for an extravagant romp, in which the human relations at the centre of the narrative may conveniently be ignored.

4 Sally Beauman, *The Royal Shakespeare Company: a history of ten decades*, Oxford, Oxford University Press, 1982, p. 189.

5 Ibid., p. 191.

6 Fiona Shaw in Carol Rutter, *Clamorous Voices: Shakespeare's women today*, London, The Women's Press, 1988, p. xvii.

7 Yvonne Mitchell, *Actress*, London, Routledge & Kegan Paul, 1957, pp. 94–5.

8 Holderness, op. cit., p. 37.

9 Yvonne Mitchell remarks in her autobiography, with justifiable heat, 'The shrew is traditionally played by a large woman, as is Lady Macbeth, though there is nothing in the text of either of these plays to warrant it. The only adjective applied to Kate in *The Shrew* which denotes her size is "dainty", and as this is said by Petruchio, it can be taken either as a fact or as a rudeness. But since the days when Kate was played with enormous success by Ada Rehan and Lady Macbeth by Sarah Siddons, critics of the theatre have decided that both these ladies must be large .... Yet in Shakespeare's day when boys played the women's parts, I'll wager neither Lady Macbeth nor Kate were played by very big boys. A shrew is in fact a small mouse, and the type of woman who derived her name from the animal might more logically be assumed to be small' (Mitchell, op. cit., p. 93). One wonders if this tradition of 'big ladies' arises from a subconscious need to see both these female characters as monsters.

10 ibid., p. 94.

11 Alexander Leggatt records that 'their first meeting began with a long pantomime in which Petruchio pretended to have only one arm.

Katharina approached him with an expression of sympathy; her reaction when the "missing" arm suddenly appeared combined indignation with wry amusement. She and Petruchio were thus established as characters who enjoyed playing games with each other . . . the effect was to soften the characters' relationship, to assure us that no real wounds were being inflicted': *Shakespeare's Comedy of Love*, London, Methuen, 1974, p. 55.

12 Janet Suzman's comment on this scene shows how even an intelligent actress can rationalise the role she finds herself playing so as to accord with the dominant paradigm: 'Petruchio, over the moon (so to speak!) that his exhausting game has been seen through at long last, joins her. Their love – combative, spirited, and until this moment, unspoken – can now flourish. Each has found an ally . . . . That hyperbolic speech at the end of the play, reviled by feminists, can now become Kate playing, in public, the exact game she has been taught in private. It is a paean to the secretiveness of real passion. And remember – Petruchio *always* stops before anything dangerous happens; no harm ever comes to Kate, does it?' (Suzman in Judith Cook, *Women in Shakespeare*, London, Harrap, 1980, p. 29)

13 Michael Bogdanov interviewed by Christopher J. McCullough, in Graham Holderness (ed.), *The Shakespeare Myth*, Manchester, Manchester University Press, 1988, p. 89.

14 ibid, pp. 91–2.

15 ibid., pp. 90–1.

16 Holderness, op. cit., pp. 85–6.

17 Paola Dionisotti in Rutter, op. cit., p. 1.

18 ibid., p. 3 (both quotations).

19 ibid., p. 23.

20 Ann Thompson, for example, 'saw this production three times . . . and agree[d] with the *TLS* reviewer, Lorna Sage, that the tone [of Kate's last speech] was "spiritless" and "unreal"' (op. cit., p. 23).

21 Sinead Cusack in Rutter, op. cit., p. 3.

22 ibid., p. 4.

23 ibid., p. 21.

24 Jonathan Miller, advance publicity release for the production, Shakespeare Centre Library cuttings book.

25 Holderness criticises Miller's historicism as 'guilty of precisely the same distortions and oversimplifications as that post-Tillyard orthodoxy which took the most dogmatic and *ex cathedra* utterances of church and state for a comprehensive formulation of Tudor ideology' (op. cit., p. 118). It is also, of course, historically naive to assume that neuroses that the modern discourse of psychology has identified would be identical in the Renaissance period, with its quite different concept of mental illness.

26 Fiona Shaw in Rutter, op. cit., p. 6. Shaw comments on the difficulty of the role for a modern actress: 'There are moments when Kate's story isn't tenable, because she doesn't have the lines. For example, when Petruchio says, "Will you, nill you, I will marry you", Kate says nothing. How does the actress occupy that silence? Is Kate shocked? Delighted? Angry? Stunned? In later plays, maybe Shakespeare would

have given someone some lines there' (p. xxv). This is a trenchant criticism of the romanticism that would see Kate and Petruchio as early versions of Beatrice and Benedick – Benedick is constantly complaining about 'my Lady Tongue', Beatrice's verbal wit, which is suggested only once in *The Shrew*, in the 'wooing scene' of II.1. Shaw wrote a thoughtful piece for *Drama* as she was preparing the role, which offers an alternative historicism to Miller's view of the play: 'There are still more than elements of a pyramidic society [today] with boys on top but our consciousness is irrevocably, I hope, suspicious of that structure. I find it hard to believe that some Elizabethan women didn't balk at the square circle theology of Eve as a rib of Adam and its resonance through to husbands as mini gods in the microcosm of the family. I say this only because women no matter what century experience themselves as fully human and any kind of developed intelligence can observe intelligence or its absence in another. So the success of this system must have needed women to collude with the notion of their own inferiority aided by various deprivations in rights while surviving by manipulating menfolk based on their sense of superiority' ('An Actor's Diary', *Drama*, 4, 1987).

27 Shaw in Rutter, op. cit., pp. 19–20, 25.

28 I offer a brief discussion of Di Trevis's *Shrew* in the Warehouse, Stratford-on-Avon in late 1985, with Sian Thomas and Alfred Molina, in the Introduction, pp. 8–9.

In 1992 there was a new RSC main-house production by Bill Alexander: according to Michael Billington (*Guardian Weekly*, 19 April 1992), a 'dullishly academic version' using the Sly framework: 'He shows Christopher Sly as a drunken bum slung out of a Stratford pub, whisked back to the manor by a group of modern aristos, and given a lesson in wife taming by an apparently unsponsored RSC mobile tour. Instead of a nakedly chauvinist comedy we get an essay in illusion and reality with the Hooray Henries and Harriets gradually drawn into the action . . . the real problem is that the frame seems bigger than the picture and that the constant presence of these toping dopes draws much of the fun and sting from the original comedy. The device, in short, doesn't make Shakespeare's play any more morally acceptable: it almost makes it worse by implying that it offers a role model to moderns with marital problems . . . . where Jonathan Miller's last RSC production directly addressed the play's biblical belief in a divine patriarchy, Alexander vainly seeks to distract us with apologetic camouflage'. Charles Spencer of the *Daily Telegraph* (3 April 1992) describes Amanda Harris's snarling Kate, extremely bad-tempered by all accounts, as 'the conventional shrew of comic literature, not a recognisable individual, and as a result neither her cruel suffering, nor her growth to love, makes much of an impression'.

4 *MEASURE FOR MEASURE*

1 Kathleen McLuskie, 'The patriarchal bard: feminist criticism and Shakespeare', in Jonathan Dollimore and Alan Sinfield (eds), *Political*

Shakespeare: new essays in cultural materialism (Manchester, Manchester University Press, 1985), p. 94.

2 Ralph Berry has a valuable short chapter on *Measure for Measure* in *Changing Styles in Shakespeare* (London, Allen & Unwin, 1981), in which he remarks, 'The play's litmus quality depends on its final action, the staging of Isabella's response to the Duke's proposal. That is a gesture of climactic significance; it cannot be masked or elided. It defines the import of the entire preceding action. And its meaning has always to be imparted by actors who must ask themselves the only question that matters at the end: Can *this* Isabella accept *this* Duke? If not, why not?' (pp. 37–8). He points to the change in expectations in recent years about whether Isabella will accept the Duke, and assigns it to the decline of 'the general esteem in which authority is held' and 'the change in the position of women . . . . Simply, a contemporary actress will not perceive marriage as the automatic close to the play; and neither will the audience' (p. 42). For further discussion of *Measure for Measure* on the recent stage, see Michael Scott, *Renaissance Drama and a Modern Audience* (London, Macmillan, 1982); Scott sees the Duke as the 'central character' (p. 61).

3 Peter Brook, *The Empty Space* (1968) (Harmondsworth, Penguin Books, 1990), p. 99.

4 On line 148 'Angelo grasps her arms, holds her against table'; at line 150: 'Isa pushes Angelo C. He falls, rises, leans on bench'; line 160: 'Angelo cross to Isab, grasps her wrist, slams door'. (Notes from 1950 promptbook in the Shakespeare Centre Library.)

5 Barbara Jefford thought of Isabella as necessarily very young: 'Any kind of sophistication is wrong for Isabella. She must believe in what she does absolutely . . . it is easy to play when you are very young – you have such tremendous certainty then' (quoted in Judith Cook, *Women in Shakespeare*, London, Harrap, 1980, p. 43).

6 Herbert S. Weil, Jr, 'The options of the audience: theory and practice in Peter Brook's *Measure for Measure*', *Shakespeare Survey*, 25, 1972, pp. 27–36 (pp. 30, 32).

7 Richard David, 'Shakespeare's comedies and the modern stage', *Shakespeare Survey*, 4, 1951, pp. 129–38 (pp. 136–7).

8 Brook, op. cit., p. 100.

9 David, op. cit., p. 137.

10 Margaret Johnston, of Australian origin, had had a successful career since before the war on the West End stage. This was her first foray into Shakespeare – she also played Portia and Desdemona in this season. The *Oxford Times* (17 August 1956) was one of several journals which spoke of her, on the evidence of these performances, as 'one of the outstanding Shakespearean actresses of our generation'. Unfortunately she did not return to Stratford.

11 'Directing problem plays: John Barton talks to Gareth Lloyd Evans', *Shakespeare Survey*, 25, 1972, pp. 63–72 (p. 66).

12 A typical example of pre-feminist thinking on the verge of becoming feminist consciousness is given by this production's Isabella, Estelle Kohler, in an interview at the time of of its opening: 'I believe it's better,

in a marriage, for the man to be successful, so I gave up the theatre. But it didn't really help.' The marriage failed and she returned to her profession. (*Daily Mail*, 11 April 1970)

13 Ian Richardson in Judith Cook, *Shakespeare's Players*, London, Harrap, 1983, p. 99.

14 Peter Thomson, 'The smallest season: the Royal Shakespeare Company at Stratford in 1974', *Shakespeare Survey*, 28, 1975, pp. 137–48 (pp. 146–7).

15 Michael Pennington in Cook, op. cit., p. 101.

16 ibid., p. 101.

17 Paola Dionisotti in Carol Rutter, *Clamorous Voices: Shakespeare's women today* (London, The Women's Press, 1988), p. 29. Dionisotti also tells the following revealing anecdote: 'It was the day after we'd opened *Measure for Measure*. We'd all read the reviews – some were awful. He [Kyle] came to me in my dressing-room and said, "I think we've gone all wrong with Isabella. I think we should be thinking about" – this glorious royal "we" from directors once you're in performance, when of course they mean "you" – "I think we should be thinking about someone very very young, very innocent." And I remember sitting there thinking, "We've been rehearsing this show for six weeks, we've had previews, and we've opened, and now he wants me to change the performance radically. Without any rehearsal or context. Tonight' (p. xx). When the production was revived at the Aldwych in 1979, Dionisotti and Pryce were replaced by Sinead Cusack and David Suchet, achieving a straight and unproblematic reading of the play.

18 ibid., p. 39.

19 Michael Pennington in Cook, op. cit., p. 101.

20 Roger Warren, 'A year of comedies at Stratford', *Shakespeare Survey*, 32, 1979, pp. 201–10 (p. 208).

21 Daniel Massey, 'The Duke in *Measure for Measure*', Russell Jackson and Robert Smallwood (eds), *Players of Shakespeare 2* (Cambridge, Cambridge University Press, 1988), p. 19. Contrast the similar but significantly different treatment of this scene in 1978: at line 114 'Isa takes head-dress [veil] off & belt & rosary'; at line 140: 'They hug'. But the Duke's 'Who's here?' is cut: evidently there was no self-consciousness suggested between the two. (Notes in promptbook for 1978 production, Shakespeare Centre Library.) The archival video of the 1983 production shows a somewhat different blocking, with Isabella weeping in the Duke's arms, both of them on the floor: following a long silence, they appear to be about to kiss, when the Duke sees Lucio and leaps up.

22 Juliet Stevenson in Rutter, op. cit., pp. 37–8.

23 Massey in Jackson and Smallwood, op. cit., p. 29.

24 Quotations from Juliet Stevenson in this paragraph are from Rutter, op. cit., pp. 40–2, 49. Stevenson does not reveal here the information given in an interview with Vera Lustig (*Plays & Players*, November 1991), that she went on a three-day retreat in a convent when preparing for the role.

25 Trevor Nunn returned to the RSC to direct a small-scale touring *Measure for Measure* in 1991. Attention was focused on the Angelo (David Haig), as a 'study in sexual repression' (the play was set in Freud's Vienna). It ended happily, 'with Claudio and Angelo shaking hands, Isabella accepting the Duke's proposal and all dancing offstage'. Isabella was played by Claire Skinner, a 'fair young English rose' (Peter Holland, 'Shakespeare performances in England, 1990–91', *Shakespeare Survey*, 45, 1993, pp. 115–44 (pp. 138, 139)). The contrast with Hytner's production, with its contemporary resonances – including the casting of a black British actress as Isabella – is striking.

5 *MUCH ADO ABOUT NOTHING*

1 Pamela Mason, *Much Ado About Nothing: text and performance*, London, Macmillan, 1992, pp. 48, 50.
2 Robert Tanitch, *Ashcroft*, London, Hutchinson, 1975. Ashcroft's voice famously retained its youthful lightness well into middle age.
3 John Gielgud, *An Actor and His Time* (1979), Harmondsworth, Penguin Books, 1981, pp. 135, 136.
4 ibid, p. 135.
5 Sally Beauman, *The Royal Shakespeare Company: a history of ten decades*, Oxford, Oxford University Press, 1982, p. 301: in 1969 'Christopher Morley created a new permanent set that, with adaptations, was used for all the plays. It was a conscious stripping away of everything extraneous, creating a stage that was like a great empty box', lit in appropriate mood colours.
6 Pamela Mason recalls the masque as threatening: 'The stage was dimly lit and the soldiers wore threatening half-face visors with long, viciously pointed noses – their individuality was genuinely masked. They brandished drawn swords which were clashed menacingly at the end of the masque. While the military were welcomed for the colour, splendour and diversion they brought to Messina, bound up inextricably with this was a potential for evil' (op. cit., p. 57). Mason clearly agrees with my recollection of the masque as aggressively phallic; it seems somewhat unfair, however, to locate the source of the play's 'evil' in this display of gender difference, when the play itself is specific about the villainous motivations of Don John and his henchmen.
7 Gielgud, op. cit., p. 136.
8 Notes in the promptbook for the 1968 production, Shakespeare Centre Library.
9 Janet Suzman in Judith Cook, *Women in Shakespeare*, London, Harrap, 1980, p. 33.
10 Suzman commented interestingly on this moment in different performances in London and Los Angeles: 'Here [London] everybody waits for it with baited [sic] breath. You can feel it and it makes you nervous . . . . But in Los Angeles, they didn't know the story, and *Kill Claudio* when it happened was an absolute shock. Usually there was an audible gasp, which was terribly exciting. And you kind of yearn for

that state of innocence in an audience, when they don't actually know what is going to happen' (*Plays & Players*, June 1973). A history of the performance of this critical moment can be found in J.F. Cox, 'The stage representation of the "Kill Claudio" sequence in *Much Ado About Nothing*', *Shakespeare Survey* 32, 1979, pp. 27–36.

11 Michael L. Greenwald, *Directions by Indirections: a profile of John Barton*, London, Associated University Presses, 1985, p. 148. Judi Dench, commenting on her own conception of the role, said that she had found Barton's choice of period difficult because of the inappropriate 'racy' language of the girls – 'but I overcame it because John did create a terribly real household' (Cook, op. cit., p. 33).

12 Judi Dench, interview in Judith Cook, *Directors' Theatre*, London, Hodder & Stoughton, 1989, p. 127.

13 The programme included quotations about the 'officers' code' and an essay by Barbara Everett on the differing 'codes' of men and women: 'this is the first play, I think, in which the clash of these two worlds is treated with a degree of seriousness, and in which the woman's world dominates': Barbara Everett, 'Something of great constancy' (first pub. 1961), repr. in J. Russell Brown (ed.), *Much Ado About Nothing and As You Like It: a casebook*, London, Macmillan, 1979, p. 95.

14 Derek Jacobi quoted in Judith Cook, *Shakespeare's Players*, London, Harrap, 1983, p. 32.

15 Sinead Cusack in Carol Rutter, *Clamorous Voices: Shakespeare's Women Today*, London, The Women's Press, 1988, pp. xvi-xvii.

16 Interview with Susan Fleetwood from an unidentified newspaper clipping, Shakespeare Centre Library.

17 Peter Holland, in his review for *Shakespeare Survey* 44, 1992, 'Shakespeare performances in England, 1989–90', pp. 157–90, comments that in his opinion the production thought women 'of far less importance than male-bonding and an awareness of social hierarchies . . . . By the end of this production the relationship of Beatrice and Benedick mattered much less than Claudio and Benedick . . . the play's climax was effectively the reconciliation of the two men with a handshake' (p. 171). I cannot agree with this assessment, as I thought Fleetwood's and Allam's performance together very strong and absolutely central, but our two responses are a good example of the way a critic reads the objective signs of a production from the point of view of what he/she finds interesting in its depiction of a society.

18 'I just know that Beatrice would take that on board, and I can't look at Benedick while we're singing it, because then it would seem as if I were endorsing it' (Fleetwood interviewed by Vera Lustig, *Plays & Players*, February 1991).

CONCLUSION

1 We should note, however, Stallybrass and White's cautionary reminder: 'The bourgeoisie . . . is perpetually rediscovering the carnivalesque as a radical source of transcendence. Indeed that act of rediscovery itself, in

which the middle classes excitedly discover their own pleasures and desires under the sign of the Other, in the realm of the Other, is constitutive of the very formation of middleclass identity'. (Peter Stallybrass and Allon White, *The Politics and Poetics of Transgression*, London, Methuen, 1986, p. 201)

2 It is worth contrasting the views on this matter of two modern directors, as recorded in the symposium *Is Shakespeare Still Our Contemporary?* (John Elsom (ed.), London, Routledge, 1989). For Michael Bogdanov, 'the principal aim of the theatre is not just to illuminate and become the brief chronicle of the time. It is also to aid the process of social change' (p. 17). Bogdanov, with Michael Pennington (both have worked with the RSC) founded the English Shakespeare Company to further this ideal; his productions are always in modern dress, thereby attempting to avoid the audience's merely indulging in spectacle. David Thacker, who has directed several plays for the RSC in recent years, says 'I understand "abstracts and brief chronicles" to mean something like newspapers, and that the actors are there to show people what the times they are living in are really like' (p. 22): this is not a consciously political agenda, but seems to aim rather for the colourful but generally bland neutrality of the 'lifestyle' magazine.

3 Fiona Shaw, letter to the author, January 1993. She added, 'They [the comedies] are imbued with compassion though and we all *need* that'.

4 '"Well, this is the Forest of Arden": an informal address', in Werner Habicht, D.J. Palmer, Roger Pringle (eds), *Images of Shakespeare: papers from the International Shakespeare Conference 1986*, London, Associated University Presses, 1988, p. 342. So far (mid-1993) Noble has not taken any productively radical steps towards change: Michael Billington observed in a review of David Thacker's *As You Like It*, 'What worries me . . . is that, with the signal exception of Adrian Noble's own work, we have not seen a really exciting production on the Stratford main stage in eighteen months' (*Guardian Weekly*, 24 April 1992).

5 Jane Lapotaire commented in an interview in the *RSC Magazine*, 7 (Summer 1993), 'I do find it disturbing to sit and have my lunch under a photograph of Buzz Goodbody and see how little we have advanced [since her debut at Stratford in 1974]. The situation has not changed one iota – there still aren't enough women playwrights, directors, lighting designers . . . . At times I feel as if I'm trapped in a time-warp and wonder what my generation of consciousness-raisers achieved' (p. 12).

BIBLIOGRAPHY

Adelman, Janet, 'Male bonding in Shakespeare's comedies', in Peter Erickson and Coppelia Kahn (eds), *Shakespeare's 'Rough Magic': Renaissance essays in honor of C.L. Barber*, Newark, University of Delaware Press, 1985.

Barber, C.L. , *Shakespeare's Festive Comedy*, Princeton, Princeton University Press, 1959.

Barton, John, *Playing Shakespeare*, London, Methuen, 1984.

Beauman, Sally, *The Royal Shakespeare Company: a history of ten decades*, Oxford, Oxford University Press, 1982.

Belsey, Catherine, 'Disrupting sexual difference: meaning and gender in the comedies', in John Drakakis (ed.), *Alternative Shakespeares*, London, Methuen, 1985.

Berry, Ralph, *Changing Styles in Shakespeare*, London, Allen & Unwin, 1981.

—— 'The reviewer as historian', *Shakespeare Quarterly*, 36, 5, 1985, pp. 594–7.

—— *On Directing Shakespeare*, London, Hamish Hamilton, 1989.

Bevington, David, and Halio, Jay L. (eds), *Shakespeare: pattern of excelling nature*, London, Associated University Presses, 1978.

Billington, Michael, *Peggy Ashcroft*, London, Mandarin, 1988.

—— *Directors' Shakespeare: approaches to 'Twelfth Night'*, London, Nick Hern Books, 1990.

Bowe, John, 'Orlando in *As You Like It*', in Brockbank, *Players of Shakespeare* (q.v.).

Brockbank, Philip (ed.), *Players of Shakespeare*, Cambridge, Cambridge University Press, 1985.

Brook, Peter, *The Empty Space*, (1968) Harmondsworth, Penguin, 1990.

Brown, John Russell, 'The interpretation of Shakespeare's comedies: 1900–1953', *Shakespeare Survey* 8, 1955, pp. 1–13.

—— (ed.), *Much Ado About Nothing and As You Like It: a casebook*, London, Macmillan, 1979.

Carlson, Susan, *Women and Comedy: rewriting the British theatrical tradition*, Ann Arbor, University of Michigan Press, 1991.

Case, Sue-Ellen, *Feminism and Theatre*, London, Macmillan, 1988.

201

—— (ed.) *Performing Feminisms: feminist critical theory and theatre*, Baltimore, Johns Hopkins University Press, 1990.

Cook, Judith, *Directors' Theatre*, London, Hodder & Stoughton, first version: 1974, second version: 1989.

—— *Women in Shakespeare*, London, Harrap, 1980.

—— *Shakespeare's Players*, London, Harrap, 1983.

Cox, J.F., 'The stage representation of the "Kill Claudio" sequence in *Much Ado About Nothing*', *Shakespeare Survey* 32, 1979, pp. 27–36.

David, Richard, 'Shakespeare's comedies and the modern stage', *Shakespeare Survey* 4, 1951, pp. 129–38

De Marinis, Marco, 'Dramaturgy of the spectator', *The Drama Review*, 31, 2, 1987, pp. 100–114.

Dollimore, Jonathan, and Sinfield, Alan (eds), *Political Shakespeare: new essays in cultural materialism*, Manchester, Manchester University Press, 1985.

Drakakis, John (ed.), *Alternative Shakespeares*, London, Methuen, 1985.

Elsom, John (ed.), *Is Shakespeare Still Our Contemporary?* London, Routledge, 1989.

Esslin, Martin, *The Field of Drama*, London, Methuen, 1988.

Everett, Barbara, 'Something of great constancy', in John Russell Brown (ed.), *Much Ado About Nothing and As You Like It: a casebook*, London, Macmillan, 1979.

Ferris, Lesley, *Acting Women: images of women in theatre*, New York, New York University Press, 1989.

Freedman, Barbara, *Staging the Gaze: postmodernism, psychoanalysis, and Shakespearean comedy*, Ithaca, Cornell University Press, 1991.

Frye, Northrop, *A Natural Perspective*, New York, Columbia University Press, 1965.

Gielgud, John, *An Actor and His Time*, Harmondsworth, Penguin, 1981.

Greenblatt, Stephen, *Shakespearean Negotiations*, Oxford, Clarendon Press, 1988.

Greenwald, Michael L., *Directions by Indirections: a profile of John Barton*, London, Associated University Presses, 1985.

Greer, Germaine, *The Female Eunuch*, London, MacGibbon & Kee, 1970.

Habicht, Werner, Palmer, D.J. and Pringle, Roger (eds), *Images of Shakespeare: papers from the International Shakespeare Conference 1986*, London, Associated University Presses, 1988.

Hamer, Mary, 'Shakespeare's Rosalind and her public image', *Theatre Research International*, 11, 2, 1986, pp. 105–18.

Harrop, John, *Acting*, London, Routledge, 1992.

Helms, Lorraine, 'Playing the woman's part', in Sue-Ellen Case (ed.), *Performing Feminisms: feminist critical theory and theatre*, Baltimore, Johns Hopkins University Press, 1990.

Hobson, Harold, *Theatre in Britain: a personal view*, Oxford, Phaidon, 1984.

Holderness, Graham (ed.), *The Shakespeare Myth*, Manchester, Manchester University Press, 1988.

—— *Shakespeare in Performance: The Taming of the Shrew*, Manchester, Manchester University Press, 1989.

Holland, Peter, 'Shakespeare performances in England, 1989–90', *Shakespeare Survey* 44, 1992, pp.157–90.

—— 'Shakespeare performances in England, 1990–1', *Shakespeare Survey* 45, 1993, pp.115–44.

Howard, Jean E., 'Crossdressing, the theatre, and gender struggle in early modern England', *Shakespeare Quarterly*, 39, 4, 1988, pp. 418–40.

Jackson, Russell, and Smallwood, Robert (eds), *Players of Shakespeare 2*, Cambridge, Cambridge University Press, 1988.

Jardine, Lisa, *Still Harping on Daughters: women and drama in the age of Shakespeare*, Brighton, Harvester Press, 1983.

Kelly, Philippa, 'Enacting Shakespeare: resistance and reception', *Southern Review* (Adelaide), 24, 3, 1991, pp. 261–77.

Leggatt, Alexander, *Shakespeare's Comedy of Love*, London, Methuen, 1974.

Lloyd Evans, Gareth, 'Directing problem plays: John Barton talks to Gareth Lloyd Evans', *Shakespeare Survey* 25, 1972, pp. 63–72.

McLuskie, Kathleen, 'The patriarchal bard: feminist criticism and Shakespeare', in Jonathan Dollimore and Alan Sinfield (eds), *Political Shakespeare: new essays in cultural materialism*, Manchester, Manchester University Press, 1985.

Mahood, M.M., 'Shakespeare's middle comedies: a generation of criticism', *Shakespeare Survey* 32, 1979, pp. 1–15.

Mason, Pamela, *Much Ado About Nothing: text and performance*, London, Macmillan, 1992.

Mazer, Cary M., 'Shakespeare, the reviewer, and the theatre historian', *Shakespeare Quarterly*, 36, 5, 1985, pp. 648–61.

Mitchell, Yvonne, *Actress*, London, Routledge & Kegan Paul, 1957.

Noble, Adrian, '"Well, this is the Forest of Arden": an informal address', in Habicht *et al.* (eds) *Images of Shakespeare: papers from the International Shakespeare Conference 1986*, London, Associated University Presses, 1988.

Onions, C.T., rev. Eagleson, R.D., *A Shakespeare Glossary*, Oxford, Oxford University Press, 1986.

Potter, Lois, *Twelfth Night: text and performance*, London, Macmillan, 1985.

Rackin, P. 'Androgyny, mimesis, and the marriage of the boy heroine on the English Renaissance Stage', in Elaine Showalter (ed.), *Speaking of Gender*, London, Routledge, 1989.

Redgrave, Vanessa, *Vanessa Redgrave: an autobiography*, London, Hutchinson, 1991.

Royal Shakespeare Company, The, London, Max Reinhardt, 1964.

Rutter, Carol, *Clamorous Voices: Shakespeare's women today*, London, The Women's Press, 1988.

St Clare Byne, M., 'The Shakespeare season at the Old Vic, 1957–8, and Stratford-upon-Avon, 1958', *Shakespeare Quarterly*, 9, 4, 1958, pp. 507–30.

Saslow, James, *Ganymede in the Renaissance*, New Haven, Yale University Press, 1986.

Scott, Michael, *Renaissance Drama and a Modern Audience*, London, Macmillan, 1982.

Shaw, Fiona, and Stevenson, Juliet, 'Celia and Rosalind in *As You Like It*', in Russell Jackson and Robert Smallwood, *Players of Shakespeare 2*, Cambridge, Cambridge University Press, 1988.

Shellard, Dominic, 'Harold Hobson and Harold Pinter', *Oxford Magazine*, Second Week, Michaelmas Term, 1990, pp. 10–11.

Showalter, Elaine (ed.) *Speaking of Gender*, London, Routledge, 1989.

Sinden, Donald, 'Malvolio in *Twelfth Night*', in Philip Brockbank (ed.), *Players of Shakespeare*, Cambridge, Cambridge University Press, 1985.

Sinfield, Alan, 'Royal Shakespeare: theatre and the making of ideology', in Jonathan Dollimore and Alan Sinfield (eds), *Political Shakespeare: new essays in cultural materialism*, Manchester, Manchester University Press, 1985.

Speaight, Robert, 'Truth and relevance in Shakespearean production', in David Bevington and Jay L. Halio (eds), *Shakespeare: pattern of excelling nature*, London, Associated University Presses, 1978.

Sprague, A.C., and Trewin, J. C., *Shakespeare's Plays Today*, University of South Carolina Press, 1970.

Stallybrass, Peter, and White, Allon, *The Politics and Poetics of Transgression*, London, Methuen, 1986.

Tanitch, Robert, *Ashcroft*, London, Hutchinson, 1975.

Thompson, Ann, 'Introduction', *The Taming of the Shrew*, Cambridge, Cambridge University Press, 1984.

Thomson, Peter, 'The smallest season: the Royal Shakespeare Company at Stratford in 1974', *Shakespeare Survey* 28, 1975, pp. 137–48.

Traub, Valerie, *Desire and Anxiety: circulations of sexuality in Shakespearean drama*, London, Routledge, 1992.

Wanamaker, Zoë, 'Viola in *Twelfth Night*', in Russell Jackson and Robert Smallwood (eds), *Players of Shakespeare 2*, Cambridge, Cambridge University Press, 1988.

Warren, Roger, 'A year of comedies at Stratford', *Shakespeare Survey* 32, 1979, pp.201–10.

—— 'Shakespeare in England', *Shakespeare Quarterly* 34, 4, 451–7.

Weil Jr, Herbert S., 'The options of the audience: theory and practice in Peter Brook's *Measure for Measure*', *Shakespeare Survey* 25, 1972, pp. 27–36.

Wells, Stanley, *Royal Shakespeare*, Manchester, Manchester University Press, 1977.

Woddis, Carole, *Sheer Bloody Magic: conversations with actresses*, London, Virago, 1991.

Worthen, W.B., 'Deeper meanings and theatrical technique: the rhetoric of performance criticism', *Shakespeare Quarterly*, 40, 4, 1989, pp. 441–55.

NOTE: Essays surveying the year's performances of Shakespeare may be found in each volume of *Shakespeare Survey* and in the annual winter number of *Shakespeare Quarterly*.

INDEX

This index includes names of actors (with their major roles), directors, designers, composers, and other theatre personnel.